WON FOR ALL

WON FOR ALL

THE INSIDE STORY OF THE NEW ENGLAND PATRIOTS' IMPROBABLE RUN TO THE SUPER BOWL

PEPPER JOHNSON

WITH BILL GUTMAN

Contemporary Books

Chicago   New York   San Francisco   Lisbon   London   Madrid   Mexico City
Milan   New Delhi   San Juan   Seoul   Singapore   Sydney   Toronto

The *McGraw·Hill* Companies

Library of Congress Cataloging-in-Publication Data

Johnson, Pepper.
    Won for all : the inside story of the New England Patriots' improbable run to the Super
Bowl / Pepper Johnson with Bill Gutman.
        p.   cm.
    Includes index.
    ISBN 0-07-140877-0
      1. New England Patriots (Football team)   2. Super Bowl (36th : 2002 : New Orleans,
La.)   I. Gutman, Bill.   II. Title

GV956.N36 J64   2003
796.332'64'0974461—dc21   2002031252

1 2 3 4 5 6 7 8 9 0   AGM/AGM   1 0 9 8 7 6 5 4 3 2

ISBN 0-07-140877-0

McGraw-Hill books are available at special quantity discounts to use as premiums and sales
promotions, or for use in corporate training programs. For more information, please write to the
Director of Special Sales, Professional Publishing, McGraw-Hill, Two Penn Plaza, New York, NY
10121-2298. Or contact your local bookstore.

This book is printed on acid-free paper.

To all our fallen soldiers who were with us during training camp and periodically throughout the season but did not receive a Super Bowl ring

Also in memory of my uncle, Archie Tinnin
(January 10, 1922–October 21, 2001)

Contents

Foreword

Pepper Johnson and I have had a kind of kinship from the first time we met when Pepper was in high school and deciding which college to attend. Being that we both came from the same area—me from Flint, Michigan, and Pepper from Detroit—I tried to recruit him to attend Michigan State. He wound up choosing Ohio State, but we spent a good deal of time together and discovered quickly that we came from similar backgrounds, both growing up and learning sports from the school of hard knocks, where toughness was as important as performance. His high school coach liked to have his team scrimmage against bigger and better schools to instill toughness and competitiveness, to get his players battle ready. Those experiences laid the blueprint for the type of college and professional player Pepper would become. He was a tough guy who understood breaking points and how to work through them, things his opponents couldn't see.

When he joined the Giants as a rookie in 1986, he was brash but not overconfident, yet I could see immediately that he understood football from both an analytical and an emotional level. He knew what it would take to be a professional long before he got there. In fact he caught most of our veterans off guard, something I found rather amusing, because I knew just where he was coming from. Nothing bothered him. He laughed at all the hazing he and the other rookies had to endure, actually enjoyed it, then practiced hard and fought hard. The more the veterans tried to break him, the more fun he had.

He made his initial contributions to the team as a special teams player, but his goals were always greater. He wanted to play full-time. To do that, he first became a leader on special teams and subsequently made everyone around him better. Pepper would always watch tape of the best player on the opponent's special teams, analyze him, and make suggestions to the coaches. Then he would get a thrill out of taking a guy's heart from him.

That was Pepper. He always took defeat personally—defeat to himself, his teammates, and his team. He just didn't want to see anyone dominate him or his teammates. Your fight was his fight. If you had a problem with a player on an opposing team, it became his problem, and that's one reason I considered him my closest teammate and still consider him my closest friend. We both played with the greatest linebacker in the game, but if I had to pick a guy to go into a fight with, it would be Pepper.

I always knew that Pepper would make an excellent coach, whether an assistant as he is now or someday a coordinator or head coach. That's because he understands the mental makeup of players, both on his team and on the opposition's. He was always very cunning as a player. He would network around the league, doing camps, playing basketball with guys, traveling around, and always recording his observations mentally. He could see a guy's mental approach to basketball, for example, and translate that to football. He could look at a player's body language and tell if a guy had high self-esteem or was a front-runner against whom you could get the upper hand right away. He would point out the guy who would quit if we did a particular thing early. All this experience continues to work for him.

I guess the best way I can put it is that Pepper understands the entire process that makes up professional football. Because he was part of the process as a player, he can always tell when a player is bullshitting him as a coach. He knows just what makes a player excel and what gives him problems, both his own players and his opponents. Yet when things get tough and there is the need for more than an analytical approach, then he's all about a good fight, too. With the Giants we were in a great situation because we had a coaching staff receptive to input. A coach who wouldn't take input from a Pepper Johnson would do it out of pure arrogance, not rational thinking, because Pepper was usually right on the money.

I have no doubts that Pepper played a huge role in the Patriots' run to the Super Bowl, because he brings so much to the table. At the same time, I know his insights into the season and his retrospective as to why the team improved, peaked at just the right time, and overcame any and all obstacles are right on the mark. As a football man, Pepper doesn't miss a trick, and as a person, friend, and teammate, he's always been a totally reliable guy in every way. When Pepper Johnson says he'll be there, he's there. Every time.

—Carl Banks
Former New York Giants All-Pro Linebacker

Acknowledgments

I would first like to thank our God Almighty and Savior, Jesus Christ.

The following are people associated with the New England Patriots, as well as friends, family, and others who supported and encouraged me throughout the long season. My mom, Maxine, and son, Dionté. My sisters, Adiva and Yvonne; brother, Alvin; nephews, Jarriel and Jumal; and nieces, Shanté and Devonne, as well as my living father, Mr. G.

The fellas and their families, Carl Banks and Mo Carthon (they help me keep my sanity), Keith Byars, Rowe and Ty Tate, Eddie Cane, Chip, Kip, Da Billy D, Keenan, Trey, Los Man, Eric, Angel, Hop, Louie, Lang, Kenny B, Greg D'Alba, Megg D, Big Dawg, Kevin G, Ingy, Purnell, McGhee, Mike the barber, Finkes, Jack, Big Daddy, Taz, Jeff, Mark Lep, Hurricane, and the Run DMC crew.

Also the dynamic New England coaching staff: Charlie, Scar, Davidson, Ivan, Ned, Coach Rehbein, RAC, E Train, Da-Bull, and the other half of the salt-and-pepper combo, Rob-O. My training buddies Mike, Marcus, and T. Shaw. Nick, Josh, and Nick, the ever-so-popular Berj, the legend Tipp and crew, Nick Saban and Mr. Mo, as well as all the employees of the New England Patriots, who made my days a little brighter and who contributed one and all to our great season in their own special ways. In addition, thanks to Erin, Paula, Michelle, Kelly, Travel Cove, Jo, Doreen, Miss Ching, and Tracey.

Special thanks to Nancy Meier and Boston's finest, Patricia, my two angels. Also to Jackie Parke, the deepest thanks for being my mold, my crutch, my direction in making all this happen. And to Bill Gutman, thanks for shaping my words. It has been an honor.

To Mr. Robert Kraft for hiring Bill Belichick and me. And to Coach Belichick, thanks for giving me the opportunity and experience. You have always been my hero and mentor. I thought I looked at football in too much detail until I met you. You have us all at a level to succeed. I have learned from the best as a player and now continuing as a coach. However, I would also like to remind you that your only loss in the Super Bowl was without me.

Additional thanks to our fine editor, Rob Taylor, as well as Brigid Brown of McGraw-Hill for her help in initiating this project, and to agents Marilyn Allen and Bob Diforio for handling business matters with their usual efficiency and expertise.

Finally, my Dawgs, the players, for buying into the system. It's yours now. Let's do it again! I need a fourth ring. God bless all of you.

All of Pepper Johnson's proceeds from the sale of this book will be donated to Raw Pep-52, Inc., a nonprofit charitable organization benefiting underprivileged children in Detroit.

1

Starting from Scratch
A New Year

A team doesn't win the Super Bowl without good reason. No matter what the talent level, you can't simply mail it in and win in the National Football League, especially in the playoffs. Looking back, I think you could say that what the Patriots accomplished in 2001 started with the last game of the 2000 season. We lost at home, 27–24, to the Dolphins after taking a 24–17 lead into the final period. Another loss and a 5–11 record. It didn't even end cleanly. There was a little discrepancy in the final seconds of the game, a problem with the clock, and what happened made it all even harder to take.

We thought the game was over, that time had expired, but the refs said no, there were still a few seconds left. So we had to come out of the locker room to try to run another play. But before we could run the play, there was more confusion about the clock. Then the refs said again that the game was over and sent us off. They really blew it. In again, then out again . . . three times, before it officially ended. It was almost as if they wouldn't allow us to let go of the season. There was heartache enough because of how the season had gone and how it ended. The Keystone Cops comedy with the clock and the refs in the final seconds made it hurt all the more.

My locker at Foxboro Stadium was all the way at the back of the room, and there was just a divider separating us from the Dolphins. We could hear them laughing the second time we went in and before we went out for the final play. It was as though they were laughing at us. That's why we wouldn't give up. We were down only three points, and if there was a chance to win the game, we wanted to take it.

I just don't think it was meant for us to win because there were so many bad elements on that team. I'm a strong believer that God don't like ugly. We had a lot of people bucking the system. Some guys were just collecting a check, and when that happens you don't stand much of a chance. When you have a majority of guys who aren't leaders, it's very difficult in this league. Maybe the best way to describe the 2000 Patriots team was that when the camera was on, it was rah, rah, rah, but when the camera was off, it became me, me, me.

The 2000 season was also Bill Belichick's first as the Patriots' head coach. The team had been 8–8 the year before, and when a new coach comes in, the media always figures you'll be lucky to get to .500 again, what with trying to learn a new system, evaluating personnel, planning for changes, coordinating your philosophy with a new staff—all those little things that go on behind the scenes. Then the finger-pointing started. Everyone in the media seemed to want to blame former head coach Pete Carroll's country-club mentality. The prevailing thought was that the players were lax. Belichick was brought in for his toughness. A cut-and-dried guy, straight line, point A to point B. The only way.

So even before the 2000 season started, I don't think the players were expecting much. Part of the problem was that they read the papers, watched the sports talk shows on television, listened to fans calling in, and heard over and over again that the team would be lucky to be a .500 ball club. Then I think a kind of losing mentality crept in. That's one of the differences in sports today from when I first came into the game as a rookie with the Giants in 1986. The veteran players knew the score and told us how it was. Our veterans, for example, didn't allow players to read the papers, at least not in the locker room. Guys like Harry Carson and George Martin set the rules, and you listened. If you wanted to read a paper, it had to be somewhere else. You didn't watch TV in the players' lounge, either—no ESPN, no talk shows, no opinions from broadcasters and ex-players. It's difficult enough explaining football to someone who wants to learn, but when you're trying to explain football to a player who already has formed his opinion based on outside sources, and he's waiting for you to agree with him, it becomes even tougher.

So I think a lot of the guys came in with their expectations already low, especially after reading all the media predictions and listening to the barrage of negatives that went with them. That's the time when the leaders are supposed to step up, take the initiative, and tell everyone that the predictions are bullshit. If they don't, everyone else will fold up. The young soldiers are too weak. They look up to the veterans who have been there, done that, and seen it all.

The Patriots had an offensive tackle named Bruce Armstrong who had been with the team since 1987. He was a longtime star, going to the Pro Bowl six times and being named to the Patriots' All-Century Team. A player like that should be an icon, someone the younger players look up to and follow. Every team needs a guy who walks and talks like an icon, a guy who sits in the locker room and always has five or six players around him while he tells his old ghost stories about when he came into the league, recounts his many wars and battles, the defeats as well as the victories. A guy like that, with thirteen years under his belt, has a much deeper impact than even a player walking around with seven or eight years on him.

When Coach Belichick came, he had to make some adjustments to the existing finances to free up some salary cap money so he could begin making the personnel changes he thought were necessary to win. One of the first things he did was ask Armstrong to take a pay cut. When he refused, he was released. That, in itself, raised a few eyebrows. Even though he was a free agent, Armstrong couldn't hook up with another team and finally re-signed with us, but now he was playing for the minimum and he was mad. He allowed his personal feelings to take over, and he decided to shut it down. Everything I had heard about him before I came over—that he was vocal and inspirational—I didn't see at all. I think it was one of those cases where he felt it was the money that made the man when, in truth, it's the man who makes the money. Whether he was embarrassed because of what had happened, or however he looked at it, he just didn't want to take that responsibility for one more year, and it killed us.

Now we had no leader. Drew Bledsoe wouldn't step up because he didn't want to step on Armstrong's toes. Armstrong had been the guy on the offensive side of the ball for so long. There were leaders on the defensive side, but even they looked up to Armstrong because of his many years in the league. I can't honestly say that if his attitude had been different we would have won six more games, but there's a chance attitude might have helped win three more. That little extra push can make a difference, especially when it comes from a player who's looked upon as an icon.

Maybe it's tough to understand how one man can have that kind of impact or inspiration. There were a number of veterans who had gone to the Super

Bowl with the team in 1996—guys like Willie McGinest, Drew, Lawyer Milloy, Ty Law, Troy Brown, Ted Johnson, Tedy Bruschi—but they were all relatively young players then. It's still the guy with the most war stories who has the most impact and influence and has the power to set the tone. A Bruce Armstrong could even tell stories about guys who went to the 1985 Super Bowl with the team, because a lot of them were still there when he came in. So he's seen it all, from a 1–15 season in 1990 to the Super Bowl in '96. It's like having a team historian in the locker room.

When I came to the Giants, guys like Carson and Martin would remind us what it was like to be 3–12, the record the team had in Bill Parcells's first year as coach. After hearing that, none of us wanted to experience a 3–12 season, and we were determined not to let it happen. So it really helps to hear all the stories, not only about the good times but about the bad ones as well.

Basically, the 5–11 season of 2000 was about a team that lacked leadership. There weren't enough high expectations. Everyone was feeling each other out. That's another thing that happens with a new coach and staff. In fact, only two offensive coaches and one of the defensive coaches knew Coach Belichick. I knew him, of course, had known him since my years with the Giants, but I was just a liaison that year, not an official coach. That gave me a lot of time to watch and listen. It was after that final game with the Dolphins when something happened in the locker room that might have set a preliminary tone for the 2001 season. It was the kind of thing I always like to see.

Normally, after each game, Coach Belichick would address the guys, then all the coaches would pretty much walk away. The players would then come together, all put their hands in, and yell "TEAM!" After the coaches walked away and before the players could put their hands together, our defensive captain and strong safety, Lawyer Milloy, stepped forward. He had something to say, and by the look on his face, all the guys knew they had better listen.

"I want everyone to take a moment and remember something, get it into your heads," he said. "Remember what you are feeling now, the taste you have in your mouths. Remember it because I'm pissed. Five and eleven. We're losers. Losers! I hope every last one of you feels the same way. Don't forget it for a minute, because I don't give a damn what we have to do until the opening kickoff next year—we're not gonna feel this way again after next season. No way. We're all gonna look back at this and laugh."

Lawyer and I spoke a lot during the off season. He wasn't the only one. I spent time with Ty Law, Willie McGinest, and Otis Smith. You could feel the pain they were carrying with them from the season. McGinest personally felt he had let the guys down. He had been hurt part of the year, and his goal was to be healthy in 2001. Lawyer had set the tone by saying he didn't care what it took. All these guys were determined to buy into Belichick's system. They were going to play the defenses that were projected for them, and they were going to win. Anyone who didn't like it could get the hell out of here. That was the way all these guys were thinking.

During the off season, Coach Belichick also began sending his own messages to the team, especially to guys who had been around and felt they would be there forever. He released linebacker Chris Slade, wouldn't re-sign Bruce Armstrong, went to guys like McGinest, Ted Johnson, and a few others and asked them to restructure their contracts, lengthen them out. By doing that he would reduce base salaries, and that would bring down salary cap numbers. I can understand why some of the guys were hesitant. They were being asked to restructure after the team had given Bledsoe an unprecedented $100 million contract. During the 2000 season, stories were leaking out that Drew was going to sign a huge contract. Bill didn't stand a chance with the Bledsoe situation because it was already happening when he got here. He was the one, though, who had to ask the vets to take pay cuts and restructure. Even though they didn't like it, they agreed. Most of them had gotten so much up front with their signing bonuses that even though restructuring chipped away at their base salaries, they were still ahead. Incentives were also added to the new contracts, both for individuals and for the accomplishments of the team.

So the restructuring and the releasing of some veterans were clear signals telling everyone that things were going to be done differently. I think one of the lessons Belichick learned when he was coaching in Cleveland was that the big-name players don't always make the best fit. We personally interview prospective players now, and it doesn't really matter how much talent each one has. If we don't feel he can be one of our guys, a guy who can fit in with our overall concept, we won't sign him. The players who were signed before the start of the 2001 season were all players brought here for specific reasons— some for specialized skills, others for leadership, still others for a winning kind of attitude, but all because we were putting together a *team*, and these were some of the elements that were missing.

Some examples: We acquired Bryan Cox, a veteran linebacker with talent but also a guy who brings an X-factor we needed for attitude. We had some outstanding linebackers returning. Ted Johnson is a helluva player, but he isn't as vocal as Cox. Tedy Bruschi is kind of between the two. His durability is his strong suit. The guy comes to play. Cox always plays with a lot of energy. Bill wanted an extra push from that position, the kind of push he gets in the secondary from Lawyer. He also brought in Anthony Pleasant, a defensive end he had drafted originally in Cleveland and a player he knew very well, one who would give us some veteran leadership on the defensive line. Defensive back Otis Smith had come over in 2000. Then we picked up veteran cornerbacks Terrell Buckley and Terrance Shaw to give us more depth in the secondary.

Otis is something special. He was with the Patriots in '96, moved on to the Jets a year later, and stayed there through 1999. The Jets let him go at the end of training camp before the 2000 season, and we picked him up just before the final preseason game. Most of these guys were players Coach Belichick knew. He didn't have to guess what they would be bringing to the table. I think the impact of our free agents must have opened the eyes of other teams. We had five guys, new faces, starting on our defense alone (Pleasant, Roman Phifer, Cox, Mike Vrabel, and first-round choice Richard Seymour), and three or four more other guys who played a lot. Matt Stevens, who came over at the tail end of the 2000 season, Buckley, and Shaw all played important backup roles in the secondary. So our defense had definitely been upgraded by the new faces.

The offense also saw a number of key changes. Wide receiver David Patten became an impact player once he got his chance. Mike Compton, a center and guard, came over after eight years with Detroit and gave us more flexibility on the offensive line. He and Damien Woody would flip-flop between guard and center, depending on the situation. For instance, Woody would be the center in most situations, but when we went into the shotgun Compton would snap the ball and Woody would move over and play guard. Compton helped in another way as well. Matt Light, our number-two draft pick and an offensive lineman, might not have survived had it not been for Compton. He spoon-fed him, mainly about blocking and making adjustments. We don't have the simplest offensive philosophy. There is a lot of communication, and it really helps a rookie to have a veteran taking him under his wing.

As coaches, we definitely felt we had substantially upgraded the team from where it had been in 2000. We didn't come in saying we had one of the most talented teams in the league, but Coach Belichick made sure all of us knew that we would have a team that was extremely strong mentally. There were changes in the staff to help us do just that. Romeo Crennel, affectionately known by everyone as "RAC," who had worked with Belichick for fourteen seasons at other stops, was brought in as defensive coordinator, a role Belichick had played the year before. The move allowed Bill to have more hands-on input with the offense. I became the inside linebackers coach, allowing Rob Ryan to concentrate on the outside linebackers. Bill also made it very clear that he wanted a lot more out of the coaches in 2001. The previous year he had to hire his staff, interview them, then teach his defense. With a year under everyone's belt and with me, RAC, and defensive backs coach Eric Mangini very familiar with Bill's system and the way he thinks, he now demanded a lot more from all of us.

The first step was to evaluate. What had we done wrong last year? What had we done right, and what did we want to change and strengthen? In areas where we were already strong, he wanted us to get better. He said that the veteran players would be the heart of the defense, and he pointed out that one of their paychecks can equal a coach's entire salary. He didn't want owner Bob Kraft wasting his money on a player because we couldn't coach him. Our job was to find a way to coach him. The way Coach Belichick put it was "If I'm going to get these players to do what I want to do, I have to start with the coaches."

His philosophy was that we, as coaches, are going to be a reflection of him, and then we have to get the players to be a reflection of us. That way everyone becomes a reflection of him. Once everyone is on the same page, we have something to work with. Now we understand each other; now we're a team. Then when we reach that point we can begin to see who is more physical, who is faster—all the individual skills, both physical and mental, that make an outstanding player.

When I first came over here—and I'm not ashamed to say this—there were only a handful of guys who really understood football. Some didn't even understand many of the basics. I was really shocked, because it was only a couple of years earlier that Parcells had been here. In three years either a lot of stuff got away or the guys were just taking it in week to week, not learning it for the duration. It was frustrating at times, sometimes sad, and there were even times when you had to keep from laughing your head off. Obviously, Belichick was aware of this as well, and that's one reason he was so firm with his coaches. At our first meeting he said, flat out, that it all starts with us.

"We must do a better job coaching," he told everyone. "If we want to be better than 5–11, we have to do a better job, all of us."

He meant it then, and he means it now. Bill will always ask for better, more from everybody. Even though we won the Super Bowl, we still had shakeups. He'll never stay with a pat hand. The free agents he brought in before 2001 were not only there to improve the team; they were there to stir up competition at a lot of crucial positions. The releasing of some of the veterans opened plenty of eyes. You could see it all begin coming together during the off-season workout program that we run every year. There was something like 90 percent attendance for a program that is pretty much voluntary. The guys work four days—Monday, Tuesday, Thursday, and Friday—and get maybe $100 or $125 a day for expenses. Coming in is definitely a sacrifice. Players living in places like Florida, California, or Texas would certainly feel a lot more comfortable staying at home than being in New England, from March until June, but they came anyway.

The conditioning program is hard work. There are more than forty workouts with two weeks off, split into a week at a time. The purpose of the workouts is to build both power and explosiveness. There is a great deal of strength training, with the concentration each day on a different part of the body and a different facet of conditioning. For instance, we have a lower-body day, where the concentration is on legs, hips, ankles, and knees. Many people don't realize that success on defense can be measured by who can get from here to there—even just a three-yard radius—the fastest. So players have to be very quick, in control, and ready to deliver a blow. It's a game of short bursts, and our training works toward that. There is also a great deal of running, the buildup of speed and coordination and, in many cases, simply teaching guys how to run. We also have nutritionists who work with players who have to learn how to eat to keep their strength at the maximum while controlling the percentage of body fat. That all takes place in the off season.

Coach Belichick allowed me to work with the strength and conditioning coaches half a day, so I was there every day watching the guys work out, and I could see the changes. For example, Tom Brady went from being a slow-footed quarterback when he began doing the drills to doing them deftly by the time the program ended. He also bulked up and got stronger. He was one of the guys who benefited most from the conditioning program, and while we didn't know it then, we would all reap the rewards of his progress during the season.

Having so many guys attend voluntarily also builds camaraderie. Many of the players were taking trips together on weekends, then talking about it when they returned. It helped the veterans get to know the new guys, and also helped the newcomers become accustomed to our system. After the workouts the players would talk to the coaches about responsibilities and also become used to the verbiage that we would be using. It was all preparation for the season, and these guys wanted to do it. All it takes is a couple of leaders to show the way. If one player told the others, "Hey, I had a great meeting with Pepper," the next thing I knew there were three or four guys in my office.

There were also some individuals looking toward 2001 to make up for things that had happened the year before. Ty Law, our cornerback who broke into the starting lineup his rookie year of 1995, was suspended the last game of the 2000 season. It was an embarrassing situation for him, and he came in determined to make amends. After the fifteenth game at Buffalo, there was a bad snowstorm, and some of the guys didn't want to get on the plane home. Terry Glenn was one who didn't like flying. Ty and Troy Brown didn't want to get on the plane either. So Coach Belichick said they could take a limo. Anyway, they decided to take a little detour through Canada. On the way back into the States, something questionable was found in Ty's travel bag, which he had recently loaned to a cousin. U.S. customs officials detained them at the border and notified the team. Pending an outcome of an investigation, the team suspended Ty for the final game of the season.

I remember Ty looking me in the face and admitting he had made a mistake by not checking the bag after it was returned to him. He was really upset with himself, and he said to me that guys were talking down to him, saying that money had gone to his head. He knew he hadn't had a good year in 2000, and now he had something to prove off the field as well as on it. I enjoyed hearing that from him because I could tell he was sincere. I couldn't know how well he would play, but I felt he was going to be a lot better than he'd been in 2000. He came back in better shape and went on to have a Pro Bowl season.

Of course, the way I look at it is that none of it should have happened. Why would a player at the top of his game get to a point where he just allowed his game to slip? I guess sometimes it does take a slap in the face, an eye-opener, to make him want to reach back and regain his status, both on his team and within the league. There are people who can't turn the switch like that, but Ty knew that he was being given a second chance, that if he didn't play well he would be benched. That's the kind of messages I was talking about, the kind Belichick sent when he picked up Terrance Shaw and Terrell Buckley, both cornerbacks. Ty knew his starting job was on the line.

Keeping jobs was probably the main reason guys were determined to get better in the off season. By the time training camp officially started, the coaches were feeling good about the things that were happening. I remember Rob Ryan telling me he had felt a lot more relaxed coming into this training camp than last, because he now fully understood the Belichick system. The players felt more comfortable with the heightened competition level and were already pushing each other harder. Ty Law who, as I said, had something to prove, was doing his conditioning test and looking back at guys, urging them on. That was the kind of key ingredient that had been missing the year before.

Then, just before June mini-camp began, something happened that at the time must have seemed like a joke to all those who were there. Was I kidding or just trying to bail out a friend? I'll let you decide. It took place at the Fox-woods Resort and Casino in Connecticut. Tony Saragusa, the All-Pro defensive tackle of the Super Bowl champion Baltimore Ravens, has a golf tournament every year. It's called the Tony Saragusa Celebrity Golf Classic, with all proceeds going to charitable organizations such as the Make-a-Wish Foundation, Grant-a-Wish Foundation, and the Ed Block Courage House, which helped underprivileged kids.

Saragusa had his coaches there, as well as a couple of teammates and some guests. We were at the party at Foxwoods the night before the golf tournament began. I was at the table with Rob Ryan, my fellow coach; Rob's father, Buddy Ryan, who was a former NFL head coach; Buddy's other son, Rex, Rob's twin brother and the defensive line coach of the Ravens; and a couple of other Ravens coaches. Now Buddy Ryan is the best. I love the guy. In fact, he's one of the few coaches I wish I could have played for, a guy not everyone always understood. Anyway, Buddy gets this thing started. He says, "Look around this table. There's only one oddball here. Everyone has a Super Bowl ring but one guy." Then I hear Rob go, "Oooooohhhh." Buddy had one from his days with the '85 Bears and another going back to the 1969 Joe Namath–led Jets, who defeated the Baltimore Colts in that monumental upset in Super Bowl III. I had a couple from the Giants. Rex and the other Ravens were picking theirs up the next week. That left Rob as the only one without a ring.

He had to be used to his father kidding with him that way, but I didn't want to let it go. I said, "That's all right, Rob-O. Next year when we sit at this table, everybody's gonna have a Super Bowl ring. We'll all have rings. Now we'll be in the same boat as they were. When we sit at Goose's table again, we'll be about a week away from getting our rings." But I don't think a single person at that table took me seriously when I said it.

Training camp can tell a lot about a team, about its spirit, its toughness, its camaraderie, its desire to win. In all my football life, starting in the ninth grade, I have never been around a team in summer camp where there wasn't a fight between players . . . that is, until I joined the Patriots' training camp in 2000. There wasn't a single fight—no pushing, shoving, no pissing contests. I'm not a big fighter, but because of the heat, the constant contact, a guy trying to cheat a drill, somebody loud-mouthing, everyone fighting for jobs, there's always a fight. Yet we went through the whole training camp without one altercation. It might seem insignificant, but it showed the character of the team. There weren't enough mean streaks; there weren't enough guys hitting other guys in the mouth.

In 2001 I noticed one difference right away. The players were a little more relaxed on the outside, yet I saw that the competition was up, saw guys motivating each other, and there were a couple of fights as well as a lot of pushing. I said, "Yeah, this is a training camp." Of course, the fights don't last long. Guys might make threats, not talk to each other for a practice or two, then they forget about it. Everyone knows that you can't let something get in the way of the team. We're professionals. In fact, the majority of time the fights at practice are awkward, almost a joke. When you see the tapes at night meetings, everybody laughs. Even the guys who were in the fight will laugh eventually. It happens in the heat of battle, but it also has to end quickly. Everyone knows they have a job to do and the real enemy will appear once the season starts.

There were other signs that things were going to be different in 2001. As I said, I watched guys like Tom Brady get better during the off-season conditioning program. Then at camp, a guy like Kevin Faulk, who had been reluctant even to talk to Coach Belichick or offensive coordinator Charlie Weis the year before, was now more confident in his position. He felt he had a chance to play and show his stuff. Guys like that now had more of a comfort zone with Belichick.

We were finally starting to become the kind of football team I wanted to see, being physical and getting leadership. Both Ty Law and Lawyer Milloy had shoulder surgery at the start of the off season. Because they were rehabbing their injuries, they had to skip passing camps and mini-camps. They didn't want to be reinjured, but Coach Belichick had asked them to come in early, to be in camp with the rookies, and they were there. All teams don't do that, but Belichick wanted them in for their leadership qualities and their attitude. It helps build character. If the young guys see a Ty Law and Lawyer Milloy in camp, they know we mean business.

The coach has this tackling drill, where he sets up a couple of cones, maybe fifteen yards apart. Then he'll set up two more, twenty to twenty-five yards away and also fifteen yards apart. It's for the offensive skills guys—running backs, wide receivers, and tight ends—matched up with defensive backs and linebackers. The drill begins by having one guy start from one end, another guy from the other end. Whoever has the ball has to try to get past the defender while staying within the fifteen-yard boundary. So Ty and Lawyer came in early, and right away they're doing the drills. Lawyer is more vocal, and sometimes he likes to complain. He has it down to a science. Some guys, for instance, complain and don't work hard. Lawyer is one of those guys who complains and still goes full tilt. I always say guys like this just like to hear themselves talk. So he's complaining about the drill, but he lines up, knocks the hell out of the guy with the ball, causing a fumble, picks the ball up, and spikes it as hard as he can. The next day he didn't have to do the drill anymore. Both he and Ty were ready, and everyone else had seen it.

In training camp we also work extremely hard on our special teams. Coach Belichick feels that special teams are the heart of the game, and they always take precedence with him. Strong special teams play can change the strategy of the game, both offensively and defensively. It's a matter of field position, and it can hamper or help you tremendously. If you consistently keep a team backed up in its own end of the field, it applies pressure. So he's always looking for guys who can do a lot of things. If a guy is a big hitter and can play on defense, but can't help on special teams, he may not make the ball club. Belichick's thinking is that the more guys you have on the team who *can't* play special teams, the more guys you need who can play *only* special teams.

Mike Vrabel, Tedy Bruschi, Roman Phifer—they all played on special teams as well as their regular positions. Patrick Pass made the team because of his special teams play, then became our backup fullback. Linebacker Larry Izzo made the Pro Bowl with the Dolphins in 2000 as a special teams player. When they didn't re-sign him, we scooped him up fast, projecting him as a special teams player. It's like keeping a caged tiger in the house. He's a small guy but a dynamo, very physical, and he wants to play. Coach Belichick felt his most valuable attribute was his special teams play, and he became the special teams captain. Je'Rod Cherry is another guy who's very physical and may be our second-best special teams guy. The philosophy is to have as many guys as possible who can contribute in more than one way.

While it may sound as if we were taking a smooth ride during training camp, moving steadily toward the start of the season, nothing could be further from the truth. Early in training camp the team was touched by a tragedy that could really have set us back. Our quarterbacks coach, Dick Rehbein, was an NFL veteran, having served as an assistant with several teams. Soon after he came over from the Giants before the start of the 2000 season, he became a very popular figure in camp. Drew was already very close to him after just one year, and he was working with Tom Brady all the time. Coach Rehbein had a quiet style but got the job done. After the first week of practice the team had the weekend off, then returned to prepare to practice against the Giants, who were coming up to our facility. Just forty-five years old and seemingly very fit, Coach Rehbein was working out on a treadmill at one of the local athletic facilities when he collapsed.

At the hospital they began running tests to see if he was fit to return to camp. Shortly after the tests he collapsed again and died. He had had some heart problems in the past, but no one had expected this. It was a devastating blow to the coaching staff and the entire team. Coach Belichick immediately called off practice and the team meetings that day. The coaching staff always had night meetings, but now it was hard to jump back in. Some of the coaches had been very close to Dick, and we all felt terrible for his wife and two daughters. It's a funny thing about timing. Had it happened a week earlier, I don't know how we would have responded, don't know if Coach Belichick would have been able to pull everyone together. It was a very difficult situation for him.

The head coach has a job to do, getting his team ready for the season. At the same time, you have to be respectful. It was impossible to disregard the fact that we had a coach who was no longer there. There's no way you can go back immediately to the way it was, guys shouting, cheering for each other, and being rah-rah. Yet we are professional athletes and coaches, and because we're also entertainers the show must go on. With the Giants coming to town to practice with us, we had to be ready. So once we got back to practice, we worked hard preparing for the Giants. It was probably easier to get the wheels back with another team coming in than if it had just been us. Then, before the joint practices started, we had a kind of memorial service at a church with both teams participating. The service was called A Celebration of the Life of Dick Rehbein. The Giants' veteran tight end Howard Cross had been very close to Dick, knew him better than any of us, and he spoke wonderfully about him. He told some stories that made the family smile—and a lot of us as well. Drew had to follow, and it was very difficult for him. I'm sure there were some guys too upset even to speak.

From that day on, Charlie Weis would always be sure to remind everyone that Coach Rehbein was still looking down on us, and when a break went our way, he'd say that the coach had something to do with it. Still, it's never something you are ready for. No one expects to lose a young coach and a friend like that. It affected the entire team and, I think, brought us all a little closer together. There was no time to hire another quarterbacks coach and teach him the system, so Belichick and Coach Weis had to assume the job. That was simply the best way to do it without taking a step backward.

A second bump in the road involved Terry Glenn, our star receiver who had caught ninety passes as a rookie in 1996 and was already the team's fourth all-time leading pass catcher. He had been hurt a couple of years after that, but in 2000 he started all sixteen games and had his second-best season, with seventy-nine receptions and six touchdowns. In 2001 he came to training camp ready to go. The way he looked during the first few days of practice, a lot of people thought Terry might catch a hundred passes in the upcoming season. Then, however, a problem arose with his contract, and as soon as he heard about it from his agent he began to slow down and start complaining about his leg bothering him and that he couldn't practice. That was the start of it.

I can't really blame him for his actions. I think he just got into a trap. Whoever was advising him, whoever was closest to him simply didn't paint a clear picture and maybe not the right picture. With Terry rebelling the way he did, it really hurt him more than anyone else. It can't hurt the organization. That's impossible. In this case the fight was between the Patriots and Terry Glenn. After the one incident occurred, more fuel began being thrown on the fire. There was a domestic situation during the off season between him and the mother of his daughter. Though the charges were allegedly dropped, the whole thing was dredged up again in the press. There was also an incident in 1999 when he was pulled over for DUI. The league put him on probation, and they also told him they would be administering random alcohol tests. These are not standard drug tests, simply a random test for alcohol use. Terry spends the off season in Ohio, and the way I understand it, he simply wasn't around several times when they came to administer the test. In fact he actually hadn't taken one for several years.

Oddly enough, after the contract dispute the random test situation cropped up again. League rules equate not taking the test with failing it, and suddenly the rule was evoked. Because he hadn't been taking the test, the league suspended him for the first four games of the season. Once he heard news of the suspension, he left training camp almost immediately. By this time everything was so ugly and out of control that he didn't really want to come back. The team thought about adding to his suspension, but the league insisted he be reinstated after four games. If there was a problem after that, anything considered as conduct detrimental to the team, the Patriots had the option of suspending him once again. He was one of our starting receivers, and suddenly his status was uncertain, the kind of situation that easily could have demoralized the team.

Lawyer was the one who squashed it early. He called the guys together and said that Terry was going through his thing and no one else had any control over it whatsoever. "We have to prepare as if he isn't going to be here," Lawyer told the team. "We don't want to talk about it anymore, don't want to address it. If you keep talking about it, it will just drag on. If no one comments, then we won't have to worry about it. We love Terry, and we hope he's here, but that's it." The media kept bringing it up, almost as if they would have liked to divide our locker room, but the guys stayed strong.

Coach Belichick also did a great job addressing it, treating it as if it were contract negotiations and letting everyone know the team had to go on, with or without him. Not surprisingly, the reporters in other cities continued to bring it up throughout the year, always asking, "What about Terry Glenn? What about Terry Glenn?" By then, however, we were strong enough to deal with it and not let it affect or distract us. So, in a real sense, the things that we went through during training camp just toughened us up for what would happen during the season.

Whenever there was a problem, the coaches and veteran leaders would step up to the plate. When Lawyer talks, it's cut-and-dried. Everyone knows where he's coming from. Without that kind of leadership locker rooms can be divided, but the unity we fostered in training camp and during the preseason would help us diffuse potential problems later in the year as well. The precedents set at the beginning carry over to the end. There is no room for thin skin. The players have to be tough, not touchy, and they can't be too sensitive. It's easy to be positive when you win, but lose a couple of games and it's tougher. We learned to respond to everything, from Terry's situation to losing Coach Rehbein to the veteran players released before the season and then to the problems that cropped up during the season. Guys have to realize this is a business, and no matter what uniform you're wearing, it shouldn't change who you are on the inside.

Signing new players and free agents can sometimes be more complicated than it appears. That's because occasionally you have a player with his own agenda, and you spend time talking with him, looking at him, trying to decide whether to make him an offer, while all the time he really has no intentions of signing. A lot of big-name free agents, such as Reggie White and Deion Sanders, would actually make tours around the league, giving all kinds of reasons why they didn't want to play here or there, all the while trying to up the ante with the teams in which they really have interest. We ran into that situation prior to the 2001 season with Tracy Scroggins, a defensive end with the

Detroit Lions. We needed an outside pass rusher and felt he might be a good fit. What we didn't know was that he would turn out to be the perfect example of a guy using free agency as a tool to get a team to up the ante.

So he came ostensibly to look at us, and I took him out, figuring I could relate to him because I knew what he had gone through, being with a team that wasn't winning and nearing the end of his career. I felt it might be time for him to leave. Mike Compton had been with the Lions, had seen the window of opportunity, and decided to sign with us, but I would find out that Tracy Scroggins was using both me and the Patriots just to get the Detroit Lions to keep him. His home was there, and he stayed. As it would turn out, he missed a chance to go to the Super Bowl and stayed with a rebuilding team that would win just a single game. I could see what was happening there, that they were bringing in new linemen for the purpose of rebuilding and that it might be a good time for him to move on.

Unfortunately, none of us has a crystal ball. If he had known his team would be 1–15 and he wouldn't play that much, he might have looked at it differently. Instead of going through a season like that, he could have been our third-down specialist and helped win a Super Bowl. That's essentially what we wanted him for. Once you get a label with the league, however, it's hard to shake it off. That's what Tracy Scroggins added to his résumé by doing what he did, trying to negotiate with the Detroit Lions through other teams. Now it will be difficult to get teams to take him seriously. Opportunities just don't come to your door looking like a wise old man with a white beard. You've got to know when to step through that door. Other guys did that as well, turning their backs on the Patriots because they didn't expect us to do what we did.

This year it will be different. A lot more people will be coming in and looking at us more seriously. They know Coach Belichick is going to play his best players to win. They also know he's a coach who tried not to have huge salary gaps. It's very hard in this league to get a guy working for $350,000 to perform when he's watching the guy who's getting paid $10 million practicing like his shit don't stink, or throwing interceptions, or fumbling the ball. Then you wind up with a team where everyone is worrying about the next man's money.

The funny thing was that after signing our free agents and throughout training camp the media was killing Belichick for trying to win with a bunch of misfits. Roman Phifer, for example, had never been in a single playoff game through his ten-year career. He left the Rams, and, bang, they went to the Super Bowl. Then he joined the Jets the year after they went to the AFC title game, and they didn't make the playoffs for the next two years. When he came here, guys were kidding him about being a walking jinx. I remember telling him how I had been to the playoffs where my teams had won the Super Bowl or lost before getting there. Losing is no fun. I would rather not go to the playoffs and lose. After the 2001 season, Phifer looked at me and said, "Pep, you were right. It was worth the wait."

The final piece in putting together the puzzle for the new season is the draft. You're always looking for impact players, but you also want to fill needs that weren't completely filled by free agency. At draft time we were still not sure about how things with Ty Law would pan out. He had filed a grievance with the Players' Association over his suspension and didn't want to pay the fine. Mr. Kraft filed a countergrievance trying to get back part of his signing bonus. Eventually the two worked it out, but before training camp Ty was on the bubble, walking on thin ice. One wrong move and he could have been gone. At the same time, the team didn't want to draft a cornerback on the first or second round, which is why they went out and got Terrell Buckley and Terrance Shaw. That was enough to put plenty of pressure on Ty, and, at the same time, we all knew both Buckley and Shaw could play.

So our first choice in the draft was Richard Seymour, a defensive tackle from Georgia, the sixth player taken overall. In the second round we took Matt Light, an offensive lineman from Purdue; in the third Brock Williams, a cornerback from Notre Dame; and in the fourth another offensive lineman, Kenyatta Jones. We felt we were weak at tight end, so we picked Jabari Holloway, also in the fourth round, and Arther Love in the sixth round. We even took a kicker, Owen Pochman, in the seventh round. That might seem strange, at first, because we had Adam Vinatieri, but he was in the last year of his contract, and negotiations weren't going too well. So Belichick wanted to apply some pressure. Basically his aim was to create competition at any position where he felt it was necessary.

As it turned out, Seymour and Light both contributed, as did cornerback Leonard Myers, our sixth-round pick. Brock Williams and Arther Love ended up on injured reserve, while Jabari Holloway was also hurt a good part of the year. Vinatieri, of course, became our kicker once again and would play a huge role in the season to come. So all in all, it was a very good draft. Seymour started out slowly, held back by a combination of acclimating to the pro game and pulling a hamstring late in the preseason. As the season progressed, however, he became stronger. It's usually the opposite with rookies. They tend to fade a bit with the longer NFL season, but Seymour would wind up making the All-Rookie Team, which meant he was an impact guy. That's what you're trying to do when a team has one of the first ten picks in the draft—get at least one impact guy.

So there was a great deal of competition during training camp. We had our roster but didn't yet have all the starters or the rotation that we would use. For example, J. R. Redmond, who had been a rookie in 2000, was listed as the starter at running back, but the team had signed Antowain Smith from Buffalo in the off season. They were alternating early, and it was J.R.'s position to lose, but in the end it's the best guy who plays. You always hear coaches talking about putting the best eleven guys on the field, but a lot of them don't. Belichick does. There are all kinds of factors when he makes a choice. One guy might have more raw talent than the other, but his game-time thought process might be slower. In the end he might not be the best guy to have on the field, despite his talent. There may be another guy who's a great practice player, great in the classroom, but there are guys who are simply better in a game. They play.

I think that overall philosophy really hit home before the start of the 2001 season. Even though there was fierce competition, the situation built camaraderie and actually made the guys comfortable. Everyone pretty much played to some extent. We went into training camp with Ty Law, Otis Smith, and Terrell Buckley rotating at corner. It was mainly Otis and Terrell fighting for the position, but if Ty had slipped, he would have been out of there. As it was, all three played and contributed. Other teams may rotate defensive linemen, but I don't see them rotating much with linebackers and safeties. We rotated everyone. Even Ty rotated somewhat during the year. Lawyer Milloy was the only guy on defense who didn't rotate all season. He came out only when we were way ahead or he had to tie his shoe.

Belichick's system really made everyone feel they were part of the team. Creating intense competition paid dividends. Guys performed at such a high level in training camp that Coach Belichick couldn't stop a Matt Stevens from alternating with Tebucky Jones at free safety. Stevens simply had an outstanding preseason. Buckley was breathing down Otis's neck. Free agents Mike Vrabel and Roman Phifer really shocked the coaches, playing a lot better than we thought they would when we signed them. Vrabel, for instance, was never a starter with Pittsburgh, but as soon as we signed him he was told he was the starting outside linebacker and it was his position to lose. In training camp there wasn't anyone close. Phifer was brought in for leadership and experience. At the beginning we rotated him because of his knees, but the more he played, the better the entire defense played, and by the end of the season he was like Lawyer—he never came off the field. Plus those guys both played special teams and contributed that way as well.

When the Giants came to town during training camp, and just after Coach Rehbein's death, I think a lot of the guys started waking up to what was beginning to happen. The Giants had been the best team in the NFC the season before, coming off a Super Bowl loss, and we saw right away what we were doing to them in practice. A lot of them were still walking around cocky, acting like prima donnas, practicing in the morning but not the afternoon. We could see their practice habits and that they simply weren't doing what we were trying to do in preparing for the season. It was almost as if they were on cruise control. I had learned a long time ago that you can't cut the hunger on and off; you have to be hungry all the time. So even though they were taking it easy in practice, we weren't. We figured they were here to give us a look.

The funny part was that we went on to beat them in our first preseason game, 14–0, and I remember Michael Strahan, their All-Pro defensive end, saying in a TV interview during Super Bowl week that he didn't think we would do that well because he remembered that week they practiced with us at training camp and didn't think our offensive line was that good. Everyone I spoke with who heard that interview laughed. The joke was on Strahan. We probably had all our backup guys practicing against them that week, so he didn't know who the hell he was practicing against. He's a great guy, but he really put his foot in his mouth with that one. There were just a lot of injuries before that week, and most of our regulars saw very little action. In fact, Mike Compton pulled a calf muscle then and missed the rest of training camp.

I know I've been talking a great deal about our defense so far, and I guess that's understandable. I was a defensive player, and now I'm a defensive coach.

Those are my guys, especially the linebackers, but it's really all of them since the linebackers are just part of the whole. I fully believe in the old saying "Offense sells tickets but defense wins championships." Still, the Patriots did a lot of work offensively in camp, and I should talk about it some.

Anytime you play where the weather changes and gets cold late in the season, you have to have a running game. At the same time, if you can get short productive passes, and have skilled people on offense who can catch and run, you're ahead of the game. In fact, catching and running are the secrets of the so-called West Coast offense, which has gotten so much play the last few years. When you run that kind of offense, all the quarterbacks are going to have high passing percentages. The only time their percentage goes down is when they get outside the offense and begin throwing deeper passes. Yet the West Coast offense will always have a receiver who can go deep.

What Charlie Weis does is try to keep you on your toes and spread the ball around as much as possible. He does it with a running attack that will run at you and around you with counterplays and draws. He will change personnel; in fact he's notorious for it. He'll go from three wide receivers to four, two halfbacks, one tailback, two or three tight ends. Week by week he tries to stay away from normal tendencies, except for the bread-and-butter plays. He does a great job that way. During the off season we knew we needed additional receivers to complement Terry Glenn and Troy Brown. We weren't looking for someone to beat those guys out, but because Troy is so valuable on special teams and as a return man, we wanted a guy who could take some plays from him on regular downs and on third downs or to run combination routes with him where the defense has to respect both.

During the off season we picked up Bert Emanuel, Charles Johnson, and Torrance Small. Emanuel was a speed guy, Johnson a possession-type receiver, while Torrance was a big guy who could do a little of both. A guy like that can hurt a defense when they begin worrying about the other receivers, but Torrance had an injury during the preseason, and it carried over. He played hurt but never really overcame it. Though I believe he stopped playing in week three or four, he will still get a ring, because he helped tremendously. He had good knowledge of the game, was a great person, and the kind of guy who got along with everyone and never created problems.

Then, when Terry Glenn's status became uncertain, David Patten emerged as an outstanding replacement. When Terry left camp, that pushed either Patten or Bert Emanuel into a starting role immediately, so now there was no one to take plays off Troy. He had to be in there, and the battle had to answer the question of who would be on the other side. Bert started off there but just wasn't the guy. We ended up releasing him after the fourth week because he simply just wasn't productive enough. David Patten, on the other hand, was in the Vrabel and Phifer category. He hadn't made an impact with either the Giants or Browns, his former teams, and was often injured in the past. So the feeling was that the more he played, the more likely he would get hurt. Glenn would come back for one game, but after that Patten stepped up and there was no looking back. He proved himself to have toughness and the ability to break down zones, the same qualities that made Troy Brown so great.

We opened the preseason schedule with that 14–0 win against the Giants at Foxboro, then traveled to Ericsson Stadium to play against the Carolina Panthers, a team we were also scheduled to play in the second game of the regular season. Because we were going to play them again so soon, it became a bit tricky. You want to have a good outing, but you don't want to show them too much. At the same time, you know you've got to throw some passes, keep tuning up the running game, begin to let Antowain get his legs under him. We won it, 23–8, with the fourth-string guys giving up a touchdown late in the game. At this point there were still young guys trying to make the final squad, while the veterans were getting their reps and looks, getting ready for the season in their own way. I think the solid outing was also the result of the kind of competition for spots that Coach Belichick had set up early in training camp.

Then there was a setback. Ideally, in the third preseason game, you want to start building the character of your team. By that time there should be a strong sense of who is going to start on both offense and defense. Instead of all those positive things coming out of the game, we ended up going to Tampa and losing badly to the Buccaneers, 20–3. It was such a bad outing that it sent us back to the drawing board. Not only did the offense fail to produce a touchdown, but the defense didn't get it done either. Tampa Bay was a team that many thought to be a possible Super Bowl contender, and Coach Belichick wanted to beat them. In fact, they had also beaten us badly the previous year in the preseason, and he wanted to see how the team would respond. The result was tantamount to disaster, and that's why we were all sent back to the drawing board. Tampa Bay was considered, at least in our eyes, a better team than either the Giants or Carolina, and we didn't look good. From a coaching standpoint you can't command your team to go out and put a better foot on the field. If we wanted to be a contender, this was the type of team we had to go out and beat. Maybe if the Bucs had still won, but the game was close, we could have handled it. It was a situation where we wanted to measure the character and attitude of our team in preseason against a high-caliber team like Tampa Bay, and we didn't show up.

It's always tough after the third preseason game and kind of scary for the head coach. This is when a team traditionally breaks camp and moves into its own stadium. I always felt a team lost some focus during this particular week. The young players who made the team, as well as the free agents, are worrying about where they'll live. Many of the players' wives come into town during this week, cars are being shipped up, guys are moving stuff out of their dorm rooms at training camp. It might sound minor, but it's all a distraction. A lot of teams just go through the motions before the final preseason game, another dangerous thing as far as I'm concerned, because there's a greater chance for injuries when you don't go full speed. It was important to us for another reason. We had Washington coming to Foxboro, and the team was coming off a terrible game at Tampa Bay. We had to start righting the ship.

Suddenly practice became more intense. Since the Giants game the first week of the preseason, we had been light on full pads, maybe just practicing with them two or three times a week. Now we were back with pads every day. Then one night when the team was scheduled for a meeting, Coach Belichick surprised us by canceling the meeting and informing us that we were going to a movie. He took the whole team, all the players and coaches, to an Imax Cinema at a mall in Providence where we saw the film about Ernest Shackleton, who took an expedition to Antarctica in 1915 only to have his ship, the *Endurance*, become trapped in solid ice and eventually break up and sink. Shackleton and a few of his men made an eight-hundred-mile journey in a twenty-foot boat, finally reaching a whaling station at South Georgia Island. They then sent rescue teams for the rest of his men. In the end, fifty-three of the fifty-six men on the expedition survived.

No one will ever confuse Bill Belichick with Knute Rockne. He doesn't scream and yell or give dramatic, emotional speeches. He made it short and brief, equating the film to football in that it showed what people can accomplish if they work together. When we were leaving the theater, he had everyone talking about it. Some of the guys understood the point; others didn't realize it at the time and just watched it for entertainment. Everyone, however, had a reaction to it and was still kidding about it at practice the next day, making wisecracks and calling each other Shackleton. The funny part was—and I don't know whether Belichick was a prophet or what—that it paid off in a strange kind of way when we ended up playing the Raiders in the snow. The guys immediately remembered the Shackleton film, and I think it was a confidence builder for us because the snow brought it all back. We wanted the snow and began hoping that the Raiders would come to town in a blizzard. I remember when we were warming up that day, guys were saying, "If Shackleton can do it, so can we." It had definitely stayed with us in the backs of our minds and gave us a push. That's just another example of how important the mental aspect of the game can be.

Anyway, after we broke camp and went over to the stadium, we had a full-tilt practice every day. The whip started to crack on the coaches, and then it went down to the players. In addition, there was another cut coming to get down to the sixty-three or sixty-four players before the final preseason game. So there were tight-assed coaches and worried players. The fortunate part was that we beat up on the Redskins pretty bad, winning 33–14 and, more important, implementing a physical game that we hadn't really seen in the preseason. No team wants to go into the regular season coming off back-to-back losses, so in that sense we ended the preseason on a good note.

But that didn't stop Coach Belichick from pulling out the whip. I went to some of the older guys who might not have been around him before and told them if they didn't know him, they had just gotten a sample of what it would be like. If they performed the way they had against Tampa Bay, I told them, the coach would work their tails off. If they performed the way they had against the Giants and Washington, he would chill a little bit.

One thing I strongly believe is that there is only a fine line between talent on all the teams in the league. The separation comes from attitude, the mental aspect of the game. There is always a difference in attitude between the elite teams, the contenders, and the teams full of guys just collecting paychecks. There is a huge difference between, say, the Detroit Lions and the St. Louis Rams or Pittsburgh Steelers. There is an aura of confidence, so much cockiness, in fact, with the Rams and Steelers that it's mind-blowing. With a team like the Lions you might have a couple of players who believe, but deep down in the subconscious of the majority a similar thought is always lurking beneath the surface: How are we gonna lose this ball game? The cocky teams will win some games where they don't play that well and could have lost. Conversely, the team that doesn't fully believe in itself from top to bottom will wind up having problems and losing games a lot of people thought they should win.

There is one final thing that I want to mention before we get into the regular season. Belichick always allowed the players to vote for the captains on offense, defense, and special teams. At the end of camp we took the vote. Lawyer Milloy and Bryan Cox were chosen as defensive captains, Drew Bledsoe and Troy Brown were named offensive captains, and Larry Izzo was chosen captain of special teams. Larry and Bryan I can sum up together and very easily. Both of those guys were free agents who came from other teams. Larry signed in March, so he had time to meet and mingle with the other players, let them see firsthand the type of player he was and the kind of character he had. It's really a feather in his cap that he made the kind of immediate impact to have guys vote him captain his first year with the team.

Same thing with Cox. He didn't come in until training camp, but the inspiration and input he gave everyone during the four weeks of camp was absolutely remarkable—to make such an incredible first impression to be named captain is nothing short of amazing. Then there was Troy Brown. One of the things that we, as a coaching staff, knew we needed was someone else besides Drew to step up offensively and help lead the team. It was a unanimous choice among the coaches that it should be Troy, and the players agreed. No one actually said that it would be a plus if he stepped up and took the offense by its horns, but he must have felt it, and he did. He doesn't talk much, just leads by example—probably the best way—and everyone loves him. Drew, of course, was the quarterback and had been a leader for several years. Everyone knows how much the quarterback means to the team. As for Lawyer, the guy wants to win as badly as anyone, and he never comes off the field. It's just a natural for him to be a captain.

So coming into the season, I think there was a lot of confidence on our part, despite the press and media saying we would be lucky to get to .500. I was panicking a bit because I didn't think every stone had been turned, but that's just me. For example, we were opening in Cincinnati against the Bengals, and I knew our defense couldn't take them for granted, especially the way Corey Dillon runs the football. Opening day isn't easy, because you have to get all the final cuts done, then prepare for the game. Even though we weren't going into the opening game at full strength, we still felt we were going to be a strong team, one capable of winning ten or eleven games. However, we didn't have the same confidence going into the opener that we would have had if all the starters on our offensive line had been healthy. We also had a couple of guys—McGinest and Seymour—banged up on the defensive unit.

All in all, we thought we were a better team than we had been in 2000, but we had battled our share of adversity in the preseason and felt that no matter what the outcome on opening day, we still weren't cooking on all cylinders. Everything was upbeat the first days of training camp, but at the end we had some wounded soldiers, enough to keep us from getting a fast start. If a team considers itself a playoff contender, they certainly don't want to suddenly wake up in week ten, find they're struggling to reach .500, and have only a slim chance to make it as a wild card. So a good start is important, especially for a team that still hadn't found that swagger, that aura of confidence. You have to earn the right to have that.

2

A Game of Transitions

Making the transition from player to coach isn't always easy. Fortunately I was able to call upon my many years of personal experience, which made things go smoothly. I retired as a player at the end of the 1998 season. After thirteen seasons the Jets weren't going to re-sign me. Bill Parcells was the coach then, and he didn't deliver the news to me personally, but I had been around long enough to have expected it. In reality I had been planning to retire before I came to the Jets, but Parcells and Belichick, who was his defensive coordinator, really seemed to want me to come over and help them set up their defense. Because of our long association with the Giants, they knew I was totally familiar with their system and knew it would help the team to have me aboard. So many people still associate me with Parcells, but I was really closer to Belichick, and he was actually the one who asked me to come back. The year I played in Cleveland when he was head coach really took our relationship over the top.

When I first joined the Giants in 1986, Coach Belichick was the linebackers coach as well as defensive coordinator, so he really had more input and influence on me than Parcells did. We had many long conversations about defense and about the game, and he was really my coach. That doesn't mean Parcells wasn't an influence and an imposing, larger-than-life figure. He had a very close relationship with a lot of his players, but I think my relationship with him suffered when he asked me to be a friend as well as a player-coach and I told him I didn't think it was a good idea. He already had that kind of relationship with guys like George Martin, Harry Carson, and even Lawrence Taylor (or as he's more affectionately known, LT) to a degree. He related to them more as a friend than as a coach, talked to them a lot about nonfootball subjects, and with them it apparently worked. I know that George Martin, for instance, always credited Parcells with helping him deal with life in general and especially life after football. You would often see them talking, even during practice. That's what he seemed to want with me, and, in all honesty, I'm probably the only person who ever responded to him in a negative way. My response, however, would be the same today, and I'll tell you why.

I know myself. Parcells always said he understood where I came from and where I grew up, that he understood inner-city kids, but I always felt you have to have lived it to fully understand it. If he was my buddy as well as my coach, our overall relationship might have suffered. If a buddy of mine, for instance, screams at me for something, I'm going to react, scream back at him. That's how we always were, and I knew if Parcells screamed at me under those circumstances my response would have been to scream back.

Maybe screaming back would be inappropriate, but I just felt that I would rather keep it strictly player and coach. Some people have said it was immature of me to think like that, but the more I look at it, the more mature the decision seems, at least for me.

In fact, there had already been an instance when I did scream back at him. It was probably one of the scariest moments of my life, and it came in my rookie year when we were playing the Chargers early in the season. I had only a few games under my belt and as I was coming off the field, Parcells started screaming at me for missing a block. Suddenly it just came out. "I didn't miss my fucking block," I said. He yelled back, "Yes, you did!" By then all my defensive teammates were looking at me as if to say "What the hell did you just do?" Then I thought, Wow, I'm talking to the head coach, and I'm cursing back at him. I played the rest of the game as if I were numb. Because of where it was located, Parcells had a habit of sitting on my stool in the locker room before we went in to meetings. The next day I turned the corner and there he was. He got up and gave me that trademark look, then asked to talk with me. I thought I was really gonna get it good, maybe be benched or worse. Instead he apologized, because he had seen the tapes and knew that I had gotten my man. No missed block. Then he told me not to blow up at him like that again and just walked away. Because he had handled it that way, my respect for him just skyrocketed. A head coach didn't have to do that, didn't have to apologize. I was just a rookie, and he apologized, so now I was kicking myself in the ass for reacting that way.

The point of the story is that when he proposed that we have more than a player-coach relationship, that incident was the first thing that came to mind and a big reason for why I responded the way I did. Looking back now, I might have had a better relationship with him if I hadn't refused him, but I'm the kind of guy who is always going to say what's on my mind. I knew then I would never have the same kind of relationship with him that Harry, George, LT, and a few others had. I probably would have if I hadn't turned him down. The result was that I never became one of the guys in the family picture, just one of his players. Yet I always watched him carefully over the years and learned that everything was motivation with him. He was always three steps ahead of other coaches with his approach, and some of his speeches, his attacks on players, and his wild flurries were premeditated. He loved to stir things up, always knew how to get under people's skin and how it contributed to winning. That's what always separated him from the rest. Even though his emotions always ran high, he took the time to treat everyone as an individual.

Being a coach now, I can see more clearly many of the things Parcells did. In fact it's also something Coach Belichick does, and I believe it is being done more all around the league—coaches getting to know each player as an individual, knowing who they are and what makes them tick. Coach Belichick, for instance, might not always play the better athlete. If, however, you're a good person and a decent athlete, then he feels he can get that little extra from you and he would rather deal with those attributes than with the guy who feels he's superior. It was sort of the same thing when I look back at the championship teams with the Giants. General Manager George Young certainly had a lot to do with it since he essentially assembled the personnel. We weren't always the most talented, but we *were* the best football team.

Sometimes a player's career takes some strange twists, going in directions he didn't expect and making it necessary for him to adjust. If someone had told me back in 1990 that I would finish my career with the New York Jets, I would have said, "No way." Yet even with free agency evolving, there were a couple of teams that every player felt he couldn't play for. I remember thinking, for example, I could never be a Washington Redskin or a Dallas Cowboy because of the intense rivalry they had with the Giants. Yet two of my good friends,

Steve DeOssie and Everson Walls, both came over to the Giants from the Cowboys. By contrast, I had always dreamed about playing on that Philadelphia Eagles defense behind that great line they had. That's something I would have welcomed. But the Redskins? The Cowboys? The Jets? No way. Lawyer Milloy resented all the former Jets joining the Patriots when Parcells came here and even after Belichick was hired. Same old thing. When you have such an intense rivalry with a team, it's hard. Maybe the classic story of a guy being affected by a rivalry is that of Jackie Robinson. He retired rather than accept a trade to the New York Giants in 1957. The old Brooklyn Dodgers and the Giants fought wars over the years, and Jackie was always right in the middle. He just couldn't see himself wearing that other uniform.

After I joined the Jets, I always looked forward to the annual preseason matchup with the Giants. It was traditionally the third preseason game, just before both teams would break camp, so there were no meetings or curfew that night. I always gave a bowling party for both the Giants and Jets players. In 1997 we beat them, and yet a couple of the Giants still came to the party. Then in '98 the Jets were starting to steal a bit of the Giants' thunder even though they were coming off winning the division. We beat them again in the preseason game, and not a single Giant showed up at the party. That really hurt me. What you have to understand is that New York City belonged to the Giants when I played there. I would go to a Knicks game at Madison Square Garden, and my feet were on the court, but if a Jets player went, chances were he'd be high up in the stands.

I remember calling some of them and saying, flat out, that even though I was playing with the Jets, until we won a Super Bowl New York City still belonged to the Giants. I knew some of their players still looked up to me because I had been a leader with the Giants when they joined the team. They were still my guys, and this is how I had to talk to them. I told them not to play second fiddle to the Jets, not to hand it over, and certainly not to hide. Football, however, is a game of transitions. Something is always changing, and players have to adjust, whether it's a new coach, a new team, or making the decision to retire.

Parcells always said, "Don't walk away from the game feeling bitter." The 1998 season was such a sweet-and-sour year for me. I had suffered the only injury of my career the year before, hurting a knee, and I wanted to come back and play strong. What was disappointing is that they didn't let me do more. You always alternated under Parcells, so I was in and out of the games. I also didn't have a contract for 1999, so the handwriting was on the wall. I pretty much read about it in the papers. No one from the Jets called, which wasn't the way it should be or the way I would have liked it. Now, however, it was time for another decision.

A friend of mine who had been helping me with my contracts began to make some calls. There were a number of players with the Giants who wanted me back there, guys like Keith Hamilton and Jesse Armstead. Both felt the team lacked the veteran player who could help push the younger guys and thought I was that man. I talked to Giants coach Jim Fassel personally, but nothing came of it. I heard later that someone thought I would be a pain in the neck in the locker room, something I hadn't been my entire career. Still, it's always hard to give up the ghost, and I didn't really pack up my cleats then. I worked out during the summer and right into the start of the 1999 season. A couple of guys from the Patriots were talking about bringing me in to help out one of their top draft choices, a linebacker named Andy Katzenmoyer. Hearing that, I worked harder, running more and trying to get into top shape. As I mentioned earlier, you get labels in this league, and by this time I was labeled a Parcells guy. Pete Carroll, who took over for Parcells in New England, didn't want another Parcells guy because he was already hearing enough about trying to fill Parcells's shoes.

The year before, in 1998, I had been part of the CBS television show "The Fifth Quarter," which aired after the eleven o'clock news on Sunday nights. Doing a sports show was always tough after a home game, and away games were even more difficult. When we were on the West Coast, they would tape my segment early, but I enjoyed it. Then, when the Jets didn't renew my contract, CBS put an offer on the table for me to continue with the show. Viacom had purchased CBS that year, and there was a change of producers, so I either had to make a commitment to them or continue to wait for a phone call from another team. There was a third option, as well, and that was coaching.

To be honest, my dream for years—the entire time I was playing—was to someday go back and coach my old high school. So while I was playing I always tried to observe every position and watch for the things the coaches were teaching the respective players at those positions. Defense was easy since I had always played there. Offensively, I tried to get some of the philosophies and techniques the coaches were imparting, as well as getting input from the players themselves. I always observed Phil Simms when he quarterbacked the Giants, watched his movement and technique and how he prepared during the off season. I also talked a great deal with running back O. J. Anderson, who was another cagey veteran and one of the best ball carriers of his era. All of this carried over from watching guys when I worked at football camps in the summer. So I was acquiring information and began to feel as if I had a pretty good football mind.

Slowly I began to think about coaching my own team. I never looked at it from an NFL-only standpoint. In fact the same things that had pushed me out of the league were the things I wasn't sure I could deal with as a coach. I had contemplated retirement after the 1994 season, and it was because of the mentality I saw in the younger players. Fortunately, I was with a pretty good group of young guys then who wanted to learn, and some of the older guys finally settled me down. When I finally came to the Jets, however, I felt I knew too much. I saw higher draft picks who couldn't get it right but who were kept around, while lower choices who had more potential were released if they said a wrong word. It's pretty much that way around the league, the first-round choice and then all the others. I kind of saw myself in the latter category.

That's why I initially thought high school would be the best place for me. Even coaching at the college level, I just didn't think I could do the recruiting, couldn't bring myself to schmooze with high school kids. At least at the high school level you can catch them young enough and maybe be part of the pipeline that eventually sends some guys to the pros. Without a doubt, though, football is my love; football is my heart. When Coach Belichick allowed me to get back into it, I was able to realize all over again how much I love the game, especially when I'm directly involved. So many people were telling me I had a good football mind, that I was wasting it and that I should do something about it. When you hear that repeatedly, it begins to weigh on your mind, and you finally decide to do something about it.

In the summer of 2000 I was in Florida coaching a YMCA youth basketball team, and I could see the positive impact I had with the kids and their parents, as well as the success they were having. I knew Bill Belichick was taking over the Patriots' head coaching job, and something kept telling me, "Call

Belichick. Call Belichick." Finally, I did. At first we played a little phone tag, with me doing more of the tagging than him. He was already extremely busy, but he finally returned my call. I congratulated him and was looking for a way to ask him about the possibility of my coaching when he asked if I could come out for the summer and help with the players, more as a liaison between the coaches and him. I was really choked up to hear him say that and knew immediately I had done the right thing. That was my blessing.

He had done this once before with me, when I was released by the Giants following the 1992 season. He called me to come play for him at Cleveland, where he had been head coach since 1991, and later called again to ask me not to retire but to join him and Parcells with the Jets. Now, for him to respect my knowledge of the game enough to ask me, in essence, to come to New England and help him communicate his system to the other coaches and players was the ultimate compliment, one of the most memorable moments in my career and my life. At first he was asking me to come in just for the summer, but I think all along he knew that if I was around it long enough I was going to stay.

We talked once a week, getting things set up. At the time I was a spokesperson for Minolta and a few other companies and had to decide how to juggle everything. Belichick said if I needed to get away during the season I could, but he was right all along: once I was in, I was in. I had no title that first year, the 2000 season, though I was listed in the team media guide as a defensive assistant. In a sense that's what I did, but I wasn't even on the payroll. I funded my being there. The NFL has a minority program to help get more minorities into coaching, and Belichick listed me as a possible coach for the future under the auspices of that program. So the NFL paid for my being there during the summer, and I paid once the season started. It was almost like a scholarship program, where you got your room and board and nothing else.

Part of my job was to help Rob Ryan with the linebackers, and sometimes that became touchy. Rob was the new guy under Belichick, and assistant coaches often get nervous. I think he was worried about my taking over his meetings and then, at the end of the year, saw himself being fired, with me replacing him. Because of that situation, I had to walk a fine line, helping all I could without stepping on any toes. So I wouldn't say some things at the meetings. Though I knew Belichick's techniques, knew what he wanted from the position, inside and out, I would never interrupt Rob at the meetings. If he wasn't explaining something correctly, I would wait to tell him afterward.

My playing background had its advantages and disadvantages. Bobby Hamilton, a defensive end, was a teammate of mine with the Jets, and he would often come to me instead of Randy Melvin, the defensive line coach. That bothered some guys. Otis Smith was another. He had been released after the final preseason game with the Jets and, as a former teammate, would also come to me before his position coach.

So you can see the tricky position I was in, being part of the coaching staff but not really being part of it. Rob Ryan should have feared the situation the most, but once he got to know me he didn't. I also got to talk with the team as a unit before some of the games. I remember going three for three before we finally lost one, and that was during the 5–11 season. Those guys were just lacking confidence before going into games, and I don't really think they knew how they were supposed to feel as a unit. So much of football is confidence and leadership. To put it in perspective, I was always taught that it didn't matter how well a quarterback could throw. If he couldn't lead, he would have a difficult time becoming an elite quarterback in the NFL.

The 2000 season was one of transition for me, coming back to the game but in a totally different capacity. I knew I couldn't spend another year as a liaison, so something had to be decided. Fortunately, it didn't take long. After the Buffalo game in week fifteen of the 2000 season, I sat with Coach Belichick on the team flight home, and he asked me how I liked being there and how I felt things had gone, aside from the fact that the team had won just five games. That's when I said, "Coach, I would really like to stay on because I don't feel I contributed in the way I know I could have." It all went back to not wanting to step on toes. That's when he said, "Well, I'm looking to bring you back to coach the inside linebackers." Before that I was going to say the only way I'd come back was if I had an equal voice in making certain decisions, but he nipped that in the bud when he said he wanted to make me inside linebackers coach. So the deal was done. I would be coming back, but this time I would be a full-time coach.

Now my duties would be changing significantly. In 2000, when I was still a liaison, I spent my mornings with the young defensive players, the first- and second-year guys. I showed them how to watch tape and talked to them in general about the league—how to act, what to expect, some of the traps and pitfalls to avoid, and, hopefully, how to be successful. In addition, I ran the defensive scout, or show, team, which emulates the next opponent's defense for our offense. The offensive coaches draw up various cards showing the defenses they want us to set up. My job was to show them the card, explain their responsibilities, then get the hell out of the way. That year we called the scout team the Ghetto Dogs. Giving them a name also gives them an identity and a sense of pride, so they want to do their job—a very important job—to the best of their ability.

Rob Ryan, as I said, was the linebackers coach in 2000. If he got overloaded with preparation—tape duties, making up show team cards, individual instruction—I would run the linebackers through their drills and warm-up. Once I became inside linebackers coach in 2001, Rob and I built a real solid relationship, affectionately calling each other salt and pepper. Rob's strength is designing defenses, while I understand the techniques of the position, having played the game for so long. I can tell guys what to expect and what to look for in different situations. So Rob would give everyone assignments, and I finish and talk about responsibilities and techniques.

Because I had been a player just three years earlier and would be coaching former teammates, as well as guys not that much younger than me, I wondered if that might be a problem and how I would handle it. Another of those transitions I had to make. When training camp started in July, I had just turned thirty-seven, and I was coaching Otis Smith, who was almost thirty-six; Bryan Cox, who was thirty-three; and a few others already in their thirties. The funny part was that it turned out to be more difficult with the young guys, who didn't know me. I felt I had to address that in training camp, because guys who hadn't played with me didn't know how I'd conducted myself as a player.

I was running the scout team again. The 2001 squad was called The Dirty Show, and we were going to be doing the same thing as the year before, getting the offense ready for the defense it would see the following week. Needless to say, this is a job I take very seriously. The scout team is extremely important. If it doesn't run the defense properly, the offense will not get the looks it needs, the quarterback and wide receivers won't get the reads they must have to be prepared, and if the defensive linemen are out of place, it causes the offense to make an adjustment and screws up the blocking techniques. Not only do the techniques have to be proper, but the scout team has to go hard. If we're not roughing up the offense, pushing them, they'll get not only a false look but false courage. They'll think they're doing everything well. I told the guys all of this before the season started, something the older guys should all know.

Then one day in training camp one of the rookie defensive backs, Leonard Myers, talked back to me. He said something that got a chuckle from another guy, something kids do, kind of mumbling it under his breath. I didn't say anything about it when it happened. At the same time, Myers wasn't really understanding the scout team card system or the importance of what we were doing. He'd been a star at the University of Miami, and maybe that had something to do with it. Anyway, the remark he made was eating at me all day and was still a sore point when we went into our night meetings. First we met with Coach Belichick, then we separated into offense and defense for another meeting. Before our defensive meeting began, I asked RAC if I could get something off my chest.

I started off just by talking about myself, telling them that I had started playing in this league when some of them weren't even in elementary school. "You don't really know me from jack," I told them, but I wasn't there to brag about myself. One thing I'm not is a bullshitter, and I told them flat out that anyone who wanted to try me was welcome and that we were going to nip this thing in the bud right now. "You don't have to talk under your breath," I told them, "so let's get something out of the way right now. I'm not here for your amusement. I'm here to make you better, and I'll do it any way I can." I told them I took pride in the scout team because that's what had made me. I had played hard on the scout team and special teams when I was a rookie, and I was rewarded when Coach Belichick began working me into the defense. It reached a point where I played more than the starting linebacker in both the playoffs and Super Bowl that year.

I didn't call out Leonard Myers or the other guy who was chuckling. I called all of them out. I said I wasn't going to tolerate this type of thing during camp or during the season. I don't think there was a person in that room who didn't understand where I was coming from, and no one gave me any shit from that point on. Yes, I basically challenged them, in a sense saying we could go into a back alley if they wanted. Guys would rib me about it later, but the veterans knew me and knew I was serious. They had also seen how I had acted in practice as a player. I felt I was the quarterback on defense. Rob told me that his dad, Buddy Ryan, always said the guy who is in the middle of your team runs your team—the quarterback on offense and the middle linebacker on defense. I liked that control, calling signals on defense. After that I had guys fighting to get on The Dirty Show. Even Ty Law and Lawyer Milloy took their turns as part of the group. Willie McGinest wanted to get on but was hurt early in the year. So was our number-one draft choice, Richard Seymour, but he wanted to get on as well. I think my point was well taken.

Coaches motivate different guys in different ways. Some needed the Knute Rockne speech, others just needed a quiet pat on the back, and still others were in between. When I was at Cleveland, Eric Turner, God rest his soul, was probably the best overall free safety I had ever played with. The way to get him to play better was to tell him constantly how good he was. So everyone is different, and I tried to get personal with every player. I knew only one way to play this game, and that was full speed. Because I played the game with a lot of intensity, I felt I should coach the game with the same intensity, full speed, and I'm very emotional about it.

When I was still just a liaison in 2000, there was another incident that I think also helped define me as a coach. Early in the preseason my only responsibility during the games was to keep guys—the linebackers and defensive linemen—together on the sideline. Because all the cuts hadn't been made, we had more bodies on the sideline than during the regular season, and Belichick didn't want guys roaming all over the place. We were playing the Redskins, and one of my ex-teammates, Chad Cascadden, a linebacker we had picked up in the off season and who was trying to make the team, was on the sideline. He was coming off an injury and had missed the first preseason game. Chad had always been kind of cocky, a very confident guy, and I noticed he was starting to wander onto the offensive portion of the sideline. It was killing me to have to supervise these guys like this, but I understood it had to be done. Both Chad and Tedy Bruschi were down there.

Bruschi saw me coming and immediately walked back to the defensive group, but Chad didn't move, and I had to tell him to get back with the rest of the defense. I guess he didn't like that and went off on one of those embarrassing tirades, demanding to know why he had to stay in a certain place. I told him if he had a problem to take it up with Coach Belichick later but to get down with us right now. He came back but didn't go over to the bench where Rob was talking to the linebackers. Instead he was standing a step behind me but a step in front of the bench.

I told him again to go behind the bench and listen to what Rob was saying, and he immediately came at me, demanding to know "what the fuck was my problem," that he had played for Coach Belichick and knew how things were run. Then he informed me that I shouldn't be telling him to talk to the coach. Well, before he said another word I grabbed him by the face mask and pulled him to me. I said, "Chad, you played for Bill Parcells. This is Bill Belichick, but I don't care who you played for. The man wants you on the sideline." I wasn't yelling at him, but he was trying to pull away. I told him again to stand his ass over there because Belichick wanted everyone on the defense in one place. "If you have a problem," I told him, "take it up with him." Then I let go. By that time a few people were grabbing at me to let him go, and he ran out on the field with the punt team.

The next day, though, he didn't show up for the meeting. Coach Belichick got a call later in the day from Chad, saying he was contemplating retirement. He ended up retiring that week, and a number of people were saying that I had made him retire, that I had choked him on the sideline. Rob was even giving me some shit about it at the time. I never spoke to Chad and didn't see him when he packed up his stuff. A year later, in 2001, when we played the Jets he was out by the bus visiting with some former teammates. I saw him coming toward me and thought we might have another problem, but he totally surprised me by apologizing. He said he had been more frustrated by not being able to play full speed then and admitted he'd been wrong to take out his frustration on me. So we shook hands and even embraced. The funny part was that after our heated encounter I thought I might have problems with guys all season and end up going back to Florida before I really got started. Coach Belichick didn't say anything about it until the off season, and even then it was more in a joking manner than anything else.

The thing is, I wouldn't hesitate to act the same way with any of those guys. I know I wouldn't want any coach putting his hands on me, but I wouldn't disrespect a guy to the point where he had to. It was the same with Leonard Myers. Don't disrespect me and I won't disrespect you. I'm not about to flip authority on everyone because I'm a coach. I'm here because I want the team to be better, the linebackers to be better. That's the only reason I'm here. I didn't feel good about the confrontation with Chad, but it was more of a gut reaction than anything else. Through my years of experience I have seen a lot of guys run over people in authority. Respect is dying, becoming extinct in our society. This, however, was the way I was raised and how I'm raising my son. You respect elders; you respect everybody until they disrespect themselves or disrespect you. Both incidents, with Leonard Myers and with Chad, were the result of my seeing an ugly situation developing, whether it's mumbling something under your breath or refusing to stand where you're supposed to stand. At first I tried to smile and play it down, maybe talk to them quietly, but it wasn't working.

If I let a young guy like Myers say one thing, other guys would try it, and it would end up snowballing. A time-out wasn't going to work in this situation. Telling Belichick and having him handle it wouldn't work either. My mother always said to me, "You can't raise other people's kids, but you can make them aware. Until they're told, they'll run over you." I think one of the biggest problems with today's players is that they don't know history, don't know the guys who came before and made it all possible for them. When I was a young player with the Jets, Parcells came up to me during mini-camp and started talking football history. He asked me how many guys on the field I thought would know who Hall of Fame Coach George Allen was. I knew because I've made it my business to know about coaches and players who came before me, even those who retired before I was born. Anyway, I looked around and guessed maybe eight, or nine, or ten. Parcells said he would be shocked if there were that many, so he started going around and asking guys, one by one. Some players didn't think George Allen was part of the sport. One guy even confused him with Woody Allen. Another thought he was an old rock star. Parcells probably went through twenty or thirty guys until one said he thought he was a coach. Parcells just shrugged. Then he went back to the player who thought he was a coach and asked him what team Allen was most remembered for coaching. The guy didn't know that one, only that he was a coach.

Well, those guys didn't know George Allen because he coached in the 1970s. It's really a shame. Maybe Parcells was wondering how many guys would remember *him* in twenty years. I haven't thought much about that because I'm just beginning. I do know, however, that football history gives you respect for the game, and that leads to respect for your teammates and coaches and ultimately for yourself.

Between 2000 and 2001 I had to make many adjustments and transitions, going from a liaison just helping a bit, learning, observing, to a full-fledged coach with many responsibilities and, I would like to think, playing a major role in helping a team come together and win. Of course, none of us knew at the beginning of the 2001 season just how it would end. By the time training camp and the preseason were over, we were all hoping just to get off fast and win from the outset. Unfortunately, it didn't happen that way.

3

The First Four Games
Beginning on a Sour Note

After evaluating our personnel for the 2001 season, one of our scouts, Jake Hallum, said he thought we would be lucky to win eight games. Jake was one of the first guys who helped me when Coach Belichick sent me on the road to scout, showing me what to look for and how to fill out the information report. Before the preseason games begin, our scouts stay in and watch our own people, then go out and begin watching other teams. Jake had watched the club through training camp and saw that the players who were competing for jobs in 2001 were more motivated than the year before. So he figured the additional inspiration would be worth three or four more games, bringing us up from 5–11 to around .500.

I think, though, that it is sometimes difficult to judge a team solely on the talent of the individual players. Football, to me, is the ultimate team game and requires contributions from each and every player. You need depth because you don't know who will be injured and which player will have to step in and pick it up. Once a ball club comes together and everyone is on the same wavelength, something special can happen. Many people tend to forget that in pro football one player can't win a game for you. If one guy can do that and what we're teaching is total teamwork, then we're full of shit. Even when someone makes a great play, it's usually because a teammate has done something to set it up. We would see that many times during the remarkable 2001 season.

Going into the season opener at Cincinnati, I think we still had a few question marks. In fact I would have liked us to have been more sound going into that game. Some of the questions involved personnel; some involved an entire unit. Our defense, for example, had a solid game plan, but we still weren't

41

sure if we were going to play more three-four defense or more four-three. We also put a lot of emphasis in practice on stopping the pass. While we didn't feel the Bengals had a strong quarterback, we knew they had some talented receivers who could make big plays. Of course, you need someone to get those guys the ball. If the quarterback is so-so and not doing the job, even the best receiving corps in the world won't help. We probably also should have prepared more for the run simply because we were facing Corey Dillon, one of the league's best running backs.

Why so many concerns when we were facing a team considered mediocre at best? First, there were injuries. Mike Compton, our free agent center/guard, hadn't practiced the entire training camp. Both linebacker Willie McGinest and rookie defensive tackle Richard Seymour were banged up. You can't really prepare for injuries, especially early in the season, when you aren't totally sure who can do the job. Later in the year, when a team is in a groove, if guys are there, great, but if they're not, then at least you know just who you will use in their place. A perfect example was our game against the Bengals the year before. We beat them, and Corey Dillon didn't have a big game. We shut down their run with a weaker defense because it was later in the season and we were prepared. In other words, there are times you can do better with a weaker defense that's prepared than with a better defense, still not confident in working together and following the game plan.

I'm not saying that this is the way it should be at the beginning of a new season. The purpose of the off-season conditioning program, the mini-camps, training camp, and the preseason—all of it is about preparedness. We had some key veteran defensive players the year before who really didn't understand the defenses we wanted to run. This year we felt we had implemented the defensive schemes at a calmer pace, took our time so that everyone would get it right. We were a team that game-planned every opponent. In the preseason games you don't really show your whole hand, but you are always moving forward and pointing toward the beginning of the regular season. I think, though, that many of the things we did in training camp catered to the offense; we were going at their pace and tailoring our defense to the things they wanted to do. At the same time, however, we were still trying to give the entire team a foundation, to let the players know that this is how we were going to continue to do things, no matter what. Remember, you can cross off much of what happened in 2000, when coaches and players were all getting to know each other. By carefully and slowly laying the foundation, we were hoping that the team would start strong, then continue to improve as the season wore on. In a perfect world we would be taking a group of mature, sound-minded players into that first game of the season.

So what happens? We go into Cincinnati and lose, 23–17. Needless to say, it was a huge letdown and the team came out of the game emotionally drained. It wasn't that we were blown out, but it certainly wasn't the way we wanted to begin. We had spent the entire off season and preseason trying to correct the wrongs of 2000, and then to open up by losing to an opponent that you beat the year before when you weren't as good a team, well, emotionally that's draining. As far as I could see, the Bengals hadn't improved that much. They were essentially the same team with the same core players, despite having some newcomers in the lineup. As a team they were doing the same things, and we didn't jump on them. They ran the ball for more than 150 yards, which is obviously something we didn't want them to do. We also didn't get a big game from our offense, our special teams didn't play well, our punting wasn't good, and, in a nutshell, it seemed as if we were still in the preseason.

There were very few pluses. We had an early 10–3 lead, then Dillon broke loose for a forty-yard run that led to the game-tying touchdown. It was still tied at the half, but they dominated the third quarter and came away with a 23–10 lead, including a seventy-yard drive that gave them their final score. We did manage a ninety-four-yard drive early in the final quarter to bring it to 23–17, but we couldn't keep the momentum going. Our last chance came with a little less than four minutes left. We took over at our own thirty but couldn't get it done, and they simply had to run out the clock to win it. Just like that, 0–1.

Our next game was supposed to be at Carolina. We had beaten the Panthers handily in the preseason, and that, coupled with our scheduled opener against the Bengals, had many of us really looking toward a 2–0 start. Now, after losing to the Bengals, the Carolina game became more important but would be far from easy. They had surprised the Vikings in their opener, 24–13, so we knew they would be a better team than we had beaten just about a month earlier, but certainly none of us wanted to think about opening at 0–2.

We were all set to go back to work when everything came to a halt. Two days after we lost to the Bengals, terrorists attacked the World Trade Center and the Pentagon, putting the entire country on edge and on alert. Needless to say, the games for the following weekend were rescheduled for a later date, which would extend the entire season by a week.

I can remember arriving at the team's offices that Tuesday and people immediately running up to me to tell me what had just happened, that a plane had hit the World Trade Center. We turned on the TV, and then the second plane hit. *What the hell is going on?* was the first thing that crossed my mind. We knew we had a big job that week to get ready, to get the team back on track. Now, all of a sudden, everyone was numb. For a while, some of us thought the entire season might be canceled or perhaps shortened. You didn't know what to think. Adding to the uncertainty were stranded players. Roman Phifer had flown to California right after the Cincinnati game to visit with his family. He called me that morning to say he couldn't get a flight back but that he would jump on a train or wait for air travel to resume.

We didn't practice on the day of the tragedy but still had our meetings, and because we hadn't yet heard about the cancellation, we gave the players written analyses of the Carolina personnel the next day. Then we found out the games were off, and I think we were all relieved. No one wanted to play that week. They said that the tragedy hit nearly everyone in a personal way and we weren't immune. Our starting guard, Joe Andruzzi, has three brothers in the New York Fire Department, and he hadn't yet heard from any of them. I remember him sweating and running out the door. Joe had worked very hard in the off season and was becoming one of the prominent guards in the league. Fortunately, all of his brothers were all right, and they came out for the ceremonial coin toss at the Meadowlands when we resumed our schedule against the Jets on September 23rd.

The Jets, of course, were a whole different situation for us. Not only were the two teams bitter divisional rivals, but the rivalry had actually been intensified over the last several years by the behind-the-scenes dramas involving both coaches and personnel. They had some former Patriots on the team, and we had a whole group of former Jets, starting with our head coach and including me. Not only did this situation make the rivalry more heated, but it also led to a potential crisis on our team that could have been disastrous.

I really don't know what had taken place between the Patriots and the Jets before Parcells arrived to coach in New England. I can, however, remember running the Giants celebrity basketball team when I was still playing in New

York. We would often come up to the New England area and always had an enormous turnout, playing at places like Brown University and Providence College. We weren't playing against the Patriots' players, just against local guys. At that time, however, there were a lot more Giants fans in the New York metropolitan area and into New England than Jets fans. When Parcells took over the Patriots, a lot of fans on the fringe areas immediately swung over to New England. That was Parcells's initial effect, giving the Patriots a big-name coach, a former Giant who had won two Super Bowls. With Parcells at the helm, the Patriots improved very quickly and eventually went to the Super Bowl in 1996 (losing to the Packers). He was like a breath of fresh air compared to what had been there before.

Then it all came apart, and he went over to the Jets. The manner in which he left, with all the animosity between him and owner Bob Kraft, just created a lot of heat on both sides. I was with Detroit when it happened, but it wasn't long before Parcells picked me up to play for the Jets. Before we played at New England in 1997, the pregame video highlights showed key players like Drew Bledsoe, Curtis Martin, Terry Glenn, and Ben Coates in action. The only Jets "highlight" to air was Parcells stalking the sideline. It had become personal, and the New England media were very hard on Pete Carroll, Parcells's successor with the Patriots. The teams split the two games they played that year.

After 1997 the rivalry seemed to become more intense, more magnified. It didn't matter what type of season either team was having; the games were always big, and usually one of them was televised nationally. Then Parcells resigned from the Jets, and Belichick was named his successor, only to quickly resign the next day. When Pete Carroll was fired and Belichick was eventually named new head coach of the Patriots, it served as more fuel for the rivalry's fire. The Jets won both games between the teams in 2000, but by this time it didn't matter who was coaching. When the two teams met, it was always war.

Besides the game of musical coaches, a number of players had swapped teams. Curtis Martin, who had been a great running back for the Patriots from his rookie year of 1995 through the 1997 season, then joined the Jets the next year, where he continued to use his considerable talents to an even greater degree. We had a number of former Jets on our Patriots roster, notably Bryan Cox, our highly vocal and tough linebacker, who has been a leader wherever he has played. Yet it was Cox who became embroiled in the controversy during the game that could have ripped the heart right out of our team, and part of that was because it happened at the same time we lost our quarterback, Drew Bledsoe.

The first half of the game was typical Patriots–Jets, dominated by defenses that yielded yards grudgingly. We scored first on a twenty-four-yard Adam Vinatieri field goal at the end of the first quarter, but they got it back when John Hall connected for three points just before the end of the half. The game was still up for grabs, but we were not pleased with the way our team was playing. We took the opening kickoff in the third quarter, started from our own seventeen, and drove right up the field, making five first downs. Now it looked as if we were really clicking, but on a second-down play from the Jets' ten-yard line, Marc Edwards carried up the middle, gained about three yards, then fumbled when he was hit and the Jets recovered. They immediately drove ninety-three yards for the go-ahead touchdown about two and a half minutes before the end of the third period, scoring on an eight-yard Curtis Martin run. That was definitely not something to make our defense proud. It was now 10–3, but there was plenty of time left, and we all felt we still had a great chance to win.

We had another good shot early in the fourth period when our offense began a drive from the Jets' thirty-one. The big play was a fifty-eight-yard pass from Drew to Troy Brown down the left sideline that brought the ball to the Jets' eleven. Then, unbelievably, we turned it over again. On third and eight, Drew threw to Charles Johnson in the end zone, only to have linebacker James Farrior pick it off. Making matters worse, Farrior then returned it forty-seven yards out to their forty-four, giving them good field position and maybe putting the crusher on us.

It turned out the day's worst moment had yet to come. With just under five minutes left we had the ball again when Drew scrambled toward our sideline. Mo Lewis, the Jets linebacker, was pursuing at an angle, and their defensive end, John Abraham, was also running toward Drew. Right near the sideline everybody sort of let up a bit. In fact, seeing that Drew was almost out of bounds, Abraham started running at Bryan Cox, who was standing about three feet from me. He was doing it as a joke with a former teammate, and he stopped before reaching him. The only one who didn't let up was Lewis, and he hit Drew with a real hard shot, jarring the ball loose and sending Drew sprawling over the sideline. I was partially obscured from seeing the play by Abraham, who was running toward us to jive with Cox. At that point Cox didn't know Drew was injured, so he and Abraham shared a few quick words, then shook hands, and Cox gave him a playful slap upside the head.

Drew got up slowly, then started to come around. Mo looked at Drew for a few seconds, and when he saw him begin getting up, he jogged back to his sideline. He knew he'd had a good hit. That's how you play the game. Tom Brady went in to finish the series, then Drew came back for one more but didn't look right. He began feeling worse and came out again. He stood on the sideline and rooted for Brady and the rest of the team. We got the ball at our own twenty-six with just over two minutes left. Brady got a couple of first downs, including a twenty-one-yard throw to David Patten, but it came down to a pair of passes into the end zone that were incomplete. We lost the game, 10–3, to fall to 0–2 on the season, but we almost lost a lot more.

At first it didn't seem as if Drew's injury was all that serious. They said, at first, that he had suffered a mild concussion. It was only later that we learned that the hit from Lewis had sheared an artery in his chest, causing internal bleeding that easily could have been life-threatening if he hadn't had immediate care. Our first concern, of course, was for Drew. Once we knew he would recover, we had to face another fact. The team had lost its first two games and would now have to play a major portion of its schedule with an untried, second-year backup quarterback running the offense. That still wasn't all. This time the rivalry between the two teams was producing some additional fallout, centering around the rumors that after the game Cox had actually congratulated Lewis on the hit.

I knew that it had been John Abraham whose hand Cox had slapped quickly, but I also knew that it was a delicate situation. Personally, I don't know John Abraham, but even if I did I wouldn't have been shaking his hand at that particular time. That wasn't me when I played. There were a lot of guys on other teams who would say hello to me before games or maybe make a sarcastic remark or wisecrack. That you can handle. The problem here was that a lot of our guys were lifelong Patriots, drafted by New England and playing here for seven, eight, or nine years. The Patriots were all they knew, and I don't think they quite knew what to make of guys who came over from other teams or, for that matter, guys who were here but left. They can still be your friends, but business is business as well.

I love Curtis Martin, for example. He helped take the Patriots to the Super Bowl in 1996, but now he's a New York Jet. If I'm playing and he's with the Jets, I try to knock him into next week. There wasn't anyone on the field who ever wanted to win as much as I did. My best friend and college teammate is Keith Byars. I wouldn't be Pepper Johnson if I didn't walk up to Keith before a game, wish him luck, and say "God bless." Nothing in the world would stop me from wishing him the best. But do I want to beat him? Darn skippy. Keith once hit me with an incredible shot, knocked me right into the air. I remember some people calling it the hardest hit of the decade. It happened back in 1990 when I was with the Giants and he was with Philadelphia. I was chasing their quarterback, Randall Cunningham, and almost had him in my grasp. As soon as I put my hand on his shoulder, Keith hit me with a perfect block. I went airborne and landed on the sideline but bounced right back up and ran to the huddle. No way I was gonna let Keith or anyone else on the Eagles know how much it hurt. It's virtually impossible to totally avoid playing against friends. A player will have some friends joining the league with him as well as making new friends over the years. Eventually he's going to find himself facing those friends on the opposite side of the ball. You just have to know how to separate friendship from the game and know that when it's over you'll still be friends. Keith Byars is like a brother to me, but it didn't stop him from blasting me to help his team. If the situation was reversed, I would have done the same thing to him.

Could Mo Lewis have hit Drew harder? I know he could have. Was Mo trying to stop Drew from getting a first down? Yes. That's the game. Unfortunately, the way Cox had interacted with Abraham on the sideline haunted us for some time. There were some guys who thought that while Cox was a Patriot his heart was still in New York. It was probably a matter of bad timing, the way we had been going, and how it all happened. A lot of guys were hurting after the loss to the Jets, and some began thinking that we had these ex-Jets on the team who didn't give a damn about born-and-bred Patriots players. Even a lot of our coaches had come over from the Jets with Belichick. We felt bad also, because these were the guys we wanted to beat more than anybody. That's how coaches feel when they are going up against their ex-team. They want to win. So everyone was extremely disappointed, very upset, because no one wants to start a season at 0–2. That's disheartening in itself, and losing to the Jets only served to make it worse, especially when some of the guys thought the defeat wasn't hurting the ex-Jets as much as the lifelong Patriots. In addition, the ex-Jets were angry because they knew how some of their teammates felt, and they thought it was unfounded.

That tough loss to the Jets and the entire situation that resulted could have easily been catastrophic. Losing Drew was one thing, but the suspicions that some of the longtime Patriots had about the new players could have done more damage. It wasn't something that would go away overnight. I think it stayed somewhere just below the surface until we began winning regularly in the second half of the season. I can remember sitting up and talking to Lawyer Milloy until 2:30 in the morning after just the sixth game of the year. It was still bugging him, and he was holding it all in. I tried to explain things from my perspective and think I got through to him somewhat. Later in the year, when the team really began pulling together, that's when I think everyone realized they all wanted the same thing—to win. No matter where they had come from or where else they had played, they were all wearing the same Patriots uniform now.

The immediate problem, however, was our next game. It was against the Indianapolis Colts at Foxboro. I had my own diversion the Friday before that game, but one that I was really looking forward to. I was originally to be inducted into the Ohio State Athletic Hall of Fame a few weeks earlier. It was quite an honor. Because of the terrorist attack, however, they rescheduled it to September 28th and 29th. So I missed Friday practice and went to Columbus for dinner and the induction ceremony that evening. Then the next day Ohio State was playing San Diego State, and all the inductees were introduced at halftime. After the game I jumped into a rental car and drove to Indianapolis, which is just two hours away. I was there in time for the Saturday night coaching staff meetings. It was a great experience for me, but one I didn't have time to savor. Now it was back to business.

The Colts had the number-one offense in the league early in the season, and many were predicting they would be making a trip to the Super Bowl that year. Peyton Manning was being heralded as perhaps the best young quarterback in the league. He had a great deep receiver in Marvin Harrison and an All-Pro running back in Edgerrin James. That gave them a bonafide big three and meant trouble for the defense.

The other problem was that a loss would drop us to 0–3, making it all the more difficult— if not near impossible—to turn things around. Chances were that at 0–3 there would have been even more bickering, more locker-room lawyers, more finger-pointing—the kind of stuff that takes down the mentality of the entire team. Games rely so much more on the mental aspect than most people think. If you have a negative mentality going into games, you're going to lose. You always have to think positive if you want to find a way to win the close ones.

A perfect example of the importance of a positive attitude was the Patriots of 2000. That team played a lot of close games. Of our eleven losses, only two could be considered blowouts. We lost a trio of games by three points or less, lost three others by a single touchdown, and lost two more by eight points. It doesn't take a genius to know that a good number of those games were winnable. Many games like that come down to last-minute drives, trying to get into field goal range, or stopping your opponent on a key series. Yet when you have the negative mentality, the majority of people on your team are thinking, whether they realize it or not, How are we gonna mess up? How are we gonna lose this game? You get enough people with that mentality and the vibes will get out there, and they spread. You've got to remember that a loss is a loss, whether it's by a single point or by thirty.

Some coaches will tell you a blowout is better. Then they can attribute it to a bad day rather than a close loss. That, however, can be a cop-out or rationalization. The team plays terribly, and the coach is sugarcoating. Some players will take the blowout loss harder, accepting it by saying, "OK, we were horrible." One of the things I've learned during my many years in the game is that you should learn something from both a win and a loss. I would much prefer to learn from winning, but every now and then you take a loss and, as bad as it might hurt, it has a positive effect. A perfect example was the final game of 2000, when Lawyer gathered the players together and told them not to forget the loss or the losing season, promising to do something about it the next year. Well, the next year was here, and we were 0–2. That's why the Colts game was huge for us, huge with a capital H.

We went in as decided underdogs, but on just the second or third play the Colts ran, Bryan Cox put a huge hit on one of their receivers, Jerome Pathon, and set the tempo for the afternoon. That's when we knew what we had to do to win, play physical defense. We wound up beating the Colts by taking their receivers out of the game physically before they could even get started. Even when they caught the ball, we were totally mistreating them, shoving them around. I don't think there was a guy on the defense who didn't have a big hit or an intimidating play during the game. The final score was 44–13, a blowout and total domination, the best way in the world to reverse an 0–2 start.

For whatever the reason, we've always played the Colts tough and have had a lot of success stopping Peyton Manning. He's never led his team to a victory in Foxboro in four tries. I believe we picked off three passes, held James to just over 50 yards rushing, while their star, receiver Marvin Harrison, caught just three passes for 49 yards. At the same time we finally ran the ball with some authority, picking up 177 yards, with Antowain Smith getting 94 of them. Brady, in his first start, played a solid game, completing thirteen of twenty-three passes for 168 yards. It was the defense, however, that really set the tone. Otis Smith picked off a pass and returned it 78 yards for a touchdown. Ty Law pilfered one and took it in from 23 yards out, while Cox continued his great play right from the opening series, winding up with eleven tackles. Did we turn our season around with one game? Some thought we did. The proof, however, is always in the pudding. Unfortunately, after our next game a lot of people were asking the real New England Patriots to please stand up.

After two games at home we traveled to Miami to play another divisional rival, the Dolphins. There may not have been quite the same intensity as our rivalry with the Jets, but the Dolphins always seemed to contend for the divisional lead and the title, and the games were always important. Our mentality going in was "Let's beat them and get our record to .500. From there, we can shoot for a winning record the first half of the season." Beating the Colts, as impressive as it may have looked, was just one small step. I think some people forgot that Miami was a team that pretty much had our number. They had beaten us twice the year before, though both games were close. There was another problem whenever we went down there. It was called heat and humidity, something we really weren't used to in New England.

It's a funny thing about that kind of weather. Somehow it becomes an issue. The week before everyone is talking about it: "Damn, it's hot down there." It gets into your head. No one wants to say it, but it's really in the back of your mind, and we always seem to play there in October. Whenever you think about something other than the game itself, you're already on the way to blowing it, another example of the mental aspect of football being so important. So we traveled to Miami and—no surprise—we wore down in the heat. They did to us what we had done to the Colts. They ran the ball, and we simply couldn't do anything. Boom! Just like that the air is out of your sails. They beat us 30–10, and now we had to win two games to get to .500.

We didn't have a good day, passing for just 86 yards while our running game netted just 80. Their defensive backs were all over our receivers, and we pretty much had a nothing game on offense. The defense didn't have much to brag about either. Lamar Smith, their running back, gained 144 yards on twenty-nine carries, part of a ground game that went over the 200-yard mark. When you run the ball like that, you don't usually lose. Bryan Cox called it a total butt-kicking, and he was right. There's really nothing more you can say. Plain and simply, we got beat.

I've got to take my hat off to Coach Belichick for the way he handled it. There was no ranting and raving, no finger-pointing, no threats to bench guys—none of that. In fact he didn't even show the team the entire game tape the next day. He made the coaches aware of what happened so we could all go back and tell our respective units. We took the blame, showed them a couple of plays, and then moved on. Belichick didn't even allow the media to come and talk about the Dolphins. We all knew the score, what 1–3 meant at this point in the season, and we all knew what had to be done. So Coach Belichick's theme was "It's done; let's put it behind us and get ready for San Diego."

The strange thing is that we kind of discovered something with that loss. The format Belichick used after the Miami game actually helped us out later, when we began winning. We treated victories just the same way we treated losses. We put them behind us. If we won a game, whoopie—it's great. But that's it. Come in Monday, begin getting the bumps and bruises out, and be ready to work on Wednesday. From that point on we didn't dwell on any game once it was over, win or lose. Remember, I said a team can learn something from a loss. This was a perfect example. Yet no matter what our philosophy was after the first four games, no one was really happy. You don't work so hard in the off season, get rid of players you feel won't work within your system, then bring in players you fully expected to contribute and expect to lose three of your first four games. Some teams can be crippled by that kind of start.

Looking back, losing the Cincinnati game was understandable. We had some injuries and just weren't ready. Then we lost to the Jets, but the events of September 11th caused the schedule to be altered and preparations to change. We knew our offense wasn't going to put up just three points in most games. The real problem coming out of that game was that we lost our quarterback for a good part of the season and had to put in a guy with virtually no experience. Then we came back and unleashed all hell against the Colts. We began playing like the team we said we were going to be during the off season and in training camp. Here we go. That game was so easy and we were so physically dominant that maybe we got cocky, boasted a bit, and didn't put the Colts game behind us the way we should. We reveled in the victory for a little too long, then went to Miami and suffered a meltdown against the Dolphins.

It was after the defeat by the Dolphins that we realized what we had to do. For openers, the players now knew they had to help Brady. There was no way they could put all the burden on him. To do that we'd have to run the ball better, and the receivers needed more separation. That wouldn't happen unless the offensive line began blocking better. Defensively, we also had to help Brady build his confidence. That meant getting him better field position, giving him the ball near midfield or even in the other team's territory, but not with his back against the goal line. The odd part was that in the back of everyone's mind was the thought that if we didn't dig too big a hole for ourselves Drew would eventually come back and get us out of it. We were all thinking about ways to help Brady, but I don't think anyone figured he would be taking us the rest of the way.

The good thing about Tom Brady is that he's a natural leader, one of the best guys in the huddle and a guy with all kinds of energy on the sideline. He talks to his teammates, always makes eye contact, and really tries to pump up his receivers. He gets everyone relaxed, tells jokes at times when most guys wouldn't be telling jokes. I think that's because he still has a lot of the kid in him. In some ways he makes everyone forget it's a business. It must be his age. In a way it's kind of a back-to-the-sandlots mentality, and he makes you want to win for him. I can remember Lawyer Milloy and Bryan Cox saying that the defense had to take more responsibility and carry more of the team on our shoulders because of Tom Brady. In fact, we all knew the defense had to do more.

The defensive philosophy is simple. You hear about teams where the offense scores a lot but the defense can't stop anybody, and they lose. I don't care how you slice it, the job of the defensive staff and the players is to stop the other team's offense from scoring more points than your offense. For example, we lost to the Jets, 10–3. Well, if our offense got only three points, our defense shouldn't have given the Jets any. Of course, it doesn't always work that way, but that has to be your goal every single week. You can't look at it any other way.

After our 1–3 start the media, as expected, were writing us off. Remember, most of them had predicted we would be lucky to be 8–8, and that would be considered a good season. Now, even more so, at 1–3 they said we would be lucky to be a .500 team, and they began questioning us, wondering, for instance, if Belichick had done the right thing by bringing in so many older veterans. Fortunately, I didn't have time to talk to the media. None of the assistant coaches do. The last thing you want to do is sit in front of a mike and be asked a lot of crazy questions. Time is consumed with preparation. While some people thought that Coach Belichick didn't allow his assistants to talk, that just isn't true.

I think there is a difference between the media in the New England area and the press in New York. In New York they're always looking for a crack in the armor, a way to suck the blood out of you. In New England the media doesn't attack as much, but they don't sugarcoat things either. They make their statements, and that's it. If they think we'll lose, they just say it. You don't see as many guys going for the jugular. There were stories about personnel decisions, bringing in misfits and not hiring a quarterback coach, stuff like that. And a lot of it resurfaced after the 1–3 start.

Sometimes the guys covering the team don't really understand the situation. For example, our quarterbacks coach passed away during training camp, and some members of the media wondered why Belichick didn't hit the phones and try to find a replacement immediately. But think about it. If you bring a guy in at that point, you've got to coach him, too. He would have to learn the entire system, and you would be taking several steps backward at a critical time. It was easier to just work with what we had, letting guys who were already there assume the duties.

At 1–3 I'm sure the majority of the media and most of the fans had already given up on us. From the standpoint of Coach Belichick and the rest of the staff, we really didn't have time to take an opinion survey. We were so dedicated and focused on trying to bring the team out of the slump that we didn't have a pulse on the media and fans. We were now at a very crucial point in the season. If anyone panicked, it would be over. Simple as that. The whole boat could flip over and sink. If we came together, there was still time to make this thing happen. That was the focus of the New England Patriots. We weren't allowing outside influences to take over our team. Everyone chose to support Coach Belichick, to support Tom Brady. I think a lot of the coaches felt the same way. They knew there was still a kind of stigma surrounding Coach Belichick, that he would always need a Bill Parcells, that he was just a defensive coordinator masquerading as a head coach. So we all wanted him to be successful. Many of the veteran players, the guys who knew the score, felt the same way. They really wanted to see Coach Belichick have a successful year and shed that stigma.

As Tom Brady began to emerge as a true team leader, the funny part was that most people didn't know that it was Bill Belichick who was coaching him. Everyone gave him credit for the defense coming around, but the coach spent the majority of his time on the offensive side with the quarterbacks. I can recall when I played for him at Cleveland. Both Carl Banks and I thought he didn't do enough with the offense. Belichick doesn't step on the toes of his coordinators but does what a head coach is supposed to do. When all is said and done, the plays called on offense are his; the guys on the field with the defense are there because of him. He is aware of everything that happens on both offense and defense, yet, for instance, he allows the defensive staff to put together the game plan for next week's opponent.

Despite the start, I think the attitude was still positive. Lawyer Milloy, for example, still had a positive attitude after four games. He's the heart and soul of the defense. How Lawyer goes, that's how our defense goes. I remember him saying to me, "Pepper, we're not going to lose too many more ball games. We'll get better. These guys are really starting to buy into the defense." Like I said, despite the losses, we still felt something would happen, that the team would click. We all faced what had happened in those first four games, faced the ways we had lost. No way we were going to put that single game we had won on a pedestal. We were proud of shutting down the Colts, and it told us we had that capability. We also knew that we had too much confidence in one another to get pushed around regularly, as we had been in the Miami game. No, that wasn't going to happen to us much longer. We all felt that in a few short weeks, 1–3 would be a distant memory.

4

Personalities and Comparisons

I've always said that football is the ultimate team game. No way I'll ever back away from that statement. The Patriots, as a team, opened the season by losing three of their first four games. If they were going to right the ship, turn it around, they would also have to do it as a team. Coach Belichick echoed that thought when he said the entire team stems from him. He's at the top of the chain, and everyone else is an extension of him and his philosophy—the assistant coaches as well as the players, each and every one of us. That, however, doesn't preclude individual personalities from thriving within the team concept. Like all other businesses and venues, it is the personalities—the individuals—that merge to build the framework of a team. Yet the individual personality remains, and that is one of the things that makes the game so interesting.

That's also one of the reasons I liked the 2001 Patriots so much. I felt as if we had begun and ended the season the same way, as a group of guys who were willing to be the first soldiers off the plane, the first ones on the beach. Even when the media and so many others were calling us a bunch of misfits, we looked at ourselves as a pack of hungry dogs. That's one of the things that brought our team together and kept it together through all the adversity—our desire to prove the prognosticators wrong.

Coach Belichick has an uncanny ability to judge personalities, read the individual players, then mold them into the team's overall personality. When he took over in 2000, he saw that a lot of guys were overweight. So he found a rusty old boat anchor and brought it out to practice, depositing it in a prominent spot near the practice field where everyone could see it. The players, of course, were wondering what the heck it was doing there. Belichick simply said that a team in shape is a team that will prosper. All the guys who came in overweight were like the anchor, weighing the ship down. If we want to go anywhere, he told them, we have to be able to raise the anchor. When the season started, he finally got rid of it, but he had kept that old anchor there throughout training camp and the preseason just to emphasize his point.

During training camp he passed out T-shirts. On the front it read "NE PATRIOTS TRAINING CAMP, 2001." On the back was a likeness of a "wanted" poster, the kind you see on a post office bulletin board, and it read "WANTED: WINNERS." It was symbolic of who would survive training camp. If you're not a winner, you're in the wrong place. A lot of guys wore the shirts on and off during the course of the year. Tebucky Jones joked about it, saying he knew he was a winner, a walking advertisement for the T-shirt, and he was going to get a lot of guys to follow him. That was the kind of mind-set we had throughout the year. Instead of sitting back and watching things happen, we always wanted to go out, take control of the season, and compete by creating our own destiny. It was a case of individual personalities coming together for a common cause, and we had a very positive attitude.

Collectively, the team had a personality on both offense and defense. Offensively, we liked to look for mismatches on the field, make the opponent start guessing. Then, for example, get it into a Troy Brown's hands and let him make a play. Like I said, you want playmakers, guys who can turn a short pass into a long gain, guys who can think on their feet, guys who fit in with the team. Defensively, we were always striving to be more physical while continuing to show opponents different looks and identities. That's why we used both the three-four and the four-three. We would start in a three-four defense but at the drop of a dime could be in a four-man line. For example, we could use Willie McGinest in a three-point stance and make him seem like a down lineman, or we could put him outside to cover a wide receiver. This creates problems for the opposing quarterback. We also wanted our safeties to hit harder, like linebackers. We couldn't have done all these different things without the various talents and personalities that made up the team.

Bill Belichick is a very intelligent man and, not surprisingly, he looks for intelligent players. A guy might be a hellacious athlete, but if he doesn't know an entrance sign from an exit sign, he isn't going to be a New England Patriot. It's not difficult to see where Belichick is coming from, at least not for me. Like most successful people, he has evolved as a coach, part of the reason being the different personalities he has been associated with during his career.

For example, he started working with Bill Parcells when both of them were Giants assistant coaches under Ray Perkins. Then the two of them, Belichick and Parcells, continued their long association when Parcells succeeded Perkins in 1983. I'm quite sure that over the years they had many long conversations about coaching, about personnel, and about the nuances of the game. When I played for the Giants, I saw the two of them talking together many times each and every season.

When I look back at the personalities that made up the Giants teams that won two Super Bowls, I don't see a lot of big names or superstars, but I do remember many players who displayed more than raw talent. For example, Phil Simms was an elite quarterback, but not solely because of his throwing arm. There were a lot of other QBs who had stronger arms, but Phil was a great leader and knew how to put a drive together when the game was on the line. Add to that the fact that he was one tough son of a bitch, and you have yourself a real winner. I don't think he ever really received the credit he deserved. His backup, Jeff Hostetler, was made of similar stuff. He started at wide receiver in a playoff game in 1986 because of injuries to some regulars. He ran back kicks for a short time and also blocked a punt. Yet when Simms was hurt in 1990, Hoss answered the call and helped us win a second title.

I don't think there was one guy on our offensive line who would ever win a tough-man competition. Parcells used to call them, collectively, the suburbanites. That almost sounds as if he was telling them they were soft, but it was his way of motivating them. They played well as a unit and could always be depended on to give a rock-solid performance, especially in big games. That Giants team is remembered for having a great defense, but once you got past the linebackers and maybe Leonard Marshall, one of our defensive ends, there were no real stars. The Giants did it with a group of collective personalities who were molded and united by a strong coach and a desire to win. Sound familiar?

No matter how good and how strong a coach is, it's nearly impossible to make a team a big winner his first year, even if the talent level is pretty high. Again, it comes down to personality. The players the new coach inherits have their own personalities, as well as the extension of the personality of the former coach. Jon Gruden will face this situation as new head coach of the Tampa Bay Buccaneers in 2002 after coming over from a successful run with the Oakland Raiders. No matter how you cut the pie, however, Gruden inherits a team built by Tony Dungy. He has maybe six months to put his program in place, to make Tony Dungy's team buy into Jon Gruden's philosophy. That isn't easy. He can't come in and immediately say this is how it's going to be done from now on, the Jon Gruden way. It might help if he could find someone to tell him exactly how Dungy ran the team and what he did. As it is, he will be coaching players who might not initially share his offensive and defensive philosophies.

Bill Belichick is already extremely familiar with the professional football player as an individual, yet even he had to work to earn respect. Guys just didn't walk up to him and say "Show us the way!" That first year, the 2000 season, there were players not listening, not doing the things he wanted them to do, and many of them were fined. Once the team began to lose, certain players began to reveal their true colors. The new coach has to see which ones are still trying to perform, still showing a strong desire to win, as opposed to those who are already taking the easy way out and, in effect, giving up on the team and the season. If one player didn't want to win as badly as the next, then we couldn't hold on to him. The coach especially has to watch the reactions of the veterans. If the veteran guys who are getting the big salaries don't respect the head coach, the young guys won't either.

When Belichick began asking some of the veterans to restructure their contracts, it was the guys who wanted to win, the ones who could see what the coach was trying to accomplish, who agreed to take a cut in pay. Another thing that we did in 2001 was to rely more on free agents than rookies. By bringing in free agents, you're bringing in known quantities, guys with track records, and hopefully guys with the kind of personalities that will add to the team. Some coaches have a motto that says "Rookies will get you fired." That's because if a coach depends on too many new guys, players learning a pro system for the first time and who won't really be ready for a year or two, he could find himself fired by then. When faced with the pressure of producing immediate results, a player like Bryan Cox, with an infectious personality and attitude, is worth more than any rookie, no matter how talented he might be.

The Patriots continue to try to make themselves a better team. Even if you win it all, you can't stand pat, thinking "We've got our guys" and that's it. You always have to look to improve, either by filling specific needs or by creating healthy competition at various positions. A prime example of this in my mind is the 2000 New York Giants. The Giants had a very successful year, making it all the way to the Super Bowl. I don't believe too many people expected them to go that far. Yet at the end of the season it was apparent the team's brain trust didn't sit back and say "Wait a minute. We made it to the Super Bowl, but we're still not complete." They failed to take the steps needed to ensure keeping the team at the same high level in 2001. With essentially the same cast of characters and some of those guys resting on their laurels, the Giants took several steps backward. A team has to keep making itself better. Belichick understands that. I'm not sure all coaches do.

Coach Belichick also has a much more low-key personality than, say, a Bill Parcells. Parcells's presence—his height, size, and scowl—allowed him to intimidate guys. I remember defensive tackle Jason Ferguson coming up to me when I was with the Jets and complaining that Belichick never said anything to him. I told Jason, "If he doesn't say anything to you, then you know you're doing well. If he's on you all the time, then you better start thinking about packing your bags." Bill Belichick is a much smaller guy physically than Parcells and has a dry way of making guys feel bad when they make a mistake. His saying is "WTFU," which means, bluntly, "Wake the fuck up!"

Belichick is also a quiet guy. Unless there is something important to say, you have to initiate the conversation with him. I've known him for seventeen years, and sometimes we just walk past each other without saying a word. If I walk past Rob Ryan, whom I've known only two years, it's always "Hey, Rob-O." "Hey, Pep." When Belichick is working on a StairMaster or treadmill, he'll be doing something like reading the paper. You always have the feeling that you don't want to bother him. It's not that's it's a bother. If you have to talk to him about something, he'll talk, but he sometimes seems a bit withdrawn. Say "hey" to Parcells when he's on a treadmill and he'll call you over and hold a conversation. Two different guys, two different personalities, both winners.

Coach Belichick has always been a stickler for detail. He has everything taped—every drill, every unit—and he watches all the tapes, every inch of them. Because his father was a coach as well, he comes from a football background and has been around the game all his life. It was his father who told him that players don't lose games—coaches do—and that coaches don't win games; players do. He believes we can put players in a position to win, but they're the ones who have to execute the game plan, make the plays, and ultimately win the game.

Neither the assistant coaches nor the players can have thin skin. If a player can't take verbal abuse from teammates telling him to wake up, that we've got to win, then he's on the wrong team. In fact a player like that will have a tough time staying in the league, let alone being successful. Head coaches have to be tough. They need to instill something of a fear factor right down the chain of command, or not very much of a positive nature will be accomplished. There's no way the head coach can do everything, so he needs our help. By the same token, if we agree with everything he says and never challenge him, then we're not doing him justice and not helping the team.

That's probably another reason a head coach wants to keep most of the same guys around him. Parcells always wanted his guys around, and Belichick is the same way. He prefers to make more work for the assistants he trusts rather than start from scratch with someone new, unless it's absolutely necessary. For instance, he decided not to hire a quarterbacks coach for 2002. If you recall, he and Charlie Weis did the job last year after Coach Rehbein's death. They met about it extensively after the season, and both decided to take the responsibility once more, instead of hiring and having to teach a new coach. Stability and continuity are the key ingredients, even when you bring in a cagey veteran like Cox or Roman Phifer or Anthony Pleasant. Guys like that are diamonds, not only because of their ability and personalities but also because they can learn a system very quickly and after one year it seems as if they have been around for five.

Coach Belichick encourages give-and-take with his players, allowing them to be individuals within the system. He's not a my-way-or-the-highway guy. Every Friday he meets with the team's captains, and a lot of issues come up. Whether players bring concerns from off the field or on it, he always listens and hears them out. If guys want to move dinnertime up one day and he can accommodate them, he will. If there's a reason not to, he won't. Last season, when things weren't going well early, a few players grew increasingly frustrated. Ty Law prefers it when the defense plays more man-to-man coverage, because that's his strong point. Lawyer, however, is a down-in-the-box safety who likes to come up and help on the run, cover tight ends, and slash like a linebacker. Something like that can become a problem. One guy wants to play man, the other wants to play zone, and both are big influences on defense. Obviously you can't play man to man and zone at the same time, so the coach has to know just how to feed all those egos.

Ultimately you have to do what's best for the team. You have to explain to them why you are playing a certain defense in certain situations, but you also have to be able to maximize the talents of the individual. So you have to find ways to give Ty enough man to man to keep him happy and still let Lawyer be the kind of safety that makes him most effective. Find the balance and the smart, dedicated player will understand. If you just tell them they have to do it your way and don't give them a reason, then chances are they'll be playing halfheartedly.

It's easier for veterans to approach the coach than it is for the younger players, almost like a chain of command. If a young player sees something he wants to bring up to the coaches, it can be a problem. If someone like Antwan Harris, a cornerback just in his second season in 2001, wanted to point something out, his best bet would be to take it to Lawyer or Ty or Otis Smith and let one of them take it to the coaches. I remember something that happened my third year in the league with the Giants. We were playing the Cardinals when I noticed we had only ten men on the field. I wanted to call a time-out, but I didn't because I felt Parcells would have snapped my head off. So I quickly backed up and played like I was a safety. I remember Belichick congratulating me for having the presence of mind to move back and fill the gap, but he also asked me why I didn't tell somebody. I just said it all happened so fast that I wasn't sure what to do.

That's the difference between being in the league three years and playing for five seasons. By 1990 I would have turned around and called time-out. I always paid attention when we went over different situations, because Parcells wanted us to be thinking what he was thinking. I knew we had two time-outs left and knew it was a crucial drive. If it's important, you best believe I'm gonna call time-out. But when you're a young player, you don't do it. In my rookie year I can honestly say my mind was numb, but by the time I went to Cleveland in 1993 I was almost a player-coach. There's a big difference when the players understand what the coaches are trying to accomplish. After I was with the Giants a few years, I was the guy who got the defense lined up and gave the secondary the coverage. The rest was cake. In Cleveland I remember Belichick telling his defensive coordinator, Nick Saban, that I could run the two-minute drill on defense because I had been doing that, too, with the Giants. Like I said, the middle linebacker is like the quarterback of the defense.

It's always interesting comparing the teams I've been with, just as it is comparing the coaches. There were certainly similarities between the Giants teams of 1986–90 and the 2001 Patriots. For openers, both teams had a lot of guts. To be honest, I didn't see the 1998 Jets falling into that category, though the team had a lot of hungry guys who were tired of losing. They were willing to do anything Parcells told them, anything Belichick and the other coaches said. It was certainly a hungry, well-shaped team. The team was so-so in 1997, then rolled into the AFC championship game the following year. A lot of pieces were in place, but they still needed a little help here and there. I retired at the end of that season, Vinny Testaverde was hurt at the start of the following year, and the team essentially collapsed in the first half. The Jets are probably the perfect example of the very good team that didn't get better, never put those final pieces in place.

When I came to the Patriots in 2000, I didn't see that hunger. There were a few guys tired of losing, but, as I've said, there were many other guys whose agendas were elsewhere. In fact there were still enough players on the team who had experienced the Super Bowl loss in 1996 and were on the divisional winning team the following year. Again, though, it was a matter of personalities going in the wrong direction. Some players were bitter and fed up, others were just cocky, and we had to remove the our-shit-don't-stink attitude. Sure, you went to the Super Bowl in '96, but you lost. That's the bottom line. You lost. At the same time, I think a lot of guys were fed up by yet another coaching change. They had believed in Parcells, just as the Jets did. When he arrived with a new team, there was the utmost respect for him and belief in him because he had always been a winner. When he bailed and Pete Carroll took over, there were many people who never believed he had had full control of the team.

It really took Belichick a whole year to begin gaining respect. The first year many of the players were unwilling to shed the country-club mentality from the previous coaching regime. The Patriots of 2001, however, found the hunger again. Guys came back wanting to win.

In some ways, though, the 1986 Giants and 2001 Patriots were not all that similar. The Giants learned a major lesson in 1985 from the Chicago Bears. The team saw firsthand how a championship team goes about things. That team was so mature, and when they played the Giants they showed them how to turn it up a notch and dominate. It was an embarrassing loss but a learning experience just the same. It was like your parents explaining why the stove is hot and not just mending your burned hand. When I joined the returning veterans in 1986, we had our destiny spelled out. Parcells told us up front that we had a championship team, but it was up to us to make it happen.

The '86 Giants relied more on rookies than the '01 Patriots. I played a great deal, and there were major contributions from Greg Lasker, Eric Dorsey, John Washington, and Mark Collins. We all saw a lot of playing time, especially late in the season. One similarity between the two teams was that the defense held up when the offense was weakened by injuries and faltered. Free agency, as I said, has somewhat diminished the role of rookies. I would say that the Patriots last year really just relied on significant contributions from Richard Seymour and Matt Light, our first two draft picks. It was our free agents—hungry guys like Cox, Vrabel, Izzo, and Phifer—who helped give the team that needed, final push.

I think you could make a case for the 2001 Patriots being closer to the 1990 Giants team. The '86 Giants just dominated, marched to the championship with incredible confidence. The '90 Giants had to take a much more difficult road, as did the 2001 Patriots. For example, I would describe the Patriots' season as on-the-job training. As the season grew, so did we. We learned something new every week and became stronger, which is exactly what you have to do if you expect to make a championship run. We would play our last five or six games of the season as if they were playoff games. After the Rams game in week ten, we were in a situation where, if we lost, we wouldn't be in control of our own destiny. Four of five other teams were also vying for that control. The road that we traveled took us from a how-can-we-get-into-the-playoffs scenario to winning the AFC East.

The 1990 Giants were motivated by getting back there. The team had won in '86 and still had many of the core players. They wanted to taste that ultimate victory once again. Guys like Harry Carson and George Martin were seasoned veterans and to me were the links to the past, reminding me of the entire New York Giants' history and tradition. The team had won a championship in the 1950s and been in the title game several times in the early 1960s.

The '86 team, however, was the first to reach and win a Super Bowl, which began after the NFL-AFL merger in 1967. That team was incredibly focused and late in the season began playing for home field advantage. We didn't want to end up in Chicago, Washington, or San Francisco. We got home field, and they could have put an NFL All-Star team out there, and we still would have beaten them for the NFC title. There wasn't that kind of confidence in the '90 Giants or '01 Patriots.

One of the similarities between the 1990 Giants and the 2001 Patriots was the change at quarterback. The Giants still had Simms starting in 1990, and we were glad to have him. I always felt for Jeff Hostetler, because it was obvious he had the talent to start for a lot of teams by then. The players knew what he could do; only the media questioned it. When Simms got hurt, a lot of the press wanted the team to go with veteran backup Matt Cavanaugh. But Hoss gave us another dimension. Now defenses couldn't load up on our running backs, Rodney Hampton, or O. J. Anderson, or our tight end, Mark Bavaro. Besides being a solid passer, Hostetler moved around in the pocket and was a threat to run.

Tom Brady also had the ability to move in the pocket, more so than Drew. I remember when Hostetler took a huge hit in the chest or ribs during the NFC title game with San Francisco. He had to come out, and Cavanaugh went in. His first pass was wild, way off the mark. He went back to the huddle, licking his fingers as quarterbacks do, then threw another way over the target. Meanwhile Hoss was on the bench, barely able to breathe. But when he saw what was happening, he sucked it up and came back in on the next series. I remember everyone breathing a big sigh of relief. It was as if the heavens began to shine. There was no way we were going to lose now. Sure enough, he drove us deep into 49ers territory, and Matt Bahr kicked the winning field goal.

When he replaced Drew in week two, Brady took a little while to grow on us, but then we began getting more confidence in him. We saw the kind of player he was. If he had to throw for four hundred yards, he did. When he had to bring us downfield and put us in a position to win a game, he did. Once he began to show us the things he could do, the defense began to play in support of the offense. We never knew when we would score ten points or twenty points. So we wanted to hold our opponents down, and we became stronger as the year wore on. As the players began coming more and more into their own, so did the coaching staff. I really think we matured as a staff during the year, found our niche, and became much more comfortable with our defense.

By the end of the season it actually became fun. We had a blitz for everyone on the defense—everyone who played, not just the starters. The third and fourth corners, for example, had blitzes designed for them with their names attached to the play call. Other formations were named after defensive linemen. If a player knew his blitz was going to be called during the game, his eyes would light up in the meeting room. Guys loved it when they had the chance to blitz, and sometimes just calling that play once would spark the player to excel for the rest of the game.

Winning is always fun, an obvious morale builder, and makes for more camaraderie on the team. As I've said before, however, you don't want it to end. Unless you win that final game, your season ends on a sour note, especially once you make the playoffs. Then, if you don't win it all, your last memory of that season is a defeat. I remember Lawyer saying that it was a lot easier talking to the coach in the captains' meetings when we were winning. No matter what the situation, Belichick always tries to keep his game face on, but he's a guy who really loves his players. No one will ever tell me anything different. However, he is never completely happy until there is a championship to celebrate. Even after a regular-season victory you rarely get a smile from him. He may throw his hands up a little after a win, but that's all. The thing he absolutely knows is that the results are much better when you have guys who want to play for you. In 2001, everyone on the team wanted to win for Bill Belichick.

There's one other sidelight that I'd like to mention here, because it shows that football players have a life away from the game, though during the season it's not always easy to enjoy it, sometimes even difficult to acknowledge it. The schedule is so totally demanding for everyone, and the season seems to get longer every year. For the coaches, in fact, it's a full-time, year-round job. At any rate, during the 2001 season we really had an epidemic of births (mostly girls) among our team. I believe Bert Emanuel was the first new father. Already a father to three daughters at the beginning of the season, he and his wife had a fourth. Then Charles Johnson's wife gave birth to a baby girl. Lawyer Milloy also became the father of a baby girl, then Kevin Faulk followed suit. Guys were beginning to ask each time, "Don't tell me you had a girl, too?" It didn't stop there. Damien Woody's wife followed with—you guessed it—another girl.

Finally, Mike Vrabel's wife broke the streak and gave birth to a boy. Vrabel ribbed the other new fathers relentlessly: "All you wussies go and have daughters. Well, I had a boy." That's the kind of thing that relieves tension, and that was great. Guys would take off, and you wouldn't see them at practice for a day. One day Bobby Hamilton left in the middle of practice. Then Coach Belichick, when he was making announcements at the morning meeting, said Bobby and his wife just had a baby. He wouldn't say what it was until somebody asked. No shock there. It was another baby girl!

Most players, however, are totally committed to the team, and when someone's wife is pregnant, almost ready to give birth, it can be tough. When my friend Keith Byars was still playing with Miami, his wife was pregnant and still wanted to attend the games, even when her due date was imminent. So just in case she went into labor, Keith had an ambulance waiting in the tunnel beneath the stadium. She was a gospel singer and sang the national anthem that day. Then he played and scored a touchdown while she was on the sideline, ready to be rushed to the hospital at a moment's notice.

I remember a story about the Houston Oilers that really made me think about a lot of things. The Oilers had an offensive lineman whose wife had a baby on a Saturday afternoon before the Sunday game. He went to the hospital, and the team owner volunteered to have a private jet pick him up Saturday evening and take him to the away game site. The guy said no, he wouldn't get on the plane, that he was going to spend the weekend with his family. He didn't play, and the team lost. Warren Moon, their quarterback then, was sacked several times. Two months later, Moon's wife had a baby on Saturday night with a game the next day. He's the quarterback, mind you, not easily replaced. Well, he made it back to the team in the wee hours Sunday morning and played later that day.

When I heard that story, I said to my girlfriend at the time that football was one of the main reasons I wasn't married. I simply love the game too much. If I was in that situation, I really don't know what I would do. I have a son who's almost sixteen now, and I know how hysterical I was when his mother went into labor and I was in Detroit. I jumped in my car and started driving to reach Ohio so I could be there with her. I was late, but I wanted to see my son. Fortunately, it wasn't during the season, but if it had been I don't know if I would have stopped and not played the next day. Look at it this way, if you really want to take care of your family, you have to continue working. I can totally understand the guys who want time off, maybe miss a game, but I think that situation would have made me want to go and play much better for the simple reason that my responsibilities just increased and I now had someone else who would be depending on me.

What some guys tend to forget is that when you miss a game you aren't the only one affected by it. It also affects your teammates and sometimes can affect the outcome of the game. During my playing career guys sometimes used to say to me, "Pepper, you don't ever get sick." It was true. I would tell myself during the season that I couldn't get sick. I didn't care what kind of weather I played in. *I can't get sick. I am the leader of the defense. Yes, I can be banged up as if my whole body is being ripped apart, but there's no way I can't come out for practice. Hell, there can't be a practice without me. It's my defense.* I didn't even want to come out for a play. That was the way I felt about the game.

Of course, not everyone feels that way, just as everyone doesn't play the same way. Different personalities make up every team in the league. Not everyone has the same agenda, the same practice habits, the same superstitions, the same routine to get himself ready. It is the combination of all these individuals that makes up a team. The trick is getting the individuals to mesh, to have the same attitude about the team, about winning, and about being a part of the whole. That's the job of the coaches, and the ones who do it the best and with the most consistency are the coaches who produce the winning teams. As the 2001 season moved into its middle stages, we were all beginning to think that Coach Belichick and the rest of us had been doing it the right way.

5

The Second Four Games
Righting a Sinking Ship

Talk about a *must* game. Our fifth game, against San Diego at Foxboro, was huge, a game we absolutely had to win. We were coming off a totally embarrassing loss to the Dolphins in Miami just at the time when we were trying to finish the first quarter of the season on a positive note. Instead, we got blown out, put up very little resistance in the heat, and came away with a 1–3 record. Now we were wondering if everything we had put into the off season and preseason really mattered.

To make matters worse, the doubters were starting to chirp a little louder. Now Coach Belichick had to tighten the noose around everybody's neck because we were on the brink of losing everything we had worked so hard to build. That's exactly what would happen if we lost to the Chargers. You have time to climb back out of a 1–3 hole, because it's a long season, not a sprint.

That's what we were trying to emphasize to the players, that the NFL season is closer to a marathon, but, at the same time, there are no easy weeks. Unlike the college game, no pro team has the luxury of playing terrible teams that are going to give you seventy points, like you see so often today in the college game. It was time to play all our cards, because, as I said, a 1–3 start can be reversed. Start the season at 1–4, however, and you might as well be staring into an abyss.

In retrospect, we really knew those first four games would be rough, mainly because of the injuries the team had suffered in the preseason. Too many guys were banged up and not practicing. A perfect example was our center/guard, Mike Compton. He was an integral part of our offensive line, but he had missed the entire preseason and was just now starting to round into top shape.

In fact, we had been alternating a number of offensive linemen just to keep them healthy, so the stability you need with that unit wasn't there.

Anyone who knows football knows the importance of a stable offensive line. In a perfect gridiron world, all five linemen work together the entire season, and that continuity has been the trademark of the best offensive lines in history. They stay together for a long period of time. The offensive line of the Giants' championship teams is a perfect example. None of the individuals were coffee-table conversation pieces, but together, when you said Giants offensive line, they could move the home that coffee table was in. They worked great together—the trademark of a good offensive line—and in the first four games of the season we didn't have that.

In week five we faced the San Diego Chargers, and we were all well aware of just what we were up against. With a 3–1 record, the Chargers were off to their best start in years. They were supposed to have had the strongest draft of any team and were coming in on a real high. When you added the fact that they were quarterbacked by Doug Flutie, who had an incredible 12–1 record playing against the Patriots at Foxboro, well, it seemed to most people that the Patriots were in for another long afternoon. Not surprisingly, the media were ambivalent about our 1–3 start. It wasn't big, bold front-page news. It was more like, hey, this is about what we expected all along. In fact, in the days leading up to the game Flutie was the main focus, not the Patriots' slow start.

The papers, however, were still second-guessing, especially our quarterback situation. They labeled Brady a third-stringer and wondered openly why Damon Huard, who had some thirty games of NFL experience and was considered the backup at the beginning of the season, hadn't gotten the call. It wasn't too late, they said, for Coach Belichick to put Brady on the bench and give the ball to Huard. A lot of them thought our victory over the Colts, as decisive as it was, amounted to nothing more than a fluke. They reminded everyone that Belichick had always done well against Peyton Manning, as if to say the one victory didn't count.

There are, however, certain aspects of the game that the writers don't understand. Manning has a great deal of responsibility for a young quarterback, and, without going into detail, he tips some of the things he's going to do. A seasoned veteran like Bryan Cox who understands the game and picks up on Manning's checks is going to kill him. We had a similar situation in the 1990 Super Bowl. Buffalo quarterback Jim Kelly called his own plays, and the offense used nicknames and numbers to make the calls.

Kelly, for instance, would say "Black 33, Monday, Monday." That meant the ball would be snapped on 1. Or he would say "Red 85, Wednesday." He called low numbers for runs and high numbers for passes. When he said "Wednesday," the snap was on 3. After halftime they started doing January, February. Same thing. We figured they would have ten or twelve plays he would run in the first half and maybe another twelve to fifteen in the second half. The snap counts, however, were the same. He would say the snap count before the play. It was just a matter of time before he repeated a name or number and then—BAM—his telegraphed call enabled our defense to make a big play. Doing that with a guy like Carl Banks was ridiculous. Banks was a devoted student of the game. He often knew what was coming. It was the same with Bryan Cox. All Manning's audibles, checks, and bluffs didn't matter. He was really hindering himself more than us.

Unfortunately, that was water under the bridge. If we were so good and so smart, how had we lost the other three games? That's what we had to correct, and now we had to prepare for Flutie, who is perhaps the most elusive quarterback in the game. Flutie is extremely difficult to defend against simply because at first glance it seems easy. That probably doesn't make sense initially, but look at it this way. Everybody says he's short, so all the defenders have to do is put their hands up while they rush and it makes it difficult for him to throw. Sure, it's often hard for him to throw passes in the middle of the field, but their offensive coordinator knows this is a problem, and he adjusts by creating blocking schemes designed to open passing lanes for him. Others try to get right in his face, only Flutie is smart enough to know you're about to get in his face, and he immediately turns into Harry Houdini and escapes.

So it's really best to let him stay back and throw the ball. Flutie isn't a pocket passer or a scrambling quarterback, per se. He's more of a modern-day Fran Tarkenton, a guy who makes things happen, so you aren't going to stop him with basic defenses. He's a student of the game and understands what it takes to get the ball to the right receiver. Rarely does he run backward twenty yards like Tarkenton did, so we try to do different things. For example, we try to blitz him when he's not expecting the blitz. We try to show blitzes and then play zone. Then we'll show zone and play man coverages. The idea is to try not to give him the same look two plays in a row. If you give him repetitive looks, he's gonna hurt you. With a guy like Flutie, I think it becomes a challenge for him to break you down. He sees you in man coverage, and he scrambles. No defense or defensive coach wants to see a quarterback scramble when you're in man coverage. That's the gift that Doug Flutie has that has enabled him to be successful.

Besides Flutie, the Chargers were equipped with other offensive weapons: receivers Curtis Conway and Jeff Graham and their outstanding rookie running back, LaDainian Tomlinson. Because they had gotten off to such a fast start while we were struggling, I don't think any of the area writers picked us to win. Maybe they had a point. We were on the verge of cracking. If Doug Flutie had come to town and won another ball game, I can honestly say I don't think we would have been able to overcome it. When coaches lose a few games in a row, they kind of run out of sales pitches. You know, the ones who say "That's OK. We almost had them. I'll take that loss. We lost it as coaches." Gradually you run out of those speeches, and the ship starts to show cracks. After the Miami loss there was a lot of hurt pride. To be honest about it, we had a little bit of arrogance going to Miami. We really thought it was the year we would go there and beat them, get even for losing that final game the previous year. We thought we were going to teach them a lesson. For them to shove it back in our face flattened a few tires.

I'm a strong believer in football being 90 percent mental. During the week leading up to the Miami game, our players drank a lot of water, and I think that adversely affected them more than the heat and humidity. Remember how I said it gets into your head? The heat, the heat, the heat. Mentally, everyone was already thinking about it. It's the same with the guys from California coming into the cold at the end of the season. That kind of stuff never washed with me. The bottom line in this sport is that you've got to be a man. We have guys who grew up in Texas, California, Mississippi, Alabama, and Florida. They talk about how hot it is and have lived in that climate all their lives. Then they go to Miami for a football game, and suddenly all those years they lived in hot weather don't mean a thing? I just don't understand that. It's the same in Denver. I never understood the mile-high thing. I didn't get any more tired playing games in Denver's altitude than I did in Detroit.

There was another topic that served as a diversion in the week preceding the game with San Diego. After serving his four-game suspension, Terry Glenn was suited up and ready to play. I think that took some of the pressure off Tom Brady. Now, instead of all the questions being directed at Tom, everyone wanted to know about Terry, how the players felt about him being back, stuff like that. He came out and practiced with us the entire week before the game. Having him back gave us a good feeling, though in some ways it was an uncomfortable one. In one sense you want to shake his hand, maybe hug him, and tell him you're glad he's back. At the same time, however, you don't want to show too much emotion toward him and treat him as if he's a baby. We knew we were going to be OK with it one way or another, but at some point we knew he had to consider us also.

A grown man has to pay his debts. In this crazy business you have to make sacrifices. At the beginning of a new season you never know what kind of sacrifices will be asked of you. In some ways making sacrifices was the story of the 2001 Patriots. Some guys had to take pay cuts, some had to lose friends, some had to turn loose idols, some had to play with pain, come through after injuries. We all had to overcome losing one of our coaches and losing one of our leaders, Drew Bledsoe, early in the season. These kinds of sacrifices were what made the Patriots succeed. Unfortunately, you don't have a choice of whether you want to lose your left foot or right hand. Suddenly it's taken from you, and you have to deal with it. So while we were basically happy to have Terry Glenn back with us, we felt he had something to prove as well.

One of the biggest knocks on Terry was that he was great at catching the ball, but his running after the catch often left something to be desired. He would either leave a defender in the dust or run out of bounds. He wasn't going to make three or four defenders miss tackles like Troy Brown or struggle for extra yards with someone hanging on him. When he was introduced to the fans before the game, the boos were as loud as the cheers. But early on he caught a four-yard hitch and wiggled one way, went the other, and ran for the extra yards and a first down. We felt maybe he was trying to prove something after all.

The game was tight early, both teams trading field goals in the first quarter. Brady smartly threw to Terry early, making sure to get his head into the game, and Terry was looking good. In the second quarter Brady threw into the end zone and Terry made a helluva catch in the corner for six points. His catch not only gave us the lead but won over the fans as well. Now everyone was cheering for him, and at that given moment no one cared a bit about the suspension or his preseason problems. The catch came from twenty-one yards out, and while it was a yard beyond the so-called red zone, Terry had always excelled at getting loose when the team was in close. Adam, however, missed the extra point, and we had just a 9–3 lead. They managed another field goal before the half, so we led by just three at intermission.

Even though we had the lead, we weren't playing well. The game was ugly in a lot of ways. Our punter, Lee Johnson, was shanking the ball all day, and our running game was still inconsistent. In addition to that, we were now about to begin the third quarter, where we had been outscored, 51–10, so far this season. I think there were a lot of reasons for this. For openers, we weren't always prepared. Teams were making adjustments at halftime and we weren't, or if we did, we just all weren't on the same page. There might have been another reason as well. In the old days a team's starters would increase their playing time throughout the preseason, right until the final game. When the season began, they were already in game shape. Today no one goes more than a half in the preseason. Maybe they'll play a series in the third quarter, then come out. So I believe part of the problem might have been game shape and game awareness.

Oddly enough, Coach Belichick is one of the best at making game day, halftime, and sideline adjustments. That's one of his key coaching strengths. He prepares so thoroughly that he totally understands the opposition, and come game day he already has all the possible adjustments in his head. In addition, he's got an incredible memory for what players and teams have done in the past. So we had the brain trust working, and that means that a large part of the problem was execution. I think it started to become a phobia. Guys began overemphasizing it. They would say "Let's not give up anything." You're supposed to come out for the third just as strongly as you finished the second, but we weren't doing that. Despite the big emphasis, we were being out-rebounded.

So it was a combination of factors. In looking at the game summaries I could see we were taking penalties, missing tackles, experiencing mental breakdowns. We would look to get a good start in the third quarter, but it wasn't happening. Once we broke out of it and finally stopped talking about it, it went away. A lot of the guys, however, continued to be wary of the third quarter until late in the season. When the Chargers scored first early in the third period and took a 13–9 lead, I know a lot of people were thinking, Here we go again. Midway through the period, however, Brady led us on a seventy-one-yard, ten-play touchdown drive with Antowain Smith scoring from just outside the goal line. It was only from a yard out, but he bounced right off a tackle from San Diego's great middle linebacker, Junior Seau, and ran it in. That's what we wanted Antowain for, that kind of power running. The year before we didn't have a dependable running back for short yardage or goal line situations. Defenses knew we would probably throw for it. With an Antowain Smith back there, the opposition knows we can score on the ground and in the air. Smith's touchdown made it 16–13, and that's how it stayed going into the fourth quarter. Only now our mettle would be tested once again.

This is where it got ugly for us. We had a couple of defensive holding penalties, the kind you hate to take, and Flutie capitalized by leading his team on a drive and throwing a short scoring pass to his tight end. The extra point gave them the lead at 19–16, with the worst yet to come. With the ball inside our own ten, Lee Johnson dropped back to punt. He fielded the snap cleanly, but with the Chargers' Derrick Harris bearing down on him, he couldn't get the kick off and tried to run. Suddenly he just dropped the ball, and when Harris scooped it up, Johnson didn't tackle him. It was a gift touchdown, and it gave the Chargers a 26–16 lead with 8:48 left. So now we're down by ten with just over half a period remaining. We were facing much more than a deflating loss; it could've been the end of the season. Quitting, however, was one of the last things on our minds because of the magnitude of the ball game. No one really talked about what might happen, because something like that is the last thing you want to mention in the heat of battle. You just don't talk about the possibility of losing. A year earlier this game would have been over. In this situation guys on the 2000 team would have had that zombie face on. Are we gonna win, or are we gonna find a way to lose? In 2001 we were calm about it. We had a prevailing sense of urgency that said, "Let's go out and win this thing instead of wondering what happens next."

So we went to work as soon as we got the ball back. This might have been the drive that made us realize Tom Brady wasn't going to let us down. He took the offense sixty-nine yards in fifteen plays, taking care of both business and the football. When the drive finally stalled, Vinatieri kicked a twenty-three-yard field goal to make it 26–19 with just 3:31 remaining. Then our defense made a stand, stopping Flutie and the Chargers quickly and getting the ball back for our offense, giving them good field position at our own forty-yard line. Doing what he had to do, Brady got us down the field quickly. It took seven plays to bring us to the Chargers' three. With just forty seconds left in regulation, Brady hit Jermaine Wiggins in the end zone for a touchdown. Adam kicked the extra point, and the game was tied with just thirty-six seconds left. They had a shot at a fifty-nine-yard field goal in the closing seconds but came up short.

Now we were in sudden death, a first-score-wins-it-all situation. The Chargers got the ball first but the defense really came through, giving them nothing but a one-two-three-punt. We started our drive from our own twenty-three, and after committing a bunch of needless penalties early in the game, we got one back. The Chargers' cornerback Alex Molden was called for pass interference on David Patten, the penalty good for thirty-seven yards. Three more Brady completions brought it to the twenty-six, and Coach Belichick sent Adam Vinatieri out to try to win it. Vinatieri was really down when he missed that extra point early in the game. He felt even worse when it was tied at the end of regulation, because that point would have been the difference. But I told him not to worry, that it would come back to him, and, sure enough, it did. He had to kick from a tough angle, but the ball went through the uprights, a forty-four-yard field goal that gave us a 29–26 win and maybe a victory that saved the season.

It was an incredible game for a lot of reasons. The defense got better as the game wore on, though our special teams didn't play well—something that just eats at Belichick—and the punting game was awful. In fact the team released Lee Johnson later in the week. On the offensive side, Terry Glenn made the most of his return to the team, catching seven passes for 110 yards, and Troy was great as usual. He grabbed eleven for 117 yards. As for Brady, he had proven an awful lot to everyone. He completed thirty-three of fifty-four for 364 yards and two touchdowns, and on the last two important drives he was ten of sixteen for 101 yards. What a lift he gave us.

As for Adam Vinatieri, what can you say about having a guy like that on your team? Everyone knows his range, so we always work hard to put on a few extra yards to make his job easier, and we're killing the clock at the same time. Then we know he's going to make the kick. Adam is a serious guy. He works out with the linebackers and has made a few tackles in his day. He's proof of what hard work can do, an undrafted player who went to Europe to play in the WFL, kept working, and finally got his chance in the NFL. He doesn't have one of the strongest legs in the league, but in a cold-weather game in December, I can't think of another guy I'd rather have kicking that football. That's the heart and soul of the man.

Was it a big win? Oh, yeah. A huge win? Oh, yeah. But it's over. Now, we're not looking at it as if we dodged a bullet, that we just beat a heavily favored 3–1 team. We're thinking that, Hey, we're supposed to win, and now we've got to concentrate on getting to .500. Everyone is also feeling a lot better about Tom Brady. He's by no means cocky, and the success he was beginning to have couldn't have happened to a better guy. You would never think it was just his second year the way he controlled the huddle in the Chargers game, how smoothly he was relaying plays. He managed the huddle with poise and confidence, which is a quality that separates the best quarterbacks from their peers. Phil Simms would call the play, then address key players individually. Brady is like that as well.

Now we were ready to go on the road to Indianapolis for our second meeting with the Colts and a chance to reach the .500 mark for the season. It seems, however, that the 2001 Patriots couldn't do anything the easy way. When Terry Glenn came back, the club released Bert Emanuel, the veteran receiver we had picked up in the off season. Terry had played a great game against the Chargers. In fact, we ended up playing him more than we had originally planned because our running game wasn't working that well. So we had a lot of sets with three or four wide receivers. The funny part was that, though he was back, a lot of the players understood what was happening with Terry, and we knew he wouldn't automatically be a fixture, only we didn't see it coming that soon. Against the Chargers he suffered a hamstring injury and was placed on the inactive list for the next six weeks. When we learned he had been deactivated for the Colts game, the team was able to adjust. We were trying to focus and concentrate on the season, so we were prepared if he was here and prepared if he wasn't here.

Unlike our previous game against the Chargers, there was no suspense with the Colts. Once again we came out strong and exploded for a 28–6 halftime lead, then coasted home with a 38–17 victory and a 3–3 record. We had achieved our first goal, getting back to .500. However, this wasn't a carbon copy of our first meeting with them. This time Indianapolis moved the ball better than they had in our first meeting, the reason being the pace of the game and the way we designed our defensive game plan. What the Colts like to do is run the ball, and then when Peyton goes to the play-action pass he wants to throw big. So what we did was kind of like catching them in the web. We weren't going to give him that deep, play-action pass. We would give him stuff underneath—give him one, maybe two, maybe even three, then jump him on third or fourth. What we didn't want to do is run around with them man to man on every play. That would catch up with us because of their speed and all their offensive weapons. Heck, their second tight end was playing better than their starting tight end. They have four above-average receivers and one very, very good receiver. In today's game, if you concentrate on stopping the star, the other guys begin to look super.

Part of the way the defense played against the Colts was dictated by our offense. Normally, we're a team that drives the ball downfield and then scores. Suddenly, we're making big plays. Patten scored on a twenty-nine-yard end around. Soon after he scored again on a long, ninety-one-yard pass-run play. Then Troy grabbed a sixty-yard scoring pass. It's great to score like that, but he puts the defense back on the field quickly. So we lay back more rather than going after them full tilt. James ran for thirty or forty yards when we were in a prevent defense formation. We weren't upset about James running as much as we were about Marvin Harrison catching passes for big chunks. We missed a tackle here, blew a coverage there. It was small, minor things, but enough to keep their drives alive.

As I said, they like to strike big. It's when they back us into our red zone— that's when the bend-but-don't-break defense comes in. We stopped them enough times when we had to that the outcome was never in doubt, despite James running for more than 140 yards and Harrison catching more than 150 yards of passes. Manning, in fact, had a big game statistically, completing twenty-two of thirty-four passes for 335 yards. He threw for only one score, though, and they had just seventeen points, so that says something for the defense, because in time of possession their offense had the ball for seven more minutes than ours did.

There were, however, some great plays that you don't read in the stat sheet. On one long pass Tebucky Jones ran down Harrison from behind and tackled him on the two- or three-yard line. We tightened, and they got just a field goal out of it. Not very many players in the league can run down Marvin Harrison, and when the rest of the guys saw his tremendous effort, they rallied around it. This was the marquee play of the game on defense. Ironically, the defense we played, sitting back on guys and trapping them in the web, was the basic game plan that the entire football world would find out about a couple of months down the road in the playoffs and Super Bowl. So we were learning, every week.

Also, let's not forget the offense. The striking power they showed against the Colts also deserves mention. David Patten had an incredible game. He ran for a touchdown, caught two touchdown passes from Brady, and, to cap it off, threw the sixty-yard touchdown pass to Troy Brown. I was told later that he was the first NFL player to do all three in the same game since Walter Payton back in 1979. How's that for being in fast company? Both Brown and Patten went over the hundred-yard mark in receiving, while Brady had another outstanding game, completing sixteen of twenty for 202 yards and three scores. He had also thrown 131 consecutive passes without an interception. How many people said an inexperienced, second-year quarterback couldn't handle the pressure?

People don't always understand that a defense is not going to look the same week after week. We might play as well, but it won't always appear that way. That's because of the adjustments that have to be made to deal with the different offenses that we're trying to stop. The Colts defense isn't that strong, and once we got the big lead early, our strategy was to lie back a little more, not necessarily go after Manning on every play. San Diego was a different story. The game plan was not to let them move the ball up and down the field because their defense is so strong. So we had to do a little bit extra, like putting them in situations where they weren't punting the ball deep down near our goal line, where Troy either had to make a fair catch or let it bounce into the end zone. We have to go hard to stop them back on their twenty or thirty. That way, when they punt Troy is outside our twenty with a chance to run it out. That's part of the overall strategy of a game, the kind of material that doesn't come out in the stat lines or even in the newspapers.

After six games we felt that we were getting better. You could see it every week. If we had a game like we did in Miami the previous year, I don't know if we could have regrouped the next week. I'm not sure that defensive unit was mentally strong enough. In 2001, even if we were losing going into the fourth quarter, players didn't stand around hanging their heads. Their attitude on the sidelines remained positive. At the same time, when we won games, guys weren't celebrating excessively. The only time that happens is in overtime, like against San Diego. That's extra excitement. Maybe the reason we don't dwell on a loss or celebrate too long after a win is because, in either case, Coach Belichick feels there is always room for improvement. In fact, until I see the day we beat someone 60–0, there will always be room for improvement. So we tried to keep things in perspective. We were finally at .500, but now we were on the way to Denver, the good old mile-high city, and we knew that wouldn't be easy.

The Broncos remind me of the San Francisco 49ers teams of the 1980s. Don't get me wrong; they have a talented team with a highly respected coach in Mike Shanahan, but their offensive linemen are some of the dirtiest guys in the league. They love to use cut blocks on opposing defensive linemen and linebackers. San Francisco did the same thing in the '80s. Cut blocks are intentional, and I think it's a chump way of playing. When you have three-hundred-pound guys diving on the legs of smaller guys, the backs or sides of their legs when they're not looking, then you know you're going to hurt them. San Francisco used to post and cut. One guy would hit you high, the other coming in and hitting low. Denver cut-blocked so much against us that they were diving on the ground like scavengers. It's second nature to them, part of the game, and I think some of them don't even realize what they're really doing.

In practice the week before the game I did extra cut-block drills with my linebackers. You can't, however, totally prepare for a guy diving on the back of your legs. Some players do it to try to soften you up, to try to get you looking for the cut block, and then they come upstairs and hit you in the mouth. Denver actually mixes it up a lot better than San Francisco did, and the Broncos are a lot more physical. I really have no problem with a guy faking a cut block and hitting you in the mouth, but when they jump on the backs of legs from the side, you lose knees. If a player dives on the back of a quarterback's legs, he can be thrown out of the game, but with linemen and linebackers, they usually get away with it.

So maybe it wasn't so surprising when the Denver game claimed a victim of a cut block, and it wasn't good news for us. Bryan Cox broke a bone in his leg and would be out some four to six weeks. He was actually cut twice in the game. After the first one, which looked worse then the second, he got up. The one that did the damage came when a lineman jumped on the back of his leg.

That, however, wasn't all. It was just a bad news day all around, though it didn't begin that way. We had a 10–7 lead after the first quarter and upped it to 17–10 by halftime. It looked as if we were in control, especially when Matt Stevens intercepted a Brian Griese pass early in the third period and Adam kicked a forty-four-yard field goal to make it 20–10. Then, without any real warning, it began to come apart very quickly.

Our defense gave up fourteen points before the third quarter ended, turning a ten-point lead into a four-point, 24–20 deficit. They simply began making big plays that we couldn't stop. Before the game we knew we had to stop their fine wide receiver, Rod Smith. Because they had lost their other top wideout, Ed McCaffery, to injury earlier in the season, we thought it would be an easier task. Only one star to stop. They have a decent tight end, but Smith was the guy. We didn't want him to get deep, or catch and run, something we had emphasized in practice all week and then right up to game time. So what happens in the third? Smith turns a short pass into a sixty-five-yard touchdown, and they're right back in it. We just could not slow Smith down. After his score they stopped us three-and-out, sacking Brady twice, then they drove eighty yards in nine plays for the go-ahead score.

Brady finally had a bad day and began doing something he hadn't done in quite a while—throw interceptions. In fact he threw four of them in the fourth quarter, but, in truth, the game was over after the first pick. He was pressing, trying to force the ball. Because the game got away from us so quickly, we wanted him to pull another rabbit out of the hat. We simply tried to make things happen too fast. We still had time, but those are the bitters of playing in Denver. What we needed was a couple of good drives and some plays, but it just wasn't going to happen. The defense put Brady in a position he shouldn't have been in. One of the interceptions was taken back for a touchdown, and they won the game, 31–20, dropping us below .500 once again.

I think the biggest blow was not *that* we lost, but *how* we lost. Defensively, we allowed Rod Smith to catch passes for nearly 160 yards. That hurt us more than anything. In practice we had put an emphasis on trying to take away the things the guy likes to do and does so well. We knew we couldn't stop him completely, but we wanted to slow him down. Say he caught six balls for 90 yards instead of six for 159. We might have won the game if that had been the case. Now we're 3–4 and feel as if we've taken a step back. Once again, that brought up a must game, one we had to win. It was beginning to seem as if we were spending the entire year just trying to get to .500. In addition, our three-game road trip was continuing with our next stop in Atlanta.

That our team was playing hard was unquestionable. Nobody was just going through the motions. These guys wanted to win. As I've said before, though, Bill Belichick always wants better, always wants more. He's never satisfied. I think the entire coaching staff from Belichick on down knew by this time that we were not a .500 ball club. We were better than that; how much better we all wanted to find out. After the Denver game Belichick gave all the players a sheet to read. On the top in bold print was the heading "99.9 PERCENT VERSUS 100 PERCENT."

That was followed by a question: "Is it too much to give 100 percent, or is 99.9 percent good enough to be considered giving it your all?" Under that it said, "Consider that if 99.9 percent was good enough in other fields . . ." Then there were bullet points:

- The United States Post Office would lose 400,000 letters each day if they gave just 99.9 percent.
- Pharmacists would fill 3,700 prescriptions incorrectly every day.
- Eighteen airplanes would crash every day.
- Doctors would drop ten babies during delivery each day.

Then there was a final question: "NOW, IS IT TOO MUCH TO GIVE 100 PERCENT?"

That was a big WOW, and I think it made an impact. Coach Belichick is notorious for doing things like this to motivate his players. He would also often show tapes during the week between games. Sometimes he shows famous highlights from other sports. He loves to show the tape of the Chicago Bulls' last championship, where Michael Jordan hit that beautiful game-winning jumper against Utah to clinch the title.

He also showed tapes of Jesse Owens running, of Jim Brown carrying the football, Bobby Thomson hitting his famous "shot heard 'round the world" home run to beat the Dodgers in 1951, John Havlicek stealing the ball and ensuring the Boston Celtics another championship, Joe Montana throwing *The Pass* and Dwight Clark making *The Catch* against Dallas in 1982. He even showed a tape of Secretariat winning the Triple Crown back in 1973.

Everything he shows has a point; sometimes he shows video to reinforce what not to do. I remember viewing a tape where Sam Cassell of the Milwaukee Bucks blew up in the seventh game of the NBA playoffs after he got upset by a ref's call. Coach Belichick's message in this instance was to keep your cool, no matter what the officials do. "You can't control what the refs call," he said. "Don't get involved. Let me do the bitching and bickering. You guys still have to play the game."

Like I said, he likes to use examples from all sports, but that doesn't mean he won't show football. In Cleveland back in '93, he once showed a highlight tape of Jim Brown running over everyone. I remember a few of the players then walking out in total awe, just watching the heart of one man playing football. Then Bill would say, "That is the mark of a champion. Look at this guy's effort. Don't tell me he doesn't want to win." I also remember, however, some guys coming out of that meeting making cracks about Jim Brown's opposition back then, that the teams weren't as good, the opposition being smaller. That wasn't true. No one could tackle that dude. Guys weren't afraid of him. They were trying to tackle him, only they couldn't. But when a team doesn't get it, doesn't buy into it because of a mentality, you just want to go around slapping guys. It was typical of that team and the reason we were 7–9.

The Patriots, however, got the point of the tapes. Much of it has to do with guys being extensions of the coaches. We can't have guys being selfish and having mental breakdowns, especially with the team back at 3–4 and again having to cross that bridge to get back to .500. So if we want to have any success in the upcoming month, we have to win this game with Atlanta. Now that Cox was out, we would have to go more with a four-three defense since we didn't have the luxury of that extra linebacker to rotate. Ted Johnson and Tedy Bruschi would have to be in for more plays, while still spending a little time with special teams. Time for everyone to suck it up and give a little more. The Falcons were a lot like us, a team at a turning point. They had already had their bye week and were at 3–3 on the year. They wanted to get above the .500 mark, while we wanted to just get there. Teams at the crossroads at this time of year, approaching the midway mark in the season, can find just a single game being a benchmark as to whether they will go up or go down in the second half. For all these reasons, Atlanta was a good game for us at this point.

Neither team generated much offense early, but late in the first quarter the Falcons broke a big one. The play that set it up was a sixteen-yard pass from Chris Chandler to Tony Martin. On the next snap, Tebucky Jones blitzed from the left side just as Chandler pitched the ball to Maurice Smith, who was also running left. Smith blew past the blitzing Jones and was off to the races, going fifty-eight yards before we nailed him. A couple of plays later, Chandler threw a nineteen-yard scoring pass to Shawn Jefferson, and the Falcons were on the board. A run like that results from either a defensive breakdown or great offensive blocking. From our defensive standpoint it was a breakdown, while from their standpoint it was helluva good blocking. There isn't an area on defense that someone is not responsible for, but by the same token you will be vulnerable in some areas. There's only so much eleven guys can do. On that run someone on our defense was blocked or cut off, and the guys pursuing couldn't get to Smith at the angles they wanted.

After that, however, we started to look a lot stronger. One thing we had going was the return of Richard Seymour, our rookie defensive tackle and number-one draft pick. A hamstring problem had forced him to miss a couple of games, and having him back on the line definitely made our defense stronger. Seymour showed a lot more toughness than some of us expected. Rookie or not, he plays a power game, a big man's style of game in the pits, where you have to be strong. By the time the game ended, our defense had recorded nine sacks. We blitzed from everywhere, with both our safeties and our linebackers. We eventually knocked Chandler out of the game, and rookie Michael Vick had to take over. He didn't do much better. As it turned out, Smith's long run in the first quarter was the only play that hurt us. We scored seventeen in the second quarter, got another score in the third, and won the game, 24–10.

In the end we held Shawn Jefferson to just the one catch. Terrence Mathis caught just one for minus 2 yards. Their passing game managed just 151 yards, and that's really shutting a team down. Meanwhile, Brady had rebounded from his four-intercept game against the Broncos. He threw for 250 yards and three scores, getting eight different receivers into the act, and Antowain Smith had his first 100-yard game of the year, gaining 117 on twenty-three carries. That was the kind of production we had hoped to get from him when we acquired him from Buffalo, and this was the kind of balanced attack our offense had been looking for all year.

The fact that Brady had spread the ball around so well showed he was continuing to learn his craft. It's no secret that Troy Brown is our best receiver, but it's hard for a defense to focus on him when there are seven other guys catching the ball. Charlie Weis uses multiple formations and calls different receivers' numbers in the huddle, which makes it harder to dial up Troy, though we usually go to him on third down. That's one of the differences people were seeing between Brady and Bledsoe. Brady would spread it around. For years critics and writers said Drew wasn't patient enough.

Every now and then when Brett Favre has a bad day for the Packers it can get ugly. He blows up occasionally. Drew used to do that when he was forcing the ball to Ben Coates and Shawn Jefferson when they played here, instead of taking what they gave him. Brady did that at the beginning but gradually learned to dump it off when the first option wasn't there. When Drew felt the whole thing was on his shoulders, that's when he would throw more interceptions, and that's what happened to Brady in Denver, when nothing else was working. Then he started to learn that it just wasn't him out there and that it was better sticking to the game plan.

Now we were at the midpoint in the season, and we were definitely happy to be at .500. We were 4–4 but gaining momentum. The nice part was that we had reached the halfway mark by playing a solid ball game against a good team. We beat them very soundly on defense. After they scored in the first quarter, we just shut them down. We even felt the few plays they made were our mistakes and the guys were standing up, admitting them, and taking responsibility for their assignments. That wasn't happening earlier in the year to the same degree. If a guy said "my fault" on a particular play, that's fine. If he said it three times, we stopped him and reminded him he had better start doing his job. But the way the guys were taking responsibility was different. You could see they were having fun.

I remember our squad meeting before we started getting ready for the Falcons. Coach Belichick was asking guys about different players on the Falcons. He'd name a guy and then ask someone what position he played. It was soon apparent that the majority of guys didn't know a lot of the Falcons players. That was Belichick's point. "We don't know this team, but we have to know them," he said. "Stay after practice and watch some tape. Take home tapes and study these guys, because we haven't played them in a long time." He just wanted everyone to be as prepared as he always was.

Even after such a satisfying win, there was something I was angry about after the game. It might sound silly at first, but it's something to think about, something that was always part of the teams I played on during my career. We had a whole bunch of guys who lived in the Atlanta area, around Georgia, from Georgia, and they had family at the ball game. Yet none of the guys had food for us afterward. No food. When I came into the league with the

Giants, if the team came close to your hometown, you were responsible for feeding the team. That included everyone from a raw rookie to Harry Carson and George Martin, the team's oldest and most respected vets. The families prepare the meal. Everyone likes home cooking, of course, but the gatherings served a higher purpose of fostering camaraderie and making guys work hard for one another.

I may not be a player any longer, but that mentality is still in my blood. In both of my two years with the Patriots I provided the food when we went to Miami. In 2000, when we played Detroit in both the preseason and regular season, I provided a meal. I said, Hey, it's only preseason, but my mother cooked a couple of hundred wings and a hundred pieces of chicken. In the regular season I just had food for the defensive guys because I was frustrated with the way the season was going. Here I was in 2000 trying to start a tradition, and I'm not even a player. Sooner or later, I figured, guys would catch on to it.

Bobby Hamilton had food in Atlanta, but his people didn't get it to us in time and had to leave with everything they had cooked. Bryan Cox lives there, but he was hurt. It's an either/or situation. Sometimes guys have food when we first get into town, Saturday evening. Cox had a spread for us when we first got there. His people brought food to the hotel, to his room. No one had anything to eat after the game. There are just too many young guys like Patrick Pass and Richard Seymour who have to learn. I was always reminding Seymour that he was always boasting about his family barbecuing. I think I made him feel guilty. In fact, not a single Atlanta-based player got away without an earful. There's too much good cooking in Atlanta for me to have to get on the flight home and eat a rotten hamburger. Besides, anything that brings more camaraderie to a team is worth doing.

Of course, I shouldn't complain because we won the game and were back at .500. Now we are one-gaming it. We had reached .500 at 3–3 and lost. By beating Atlanta we were back again, and the next step is to get above it. I still don't think the team had sold anything to the New England media. They knew we had beaten a team considered to be of our caliber, but most of them were still thinking if we got to 8–8 we would be successful. We really hadn't changed too many minds. Though we felt good about our victory over the Falcons, I don't think anyone thought of us as a possible Super Bowl team, or even "Hey, watch out; this team will make the playoffs." Of course, we had stopped some pretty good teams already and then didn't respond the next week. We beat up on the Colts, then were soundly beaten by Miami. We had, however, won three of four in the second quarter of the season, but there was still a long way to go.

Football is different from the other sports. In baseball they play 162 games, basketball 82. Yet what we have to do just to play that one game at the end of the week is more draining than a West Coast swing in those other sports. Basketball players have a game one evening, then don't have to come back to work until the next afternoon, because they aren't playing until maybe seven the following evening. So they come in and shoot around and practice for an hour. We're just getting started after an hour on the field. That's why I think I'm justified in calling a 16-game season a marathon. Take in everything from training camp to the playoffs, and you are putting in a solid seven months of intensity, not to mention the beating you take. Throw in the off-season conditioning program and the mini-camps, and the life of an NFL player, as well as the coaches, is extremely demanding.

So we still had half a season left, and our mentality was to win one game at a time. We were 4–4 with no assurance that 10–6 or even 11–5 would get us into the playoffs, so the margin for error was very small. Coach Belichick likes to slice the season into quarters. He acknowledged that we had a very good second quarter, but we simply couldn't afford a bad third quarter. That would finish us. So our goal was to put together a couple of victories, with the big picture being to reach a point where we could control our own destiny at the end of the year. The only way to do that was to begin by beating Buffalo the following week. After that we knew we had a tough one with the Rams, already considered the league's best team and the early favorite to win the Super Bowl. So nothing would be handed to us.

You also want to be winning going into the playoffs. I remember the 1990 Giants stumbling at the end of the season, losing to both Philadelphia and San Francisco after a ten-game winning streak. We sneaked in a win against Minnesota before losing to Buffalo, and then we ended the regular season by winning a very close game, 13–10, against a New England team that had only won once the entire year. Fortunately, we were able to get it back together for the playoffs, but that's definitely *not* the way you want to finish a season. I know I've said already that a team should find something positive from a loss, something to motivate them the following week. I've got to admit that it took a long time for me to say that because I never found anything positive about losing. My philosophy was "Let's go beat somebody." I always dreamed about that undefeated season, like the Miami Dolphins of 1972, who were 17–0. Man, that would be the ultimate.

We didn't show the team tape of our losses to Miami and Denver in the first half. You can't totally ignore it, or guys will think it was OK, but the coach sometimes has to turn into an artist when he addresses the team after a bad loss, finding ways to keep the players focused and wanting to win the next week. You also have to show them what they did wrong, maybe put some new plays in, even if you don't let them look at the tape. It's when you show a team what was wrong and they go out the following week and repeat the mistakes—now that's really disheartening. It's a total pain for a coach when his players aren't taking the things you want them to do out onto the field. That hurts.

My high school coach and I had a falling-out some time ago, and we barely speak now, but there are a lot of things that he instilled in me that I still live by today. It all begins with working hard. There's no substitute for that. Then you simply line up and kick the guy's ass who's in front of you. Even when the other team knew our plays, we didn't care. Just get the guy in front of you and go. With the Giants our front seven had so much pride in being able to get the job done, that when the coaches would design plays to bring the strong safety down to help stop a runner like Bo Jackson, we would really get mad. In fact we wouldn't allow it. No way you're going to bring the damned safety down to help our front seven guys. Belichick tells me now they used to do it just to make us mad.

There are all the little things that go into winning, into motivating players as you try to build not only a winning team but a winning tradition. We had played .500 ball over the first half of the season. To get there, however, we had won three of four in the season's second quarter, and that gave us something to build on. Now it was up to all of us to continue because to play .500 for the second half and the entire season was simply not acceptable and certainly not good enough.

6

A Week in the Life of an NFL Coach

Coaches in the National Football League are known for working long hours. I don't know if it was that way fifty years ago, but like everything else the business has changed over the years and has certainly become more complex. The most intense pressure, of course, is on the head coach. It is from him that everything emanates, with the entire staff following his lead. Bill Belichick has always been one of the hardest-working coaches in the league, a guy whose evaluation and preparation leave no stone unturned. His strong work ethic is imparted to us, simple as that. Fans who watch the games on Sundays don't always realize the amount of work coaches put in each week to have the team ready and give it the best chance to win.

It's funny, how I prepare for a game as a coach differs from what I did as a player, but they say that old habits die hard, and I still find that parts of my daily routine carry over from my playing days. Some of it stems from superstitions that I have followed for years. For instance, I can never set my alarm clock for 6:00 or 7:00 A.M. It always has to be 6:05 or 7:05. I always roll out of bed on the right side, away from the clock, wash up first, then get dressed. It's always the same. When I played, I always put my game uniform on the same way, and now I do that with my coaching clothes. Left to right. Left sock first, left pants leg first, left sleeve first or left arm first into a pullover. I also was superstitious about arriving at the stadium too early. As a player, dressing too early and standing around in my uniform made me feel uncomfortable. I preferred to dress and go, didn't even like a lot of pregame warmups. If I was stretching before a game, I was just killing time.

The routine used to work for me and somehow made me angrier at the guys we were playing. Now, as a coach, I can't take out anger on the opponent, but that fire inside doesn't really go away. Before a game, when the guys are getting ready to play, I try to stay out of the locker room and away from them. Being in that highly charged atmosphere just gets me too pumped up, and I have to stay focused on my coaching duties. I guess some of the players can see that I become antsy, almost like I want to play. Bledsoe once came up to me before a game and kidded me about not having my mouthpiece, not having my helmet, and asked me when I was getting my ankles taped. "I can see it in your face," he said. A few times during games when opposing players ran toward the sideline I had to restrain myself from wanting to sneak an elbow in.

In a strange way, it relaxes me to know that other guys are fired up. I see Bobby Hamilton, a former teammate of mine, getting ready, and I live vicariously through him. Or I'll approach Je'Rod Cherry and ask him if he's mad yet. I can see it in his face. Those are the things that begin calming me down. Then I can relax and watch. When Coach Belichick first brought me in as a liaison in 2000, I always wanted to dress and go out on the field. When the linebackers were doing drills and hitting the blocking sled, I used to hit the sled, too. When I instruct the guys as a coach, I go though the workouts with them for the most part. It draws me a little closer to them. I remember that from my Giants days, how good I felt when the team's strength and conditioning coach, Johnny Parker, used to work out with us. He was slender but strong, and having him work alongside made us want to go harder. It motivated me, and I try to do the same thing with the Patriots.

As a coach, my week never really begins and ends. During the season it all runs together, seven full days and very little rest. When the game ends on Sunday, I'm already beginning my routine for the following week. I won't leave the stadium until our video director, Jimmy Dee, has finished transforming the tape and making a segment to give me. When teams tape the games, they have to make copies for several reasons. Some copies go to our opponents. Jimmy works out the schedule with the other clubs prior to the season. When we're getting ready to play our next opponent, we always have video of at least their previous three games. If it's at the beginning of the season, we have tapes of their preseason games. Once the season wears on, we have tapes of even more games. From these taped games Jimmy makes additional copies for the coaches that are downloaded into a computer system called Advid. It's great. Whatever Jimmy puts into the system can be viewed by every coach at his own station. If a coach wants you to have a particular game sequence, all you have to do is note the play numbers, send them down to Jimmy in the video room, and he'll cut the tape with just what you need. In the past, you had to watch a tape and time-code the plays you wanted. With the Advid, you just punch in the numbers and take the plays. If I want plays three, seven, eighteen, and twenty-one, it takes just five minutes to get them. With the old system it took fifteen or twenty minutes.

One of my responsibilities is ball disruption, which means creating a turnover or a big play on defense. Block a pass at the line of scrimmage, force a fumble, or intercept a pass—all examples of ball disruption. During a game I keep track of every player who makes a big play like that. If we have seventeen ball disruption plays in the course of a game, I save the numbers, send them down to the video crew—Steve, Fernando, and Matt—and they send me the plays back on a beta tape. I want it on hard copy so I can show it Monday afternoon when the guys come in and also save it for my own collection. I'm still old-fashioned. I know if I have the tape in my hands, I can't go wrong, even though Jimmy could have easily sent the plays directly through the system to the defense meeting room.

There is just a single road in and out to the Stadium at Foxboro. Since you can't get out without sitting in heavy traffic, I always stick around maybe two hours after a game and wait until Jimmy is ready with the tape. He always gives me the first copy because he knows I'm waiting. Then, after I view the entire tape, I grade my guys. As I'm grading them, I also view each play for ball disruption. So if a one o'clock game is over around four, I'll usually remain at the stadium until about eight o'clock. The reason I do it this way is that I'm always still kind of high after a game and it's nearly impossible to relax. So instead of fighting the traffic, I'd rather watch the tape and grade my guys, stay up late, then sleep a little later on Monday.

On Monday some of the coaches arrive as early as 6:00 or 7:00 A.M. to review game tapes and prepare for the staff meetings. The defensive coaches meet at 9. By that time, all the coaches should have graded their players. For example, I will give plus and minus grades for each inside linebacker on each play. Then each one ends up with a score. We keep count of how many plays each played that week, and their total production—how many tackles they made, how many they missed, if they knocked down a pass, picked up a fumble. Each defensive coach has to be ready to talk about his players individually to RAC, the defensive coordinator. Then we watch the tapes again as a unit, and talk about every single play, what we did well and not so well as a unit. By the time we meet with Coach Belichick at eleven, we've already gone over everything as offensive and defensive units.

Coach Belichick meets with each of the assistants, asking who were the best players on offense, defense, and special teams, what we executed well, what we did poorly. Then we talk defense—what we did individually and as a unit—then move over to the offense. That's when we go over everything, including player grades, strengths and weaknesses as units, both offensively and defensively. After that, we gather for Coach Belichick's 1:00 P.M. meeting with the players.

At this meeting Coach Belichick stresses what went well and where we need to improve, what each unit and the special teams did to contribute to winning the game or didn't do if we lost. After he's finished, the coaches and quarterbacks leave, but the rest of the team stays to watch tapes of special teams. As I said, nearly all the players have to play some kind of role with special teams at some point in the year. Then, a half hour to forty-five minutes later we go into offensive and defensive meetings once again.

First RAC talks to the entire defense, this time going over for the players the things we were pleased with and then things that we have to continue to work on the most. At that point he has me talk to the guys. I tell them who was productive and why and go over the big plays, citing the guys who made them. We do all this as a unit because we feel that defense is a collective effort, and even if the defensive backs are getting corrections from their position coach, we like the entire defense present, even when we're addressing the linebackers or defensive ends. Then everyone knows who made a mistake or why a play was successful. After that, I show the ball disruption tape, pointing out what made the plays work. In fact, during a positive week we may show only the positive plays and work from that. So it varies a bit from week to week.

By 3:00 P.M. on Monday the players are out on the field, running and loosening up their legs. The best way to get the bumps and bruises out is to go back to work. Some guys will also lift some weights, while others just prefer to run. Then, by 3:30, the defensive coaching staff is together again, and we begin analyzing our approach to our next opponent. This time we have the tapes segmented into what we want to watch. Sometimes it's a four-game breakdown, and late in the season it can be a seven- or eight-game breakdown of our opponents. When we're halfway through the season, for instance, we'll have the eight previous games our next opponent played before we get ready for them. I'm going to watch every one of those games just to see which of their players I want to target for ball disruption opportunities. It might be a running back who handles the ball carelessly. Maybe he carries the ball low on his body, or he doesn't protect it in traffic. Quarterbacks who wave the ball around a bit too much are also vulnerable.

Those are the kinds of tendencies I'm looking for. It may also be a receiver who catches with one hand or pins the ball against his chest. Some players are prone to fumbling, and I look for ways to make that happen. I might pick out fifteen or twenty plays with turnover potential from each game, then list the players and see which ones were involved in most of those plays. Most times it's the quarterback, because he handles the ball on each play. There might be a receiver who doesn't show up on my play list, because he is very protective of the ball. When you face a team like the Rams that frequently turns over the ball, the play list grows. Not only do their starters wave the ball around; all of them do it. At any rate, once I make my play list for potential ball disruption, those plays are fed into Advid. The rest of the day is pretty much worked around Coach Belichick. Most Mondays he wants us back together as a staff around 6:00 P.M. That's when we'll talk once again about our upcoming opponent. After that the defensive staff has yet another meeting, and all the coaches are assigned a project for the week. We really don't get started on our game plan until Tuesday morning. That's when Coach Belichick begins describing Sunday's strategy. By the end of a late Monday evening—I'm lucky if I get out of there by 10:30 or 11:00 P.M.—we've done all the preliminaries and we're ready to get the game plan.

Tuesday the players are off but not the coaches. The defensive staff begins with a meeting around 8:30 A.M. Because Wednesday's practice concentrates on defending first- and second-down plays, we watch tapes of our opponent's first- and second-down tendencies and begin putting together our defensive package to stop them. Early in the season, the first or second game, you have to use tapes of the preseason or even the previous season. By midseason, however, you have a lot of recent tapes to review. So on Tuesday, from 8:30 A.M. to 1:00 P.M. with just a few short breaks, we watch tapes and get together our first- and second-down packages. We don't meet with Belichick until 3:00 or 4:00. That's when we talk about Wednesday's practice, the status of the players, which guys are injured, which ones are all right. We do this every day because we have to firm up the fifty-three-man roster. In a team's weekly preparation, injuries always play a significant role. You have to know who's active, how long players will be out, if anyone is suspended, as well as other circumstances that may dictate the need to bring another player in.

After the meeting with Coach Belichick, we go back into a defensive meeting and once again study our opponent's various offensive formations, this time identifying the alerts, the things we have to be prepared to counter with our defense. We play both our three-four and four-three packages. If they bring in an extra wide receiver, for instance, we have to determine whether to stay in our regular defense or bring in the nickel package, with an additional defensive back. This depends on the team we're playing and how we match up. If our opponent brings in four wide receivers on first or second down, then we go right to our third-down package, which we won't be working on until the next evening.

At this point we'll usually break for dinner. Because of the long hours we work, the team feeds us breakfast, lunch, and dinner. Coach Belichick's father says we're the biggest defensive staff in the league, and they always set the food up outside the defensive staff's meeting room. We fill our plates and go right back to the meeting.

The evening hours on Tuesday are spent making up play cards. We diagram offensive plays on eight-by-ten cards, plot their various blocking schemes with everything scripted out for the show team to follow in practice. Every aspect of the opponent's offense is charted on the cards—straight running plays, play action, straight drops, and trick plays. By late Tuesday evening we have maybe sixty cards made up. No one leaves until they are done so we won't have to carry Tuesday's work into Wednesday. We like to stay a day ahead, and sometimes I don't leave until midnight, but by then the cards are done.

One of my other responsibilities besides ball disruption is being in charge of the younger guys: our rookies, other first-year players, and the players on the developmental squad. Coach Belichick wants me to more or less help them adjust to life in the NFL and feels it's better coming from an ex-player who's been there. He's an old-school coach and doesn't want rookies walking into meetings late. So we ask them to be at the facility early on Wednesday. I have the defensive rookies come in at 7:30 in the morning. One of the things we do is assign them a particular player on the upcoming opposing team. Their job is to find out something about that player that RAC didn't talk about on Monday. Our defensive backs will usually get an offensive running back. For example, I'll assign Leonard Myers to find out something about Edgerrin James. The two were teammates at the University of Miami.

Our defensive linemen and linebackers are assigned the opposing offensive linemen and tight ends. Each day they have one person to review. They have to watch his tendencies and try to pick up something different from each player they're scrutinizing. This is a way to gradually teach them to watch tape. When a guy hands me a bad report, I've got to tell him how to improve. I'll usually keep the young guys about a half hour. Then at 8:00 A.M. our special teams coach takes all his guys to go over their assignments and schedule. I will still have some of the defensive linemen with me, and we might watch tape for a short time, focusing on the opponent's defense. If we're preparing for the Miami Dolphins, I'll already have briefed them on the Dolphins' defensive line, then they'll get to see a couple of plays to show them how this particular person is playing. All this is preparation for the show team, those players emulating the Miami defense against our offense in practice. I like to think I take more pride in our show team than any coach in the league. The guys loved the name we picked in 2001—the Dirty Show. All the players loved being part of it, and even the so-called big-name guys came out. Before the Raiders game, Ty Law played Rod Woodson for the week on the show team. It's extra work for someone like Ty, but he does it willingly, like the rest of the guys.

When our offense had a productive game, it was partially because of the Dirty Show. We take great pride in that. Some of the guys that make up the Dirty Show are members of the Patriots' developmental squad. They don't dress for games, and some are borderline as to whether they'll make it or not. But they work very hard every week and don't let up. Every now and then we get a starter who comes out to play with us, and he takes great pride in it as well. If I ask Lawyer to help us out, he'll sprint out there, ready to go. Otis Smith doesn't go a week without taking a turn with the defensive show team. One week Roman Phifer came out to play with the Dirty Show in spite of a bad knee. It helps keep practice fun and gets us ready at the same time.

Anyway, by 8:30 on Wednesday we're all ready for another team meeting, where Coach Belichick will address the team. By then we've put our previous opponent totally behind us, and we're all thinking about the upcoming game.

This is the meeting where Belichick asks guys how well they know players on the opposition. Then we break for twenty minutes while there is a special teams meeting. That's when I have a little breather and prepare for another long day. Belichick's meeting ends by 9:00 A.M., and at 9:20 we go into separate offense and defense meetings once again. This is when we hand out part of the game plan. It contains first- and second-down plays, and we go through all the personnel on the upcoming opponent as well as go over tips and tendencies and how we think they'll attack us. All of this is done collectively, with all the defensive coaches taking part in the meeting.

Normally Rob Ryan begins by giving his top ten tips of the week, telling the defense what they must be on alert to defend against. Next the defensive line coach, Randy Melvin, talks about all the different running plays our defense will face. After Randy, Eric Mangini, the defensive backs coach, will give tips on their favorite pass plays and how they normally try to attack with the passing game, which receivers have to be watched the most carefully, and whether the team will more likely go to a deep passing attack or use the short- and medium-range stuff. Finally, RAC sums up everything the assistants have said.

From there we have about a half hour of individual time and break up into smaller groups, of linemen, linebackers, and defensive backs. By about 11:00 A.M. the week's rigorous meetings are getting monotonous, so we go out to the field and do a walk-through, showing the guys physically what we were talking about on paper. We don't actually go against each other, just show the look of the different formations. We're not running plays but making adjustments. So everyone is shifting, walking through the different motions. There's no running, and the guys aren't in pads. We do this for two periods of about ten minutes each, maybe twenty to twenty-five minutes at most. Going out like this helps the sleepyheads, the guys who have a hard time staying awake in meetings.

Then we break for lunch. It's now about 11:30, and we'll take maybe thirty to forty-five minutes. After lunch we head to the practice field. Special teams begin doing a walk-through at about 12:45. This isn't considered real practice time yet, but last year's team was made of mature, professional athletes, and often players were out there early doing individual work. Anthony Pleasant, for example, likes to work with his hands doing pass rush moves. He's slapping bags and doing things he might not be able to do in practice because it's so scripted. Richard Seymour is out early watching the veterans. Everyone is getting ready in his own way.

In practice I have two responsibilities besides the obvious. I'm in charge of the show team and also the rotation of my linebackers. During the offensive part of the practice I run the show team. During the defensive portion I'm in charge of the opponent's personnel. I give the offensive numbering system, letting the defense know what the offense is about to run. Everyone has to get the signals. The linebackers and defensive backs look to RAC for the defensive signals. Linebacker Tedy Bruschi normally calls the signals on the field. If he calls a certain defense, all the other guys are watching to make sure his signals are relayed.

There are two ways of scrimmaging in practice. One is full contact, where the defense takes the offense to the ground. With the other they just butt up to the ball carrier, not tackling him but just stopping his momentum. Practice is always very scripted. The offensive show team has the play cards we drew up the night before. So we have the script in hand, knowing what offensive plays will be run, but the defensive players don't. They have to react. For example, if we change from a three-four defense to the four-three, I'll put up a signal, then scream it out. The free safety always has to know the down and distance, then relay it to everyone else. We'll use hand signals to let him know. If I send two guys onto the field, I have to make sure two guys come off, and I have to know which guys are in the game for each type of defense we use— nickel, dime, goal line. We also change from week to week. The personnel is not always the same, so it's a constant process throughout the entire season.

Wednesday practice lasts from one hour and fifty minutes to two hours and fifteen minutes. After practice the rookies and developmental guys stay out, and we do some extra work with them. Some of the veterans, like Ty Law and Otis Smith, will stay to run additional wind sprints, the quarterbacks will stay to throw more passes, and some of the defensive backs are catching passes from the jugs machine. Some of the receivers get extra work that way, too. The extra work takes maybe ten to twenty minutes. The players finish by lifting some weights and then shower. That takes about another forty-five minutes, and then the coaches meet with the players to watch the tapes of practice so that Thursday morning we won't have to return to anything to do with Wednesday practice. We don't want anything to stop us from moving forward.

Every single moment of practice is taped. This way the corrections are fresh in everyone's minds. So players will come in on Wednesday morning and get the game plan. By evening they have their practice corrected, and everyone feels more comfortable coming back in on Thursday. After that the players leave and we watch the practice again as a staff and with Coach Belichick. This is at about 4:30 or 5:00 P.M. When the players are in, we watch only the team working together. As a staff we watch everything, go over the calls, discuss what we want, and go over everything with Belichick. That evening we hammer out the game plan for third-down and red zone defenses. The day ends about 11:00 P.M.

Wednesday and Thursday are our heaviest days. There are no breaks on Wednesday. Before we leave, we plan Thursday's practice, then do the notorious play cards once again.

Thursday morning I start with the young guys again—both active roster and the developmental squad—showing them Wednesday's practice tapes. The developmental squad guys are required to do everything the active players do, attend every meeting, and practice right up until Saturday. When Coach Belichick sets the active roster and traveling squad, the inactive guys and those who can't play because of an injury leave. While we're in Saturday meetings, they're working with our strength and conditioning coach, Mike Woicik, or rehabbing their injuries. Back at practice, I'll critique the defensive linemen on their blocking techniques and execution. I also tell them whether they've been improving or not and whether their show teamwork is helping the offense. They are, in effect, my projects, and they have to improve or Coach Belichick will get on me. He may sometimes go directly to a player and read him the riot act, or I'll either hear it or get that look. Oh, yes, the coach has a penetrating look, and everyone knows what it means.

Since the beginning of training camp, one of the things I liked about this team was that the players help each other out. Like I said, while the show team is made up mostly of developmental guys, backups, and special teams players, a lot of the starters and veterans contribute throughout the year. When a veteran comes out to work with the show team, it's strictly on a volunteer basis. I've been with teams where the so-called big-name guys laugh and turn away from doing scout team duty. They're too big for it. Yet they are the first guys to cry and complain when someone runs back a punt for a touchdown and no one tackles him.

There was one thing about Lawrence Taylor that I'll never forget. The only time he ever played on special teams was when we needed a field goal blocked. He substituted for the regular wing player to try to block the kick. He did it once in Philadelphia, the first time since I had been there that I saw him on that unit. He tried it again in the 1990 Super Bowl against Buffalo, the final kick that could have won the game for the Bills but went wide right. If the kick had been straight, he might have gotten it. The point is that when we really needed a big special teams play he came out there and tried to make it happen. Almost all the guys on the Patriots are like that as well. When teams have what we call a *gunner* on their punt coverage, a guy who runs down wide and often makes the tackle, he's often difficult to stop. When we faced teams with a good gunner, Ty Law and Lawyer Milloy would come out with the receiving team to block and hold up the gunner. Whenever Brad Seely, our special teams coach, called on them, they were ready and more than willing.

You want to see that kind of thing. It gives the entire team a good feeling. The guys whose positions they take in those situations will get pissed off and even more fired up. Then you rotate them so you get more out of the normal guys who hold up the gunner and benefit from the skills of a Ty Law or Lawyer Milloy as well. I've already mentioned how important special teams are to Coach Belichick, so he loves to see that kind of thing as well.

After I work with the developmental guys first thing Thursday morning, our day becomes pretty similar to Wednesday. There are meetings, walk-throughs on the practice field, this time emphasizing third-down plays and plays we run inside the red zone. Unless we struggled in a certain area the previous week, we might do a couple of other things. If the team we're going to play has a no-huddle offense, for example, we might work again on that for a time. While we were in full pads about 90 percent of the time on Wednesday, Thursday is more a day for half pads, and the majority of Fridays we're not in pads at all.

Most of the contact in practice is between the two lines in the pits. We're not going to tackle Antowain Smith during the week; it's just too risky. The Dirty Show guys will try to strip the ball from him, tugging or slapping at it, or hit him just enough to stop his momentum. If we have pads on, guys like to get in the way and thump him a little bit. When we started practice, Antowain was running kind of upright in practice, and we butted him up. The next time he was bent more at the waist. In my eyes we made him better and got him ready for the game. Without that he will be too relaxed and can be stripped of the ball. So in practice contact is there, but it's more controlled. Guys are hit and bumped every now and then, and in the end they benefit from it.

When Charlie Weis is ready for a strong practice, he'll draw up the defensive cards for the plays he wants to see. Sometimes he wants to curse me out because I have the linebackers going so hard, but I know he appreciates the effort because it gets his guys ready. Coach Belichick has the final say with the offense. If a play looks good in practice, he'll want it called in a game. If it doesn't look good, he won't use it. Frequently he'll draw up defensive plays to test his offense. For example, he tells us to use a defensive formation that is more difficult for the offensive line to block against—say, on a certain running play. This is his way of perhaps testing center Damien Woody or one of the offensive tackles. It's better to do it that way than to just scream at a guy in practice and then have someone blindside the quarterback or hit Smith in the backfield for a five-yard loss because Charlie was drawing up cards simply to make the offense look good and not really test them.

On Thursday the emphasis in practice changes. We stress different game situations. After practice there is no tape or meetings for the players, but the coaches still gather. Practice is over at about 3:00 or 3:15, and the players are pretty much out of there by 4:00. Some guys stay to lift some weights after practice, and the coaches stay for more meetings. We have to watch the practice tapes separately again, as offensive and defensive staffs. When we finish at about 5:30 or 6:00, Coach Belichick comes in, and we watch the tapes again with him. Then we go over the corrections we have to make before getting ready for the Friday practice schedule. Thursday night's meeting is a cleanup of everything for the coaches. Finally we set up Friday's installment and leave about 11:00 P.M.

Friday is a shorter day. We work on short yardage and goal line defenses and two-minute drills. Also, if we have any play that we want to correct from Wednesday and Thursday, we put them in again on Friday. The schedule is also different. Friday morning I meet with my young guys again. Each one has to report on the opposing player he was assigned, standing up in front of his peers and coaches and telling them what he learned. For example, if Cincinnati were the next opponent, one of my young defensive backs would have to report on their star runner, Corey Dillon. What he should know by this time is that Dillon likes to have the ball in his left hand. When he breaks away and runs left, he often gets away because his right arm is free to knock hands down and stiff-arm defenders. But when he cuts to the right, the ball is still in his left hand, and without a free arm to protect himself he's often easier to bring down. Knowing this can help the defender position himself when he's going after Dillon in the open field.

If a guy does well with his report, he gets moderate applause. If he didn't put too much effort into it, he gets one clap and we sit him down. It isn't forgotten, either, because it will eventually get back to Coach Belichick. Suppose RAC asks one of the young players a question and he doesn't have an answer. I feel responsible. That's a big part of the developmental program, helping the young guys get better during the course of the season. Part of that is making them arrive very early in the morning, become acclimated, watch tapes, and learn throughout the year. If one rookie is late for a meeting, Belichick makes them all come in a half hour earlier the next day. They'll have to be in at 7:00. If another rookie is late, it becomes 6:30. The player who is late is also fined. That's one way to teach *team*. If one dies, we all die. If one guy blows his responsibility on the field, we all pay the price. That's because it says "Patriots" on the scoreboard. Making guys come in early doesn't bother Belichick at all, because he's there between 5:30 and 5:45 every morning. Enough said.

After Belichick's morning staff meeting, the special teams meeting lasts a little longer, going right through lunch. We're out on a practice field early, but practice is a little shorter. We'll just go over the final corrections. It may take two hours, and we sometimes finish by 1:15. Then I'll often have the linebackers line up on the sideline while I'm standing on the numbers at the hash marks. I'll fire the football as hard as I can at them. Sometimes I'll look at one guy and fire at another. If a player drops the ball, he has to do ten push-ups. If they all catch it, I do push-ups. If I make a bad throw, I do push-ups again. The drill reached the point where the offensive coaches were standing around gleefully watching it. Then Drew wanted to throw to the guys. Funny, my superstitions came into play again. We were winning then, so I wouldn't let Drew throw to them. I had to keep doing it.

This was something I started last year, doing it with the linebackers every Friday. We had a linebacker named Rob Holmberg who was with us in 2000. He returned to training camp in 2001, then was released. We brought him back during the early part of the 2001 season when a couple of special teams guys were injured. He wasn't used to the drill and didn't listen to me when I told him to put a helmet on. I fired the ball, and it went through his hands and hit him on the side of the neck. He had a pretty good bruise from that one and didn't try it without a helmet again. Some guys would challenge me by walking closer and asking, "Is that all you got?" Here I am throwing my arm out, but there was just one time when all the players caught the final passes and I had to do push-ups.

Friday we're off the field early, getting guys off their feet and allowing them forty-eight hours to get their rest before the game. They're finished with practice by 1:30 or 2:00 P.M. and really appreciate it. Friday is also pizza day, and guys will grab a whole pie, eat a couple of slices in the locker room, and take the rest with them when they leave. Because the guys are out early and we don't have anything planned for them on Saturday, Belichick will meet with the Patriots' owner, Bob Kraft, that afternoon. The offensive and defensive staffs watch practice tapes, starting as soon as they can. There are no more cards to draw up. We just might watch a couple of plays that we feel we didn't get quite right and see what last-minute corrections might be needed. So when we leave on Friday we want to have all the *i*s dotted and *t*s crossed. Come Saturday, everything should be verbal.

There was another tradition I started last year, almost by accident. When we got out of practice on Friday, I would get in my truck and drive to New York for a haircut. This probably sounds strange, but I couldn't find anyone in Providence to cut my hair the way I liked it. I even tried one in Massachusetts, but it didn't work out. From that point on, I went to New York every two weeks to a barbershop in Harlem, the Den, to have Mike the barber cut my hair. There's a regular Friday night crew there, and Mike doesn't close until everyone's hair is cut. Soon the guys got wind of it, not because they noticed my haircut but because of what I was bringing back.

Everyone loved my trips to New York, because I returned for Saturday morning's practice with Krispy Kreme doughnuts. While getting my hair cut, I would order the doughnuts, leave the barbershop around 11:30, and go pick up twenty dozen donuts on 125th Street. Our two top draft choices, Richard

Seymour and Matt Light, buy breakfast Saturday mornings. Richard Seymour was in charge of the doughnuts, and he was getting Dunkin' Donuts until everyone tasted the Krispy Kremes. Best doughnuts in the world, and they are gone in no time. They're kind of small, and you can eat them like potato chips. So my haircut trips to Harlem had the unintended effect of my replacing Seymour as the doughnut guy. It got to a point where I would pick up the doughnuts just for certain players—Troy Brown, Anthony Pleasant, Bobby Hamilton, Brandon Mitchell, Otis Smith, Lawyer, Ty, Adam, and Riddick Parker. Riddick, one of our defensive tackles, got me started on them. He's a southern guy from North Carolina and had them sent to us.

Like I was a little Santa's helper, I placed a box in each of the guys' lockers Saturday morning. Then I gave doughnuts to the coaches, maybe two or three boxes for the offensive and defensive coaches and, of course, a box for me. One trip I drove to New York with some friends and returned by train. I was on the train loaded up with fifteen Krispy Kreme boxes, sleeping with one eye open so no one took them. Great doughnuts and another tradition that continued throughout the season. But back to our routine.

Saturday morning we have a straight walk-through. No pads and no helmets. The coaches might put in some trick plays with Charlie and RAC drawing them up. The coaches also take Saturday to begin getting an early start on the following week's opponent, which helps make our Monday easier. If we don't do the extra work on Saturday, we might not get out Monday until midnight, instead of by 11:00 P.M. Charlie, for instance, has a blow-up bed in his office and often stays over if it gets too late. In fact we've all slept over at times. I'll sometimes stay in a nearby hotel.

I don't do anything with the young guys on Saturday. Before the walk-through we have a full squad meeting for about forty-five minutes, maybe keep special teams a little longer. Out on the field we do some special teams callouts and work with the punting team, making last-minute adjustments. We also go over the game plan, making sure we know who the backups are, then once again go over kickoffs, kick returns, field goals, and field goal blocks. Then we work briefly with the offense and defense, but no one breaks a sweat. If we have a home game, we'll all stay at a hotel that night. All the guys who are on the active roster go to the hotel and have a squad meeting at 8:30 that night. The coaches meet earlier, at 7:45. That's when we finalize the active roster. There are always a few game-day decisions if we're not quite sure whether a player will be ready to go or not. Coach Belichick will outline some offensive plays he wants Charlie to call early in the game. It's all touch-up.

The 8:30 meeting is broken into offense and defense. At our defensive meeting RAC talks to the team and reviews the game plan. He then lets me talk again about ball disruption, and I'll show fifteen to twenty-five plays, once again pointing out opposing players I feel we can get the ball from. I may point out why a certain running back fumbles or why a particular wide receiver drops a lot of passes. There are times when I get carried away with the disruptions, especially if we're playing a team I really want to beat. I'll also try to sneak in a little motivational talk. I often introduce it by throwing in a tape from my playing days. When the playoffs neared, I kept showing the tape of William Roberts and me from the 1986 season, dancing on the field after the Giants' Super Bowl victory. Some of the guys know the history, some don't, so I let them know I was there and that we won it. And I tell them I want to dance again. It got to a point where Lawyer would put some music on the boom box, jazzing it up a bit before I showed the tape, calling it a Pepper Johnson production. Anything for motivation and camaraderie. It had been a long week for everyone, as they all are. Now we could only hope we hadn't left any stones unturned and that we were ready for the game.

This past year I couldn't stay at the hotel with the rest of the guys the evening prior to home games. My room was right next to the swimming pool. It's funny, I try not to have some of the habits I had as a player, but they just don't go away. I normally can't sleep well. As much as I like to relax, I just couldn't get to sleep in that bed. Maybe it was the chlorine odor from the swimming pool. During the 2000 season I gutted it out, but last year I just couldn't do it, couldn't stay there. So after our Saturday meeting I would return to my apartment in North Providence, Rhode Island. It's about a half hour from the stadium, the same distance as the hotel but in the opposite direction. There I have so much peace and quiet. So for peace of mind I watch a movie, relax, and think about the game. All the other coaches are married with kids. I think they would rather stay in the hotel because that's where they find the solitude they need. I find mine in my apartment.

On game day some things just don't change. When I played for both Bills, Parcells and Belichick, they wanted everyone to arrive an hour and a half before the game. That was enough time to get things done before pregame warm-ups begin. If you're late, you're fined. I was one of those guys who got his rush from making it there an hour and thirty-one minutes before kickoff. Sometimes I was right on time and a few times five minutes late. That would get me going, give me a sense of urgency, a buildup. As a player I didn't give a hoot about pregame warm-ups. I would stay in the locker room until the coin toss if I had my way. I always felt uncomfortable at pregame. I'm not real flexible, so I avoided the stretching if I could.

As a coach I still arrive at the stadium in the nick of time. I'll go down to get dressed with the same old superstition, left to right. Socks, pants, arms through sleeves, and no watch. As a player I never wore jewelry. As a coach I won't wear a watch on the field. As I said, old habits die hard. When I get to the stadium, I have fifteen or twenty minutes to dress, then Coach Belichick has us come in for offensive and defensive meetings for both players and coaches. More superstition. Last season, before the regular-season game against New Orleans, I was sitting in the locker room talking to Scott Pioli, our director of player personnel. Suddenly I realized I was late for the meeting. The door was already closed, but I felt I wasn't missing anything because RAC had already talked to us. I like to leave my guys alone, because I know how I was on game day. So when I was late I just went back into my office. We won the game that day, and after that I never went back to the meeting until the playoffs.

It's actually a very short meeting, barely five minutes long. Just a check of the players to get the guys together, to see if there are any questions on the game plan or personnel. RAC will talk about which opponent's players are inactive. A team has to make its final roster announcement two hours before game time. For example, if a running back like Curtis Martin of the Jets is listed as probable all week, we don't know if he'll play, but we have to prepare for him. If it's announced that he won't play, it's good for the players to know so they can click him off in their minds and think about the style of runner that will replace him. Same with the defensive linemen. If Anthony Pleasant expects to go up against a very strong offensive tackle, and suddenly that guy is out, he should know that the replacement isn't a power blocker but a guy who might have very quick feet. So it's just another last-minute adjustment. Then RAC releases them. It's almost just for the purposes of taking a head count, a comfort zone for the coaches and coordinators to know all the guys are there. It's easy for each coach to spot his guys, because they're always in the same place. Then an hour before the game I'm back in my office, sometimes going over responsibilities again, maybe just reading a book, anything to relax.

Some fifty-five minutes before game time the kickers go out. Ten minutes later the early birds—guys who catch the kicks, the quarterbacks throwing the ball, and anyone else who is dressed—might decide to go out. Now guys are going out with their pads on because they aren't coming back until we come back in as a team. The quarterbacks return, the holders, long snappers. Next are the receivers, the defensive backs, running backs—the little guys. They get together and go out, still on their own. The wide receivers might sprint a little, jog around. At this point the players are on their own schedule. They're getting their legs loose, doing some extra stretching. Then the linebackers and tight ends take the field. The tight ends might catch a few passes while the linebackers practice some moves, run back and forth, and stretch. Five minutes later the big guys come out. When the others see the linemen at the edge of the tunnel, they come back and meet them. Now our captains— Bledsoe, Izzo, Cox, Brown, and Milloy—lead us out and run toward our sideline for the official team warm-up.

Now we're all out there as a full team. Mike Woicik, our strength and conditioning coach, leads the team in stretching. By then I'm out on the field loosening up, listening to music, watching the players, walking up and down, high-fiving guys. Some of the coaches move back and forth, wishing everyone luck. Others just wait in their corners for their units. The offensive linemen gather on the same side as our team bench, while the defensive linemen always get together at the back of the end zone. Defensive backfield coach Eric Mangini is watching our opponents, especially if they're warming up throwing passes. He likes to see how the receivers are moving, but eventually he will go to the opponent's sideline and wait for his guys. After they finish stretching, our quarterbacks and receivers do what's known as a pat-and-go. The quarterback pats the ball to simulate a snap, and the receivers run a straight go-route. All the quarterbacks are out there on the forty- or forty-five-yard line, throwing toward the end zone to the running backs, wide receivers, and tight ends.

Next they throw to the defensive backs and linebackers, moving them around and getting them used to tracking passes in the air. Then we break up, and guys go to their own coaches to warm up. We all do our own drills. Rob and I have the linebackers make a little contact, then we do shadow coverage on the wide receivers, running backs, and tight ends. We're not trying to intercept or knock the passes down. We let them catch and just work on our breaks, simple routes. We do about six plays, then call the defensive and offensive linemen back. We're building the family back together. Everybody head-butts each other to get loose, then we run one play so that everybody gets that one thud, to motivate and get it out of the system. We run a full formation, eleven on eleven. We do two or three more plays, and then the second unit comes out and does the same thing.

We punt the ball, let Troy field a few punts, then Adam kicks a few field goals, and we're off the field. The warm-up lasts about twenty-three to twenty-six minutes. Then we return to the locker room with enough time for guys to get taped, change their shoes, and take care of anything they need in the training room. There are about five to seven minutes to get situated, then the offensive and defensive coordinators speak to the team, talk about adjustments, little reminders. They'll tell us if they noticed anything in pregame warm-ups. We get a two-minute call four minutes before kickoff and two minutes before we have to go out and be introduced. Finally we come together for the Lord's prayer, and Coach Belichick delivers a short speech, reminding us of the point of emphasis for that given week. Then the players circle around one another, put their hands in, and say "One-two-three TEAM!" Then we're out of the locker room, heading for the walk through the tunnel back to the field.

We started something this past season that I think also contributed to us coming together as a team. Playing on the road, the home team public-address announcer is often somewhat careless when introducing the opposition. Our names are typically announced very quickly, and the next thing you know the player being announced isn't the guy running onto the field. So instead of us rushing on the field one after another and getting disorganized, our guys began coming out together. We started doing it early in the season, beginning with the defensive unit. Every week they would switch off which unit would be introduced, and in one of the early games—I can't quite remember which one; I want to say it was the Colts in week five—the defense ran out together.

The offense continued to come out individually for a few more weeks, but once we were winning later in the season, they did the same thing. After that they all came out together in the Super Bowl.

During the intros the coaches are already wearing their headsets. I leave mine on the table by our bench. Superstition again. I won't put it on until I go up to each coach and shake his hand. On the defensive side, Rob Ryan and coaching assistant Brian Daboll are up in the booth, where they will watch the plays, especially pass plays, and document them. Rob takes one side of the field, Brian the other. They document what the opponent's receivers and our linebackers are doing during the course of the game. They talk over the headsets to me, to RAC, to Eric Mangini and Randy Melvin. RAC and Eric use the microphone affixed to the headset, but I flip mine up in the air. In a preseason game I screamed so loud that everyone was telling me to cut my mike off. Even when mine was off, Eric's mike still picked up my loud voice.

We have two offensive coaches upstairs, Jeff Davidson and Ned Burke. Charlie is on the field along with Dante Scarnecchia, our assistant head coach and offensive line coach. Special teams coach Brad Seely and wide receivers coach Ivan Fears are also on the sideline. Ivan is in charge of substitutions on the offensive side. My job during the game is to signal our safeties as to which players the opposing offense has in the game—whether it's two backs and one tight end or other formations. The linebacker in front of the defensive huddle—Bruschi or Phifer—gets the defensive signals from RAC. To eliminate too much verbiage, the safety calls out the personnel. Now everyone knows the personnel in on offense and the defense we're calling. In most situations Bruschi would come out on third downs and Phifer would take over calling the defensive signals, but I'm still giving personnel to the safeties. We don't want our signal caller first looking at personnel, then having to look for the defensive signal. So I do it, and I usually know it before RAC because I'm getting it from Rob upstairs. Sometimes I see it before Rob sends it down. Some teams try to fool you by having a guy run halfway on, then run off again. That can backfire, because they're so busy trying to trick us that they end up hurting themselves.

Sometimes during a game the headsets can become a Comedy Central show. The head coach's headset can switch from offense to defense, so Belichick listens to both sides. He always knows what we're calling, and his mike goes through our headsets. Sometimes in crucial situations he'll interrupt RAC and may have a call he wants to make. He may just make the call, or he might say, "What are you thinking, RAC?" or ask about another play. If anyone else opens his mouth during this exchange, all hell will break loose. It's just between Belichick and RAC. Unless you're asked, you keep quiet. No adding your two cents or making another suggestion. Sometimes Belichick comes in and changes the call late, and we don't get it out there in time. That's rare. If we dodge the bullet and the original play works, then it's funny. If not, we all go on the carpet.

Coach Belichick always has a strong grasp of the game. He may see that the opponent is getting ready to run a certain play, and he'll ask what we have in our defensive game plan that defends that play. It might not be a change of defense, just a matter of alerting the guys to a certain play or to protect a specific area because that's where he feels they're going to attack. RAC will go to the game plan to see what we have. That's when it can become chaotic. When Belichick wants to change a play, he usually makes it in time, but once in a while he's late.

I'm also responsible for our personnel. We have as many groups on defense as they have on offense—the regular defense, nickel and dime packages—and I'm responsible for getting those guys out there. The safety will look over toward me for a signal, and the guys running onto the field are also using hand signals and screaming the play out, so the guys who have to leave will come off in time. Last, I give the alerts. Let's say RAC thinks they're going to run a screen. Then I alert the defense for a screen with a hand signal to the safety. The linebackers also watch me. So when Bruschi is calling the defensive signal, Phifer and Tebucky Jones are watching me. When Phifer is calling the defense, sometimes I get a cornerback or Lawyer to watch me.

If there is a play or two where I feel the guys looked confused and simply didn't make it, I will address it on the sideline during the course of the game. If Rob sees an adjustment from upstairs, he'll tell me through the headset, and I relay it to the players. Both Bobby Hamilton and Anthony Pleasant, who were teammates of mine when I played, still come to me now and ask about specific plays during a game. Willie McGinest also has a comfort zone with asking me things when the game is under way.

NFL rules prohibit viewing video during a game, so teams take still photos of formations while the game is still in progress. The cameras won't work until two seconds after the ball is snapped. You can shoot tape only before and after the snap. Jimmy Dee, our video director, takes the photos, and a runner brings them down to us on the sideline. RAC gets them, numbers the plays, and it helps us plan our defenses. We do this for the entire game.

At halftime we have only twelve minutes in the locker room, so we have to move fast. Guys with bumps and bruises or those who have to be taped see the trainer immediately. Then we try to make adjustments. If the offense has the ball in the closing seconds, Brian Daboll comes down from the booth early and begins drawing out plays that have hurt us in the first half. Whether they are pass or run plays, he has them on the board. When the rest of us come in, we're already gathering our thoughts as RAC begins talking to the defense. As always, the offense and defense are on separate sides of the locker room. Rob Ryan is very good at putting together the tendencies our opponent was showing in the first half. If they ran 70 percent on first down, it's been documented. In any case, the twelve minutes go by very quickly. Some stadiums have visitors' locker rooms pretty far from the field, which makes it a long walk. Never underestimate an opponent's inclination to frustrate a coach or staff, even if it means creating a three-minute walk to the locker room. You have only twelve minutes to make your adjustments, so the quicker you get there, the better.

We also look at personnel. If a guy doesn't seem right and isn't playing well, Belichick will see it first. We alternate so much, but if someone isn't cutting it, he won't be back on the field. If a player needs a pep talk, you have to do it individually. For example, some guys have thin skins on game day, and you do not want to make it worse by screaming at them. But if a guy needs someone in his face to wake him up, you do it. The head coach will address the team collectively, let them know how he feels they are looking. For individuals he delegates. If Belichick sees a problem with an inside linebacker, he'll tell me to talk to him.

You can't just win with eleven good guys in today's NFL. You need at least eighteen to twenty players on both offense and defense. Some guys will continue to play with minor injuries, even if they aren't 100 percent. The adrenaline just helps to get some guys back on the field, but others will shut it down for the day. Offensively, you want your linemen to stay in there. The so-called skill guys you can alternate more. Some teams now have second- and third-down running backs, three wide receivers who can get eight to twelve yards.

You still need at least five receivers, because if one of the first four goes down, you don't want to be out of four-receiver plays. When we see our opponents bring an extra wide receiver in, we'll counter with an extra defensive back, taking a linebacker off the field, especially if he's more of a first- or second-down guy. The game has become very situational. We have defensive linemen who are first- and second-down guys, then alternates who are pass rush specialists.

Coach Belichick never takes anything for granted. If we have a 20–3 lead at halftime, he'll tell the team that there's no guarantee that our opponent won't score 21 points in the second half and hold us to 3, winning the game. The only thing that can stop them from doing that is us. He expects us to maintain what we established in the first half or play even better. Thus the second half is always more intense. If our opponents just had a two-minute situation before the half, nine times out of ten we're just trying to avoid having them score a touchdown. The main objective right before a half is to keep them from getting six. No one is playing for a field goal before the half. Settle for it, but don't play for it. So, in the second half, the thinking process is a little different. It all depends on the score. Is this team playing for a field goal tie or win? Or are they down four points or more and need that touchdown? Or are you up by several touchdowns and they're just trying to make it look good? These situations determine how our defense is going to play.

As coaches we really don't relax for a second during the game. And, as I said, after a home game I don't leave the stadium for hours, waiting for tapes and beginning next week's preparation. There is one other thing, however, that determines how I feel after a game: the matter of winning or losing. I remember a friend telling me that Larry Bird once said he hated losing more than he liked winning. Until I heard that, I didn't look at it quite that way, but now I totally agree. I've won two Super Bowls as a professional player and now one as a coach. Never reached the Super Bowl and lost, but I have lost big games, like the 1998 AFC Championship game with the Jets versus Denver.

When I lose a game, any game, the first thing that hits me personally is how I came to this situation where I'm sitting here with my head down. The only way I can soothe that hurt is the next week, when we play again. If it's a title game, you aren't soothed until the next year. It's the whole season when you lose the last game or a championship game. Once Larry Bird's statement sank in, I realized that it didn't matter how many games you won; you're always going to look back at those losses. You look back at them more than the wins.

The 1990 Giants started the season 10–0, then lost to Philadelphia in that game when my friend Keith Byars put that big hit on me. We played San Francisco the following week, and both teams had identical records at 10–1, but all I could think about was that one loss. When we lost to the 49ers, the pain just intensified. I blamed the San Francisco loss on the previous week's loss to Philly. I really felt we would have found a way to win the 49ers game if the loss to Philadelphia wasn't still lingering in our minds, our bodies, and our souls. Even after we won the Super Bowl by beating Buffalo, I found myself looking back at the three games we wound up losing toward the end of the regular season.

I've always hated it when people have walked up to me and said "Good game" when we've lost. When I see a guy not affected by a loss, it's painful for me all over again. This bothered me to the point where I considered retiring after the 1994 season, because there were too many players who didn't care or seemed unaffected by losses. Like cancer, this mentality spreads to the older guys, and when you start seeing the older guys acting like the younger guys, it's bad. Finally, wherever you look, no one cares. Now guys begin complaining, but no one wants to take personal responsibility. After a heavy dose of this I found myself coming home and digging my own guts out for answers. I didn't know whether this was a new era or maybe because I was on a different team. Belichick was the coach in Cleveland that year, and we had fun but then didn't have jack to show for it. The little creeps who were coming in and not caring—wow, I just couldn't stomach that. I tried talking to them, but it was wearing me down, almost killing me.

It reached a point where I wasn't sure whether I fit in the game anymore, that my concern and passion for the game and for winning weren't appreciated. I couldn't hide who I was, and the losses hurt even more, because you didn't know who was feeling that pain. If you win a game, well, that's what you're supposed to do. You win the first game of the season the same way you win the last game. You're not hysterical until you win the championships. We, the Giants, were champions of the world, and no one can take that away from us. So you feel rewarded for all the hard work you put in all year. When we won those championships I was even happier for my family and friends than for myself.

Maybe my curse is that I don't enjoy it enough. As soon as we won the first Super Bowl, the thing that crossed my mind was repeating. I remember in 1990 when we won again. I got down on a knee to thank the Lord, then asked, "Please, let us repeat." I would love to be part of an undefeated team, like the 1972 Miami Dolphins. That's the ultimate goal. The thrill of victory takes a little longer to hit you. I was dancing on the field when the Giants won it in 1986, but I was happiest when I got back to Detroit that summer and handed my Super Bowl ring to my mother with the rest of the family gathered around. That's when I was really floating on air.

Fortunately, most of the players on the 2001 Patriots had the same attitude. We had weathered the storm of a rocky start, never losing faith, never letting our work ethic slip even a little bit. And once we started winning, we just didn't want it to end. Anything less than a championship would have left us trying to fill a gaping hole, and we simply didn't want to go there. Not this time.

7

The Third Four Games
The Playoffs Become Reality

It didn't take a rocket scientist to tell us the second half of the season couldn't be a repeat of the first. Sure, we were at .500 with a 4–4 record and coming off a big win against a good Atlanta team, but it had been a battle to get there, and the future was still uncertain. We weren't out of the playoff hunt by any means, but we weren't in the thick of it either. Since we had won three of our last four to reach this point, the consensus among the coaches and players was that the arrow was pointing up. The coaches were working their tails off, and the players were following suit as the connective arm extending from Coach Belichick on down was getting longer and longer. Everyone knew we needed a big second half, and that wouldn't be easy. Not only did we have the Rams on the schedule, but we had a pair of divisional games with Buffalo, then the Jets and Dolphins again. I don't know if anyone was counting, but we all knew that a couple more losses and it might all be over.

In week nine we played host to the Bills at Foxboro. They were a dismal 1–6 for the season, but whenever divisional rivals meet, the records can be tossed out the window. In fact the last time we had met, in week fifteen of the 2000 season, the game was decided by a twenty-four-yard Vinatieri field goal in overtime, in the snow. Divisional games are always played tight for the simple reason that the teams know each other so well. As a rule you aren't going to fool anyone. It's straight-to-the-vest football, with the winner being the team that plays better on that given day. The way it unfolded, the game was a big plus for us, perhaps an important turning point. We played with confidence and executed extremely well. Our defense had really pushed the Falcons around the week before, and when we began to establish a running game against Buffalo, the identity of the entire team became more sharply focused.

We won 21–11, but the game was closer than the final score indicated. We didn't wrap it up until there were less than two minutes remaining in the final quarter. Despite the score, this game was more of a defensive struggle. We had just too many offensive breakdowns, and Brady was sacked seven times. He also threw an interception and fumbled twice, so it shouldn't be surprising that we barely passed the hundred-yard mark in passing. Antowain Smith chipped in, playing against his former team and responding with a great game, gaining an even hundred yards on twenty carries.

Defensively, Terrell Buckley sacked their quarterback, Rob Johnson, and put him out of the game with a shoulder injury. Terrell isn't the type of player who wants to hurt someone, and he felt really bad about it. We're a physical team, but we play a clean game. Our players don't do those kinds of things intentionally. It's simply a result of their competitive nature, of playing hard. In fact our entire defense played a tough, physical game. Willie McGinest had his best game of the year, while Ted Johnson and Richard Seymour, our top draft choice, were credited with seven tackles each.

We scored first in the opening quarter when Brady hit Kevin Faulk with a six-yard scoring pass. The Bills came back with a field goal in the second quarter, and at the half it was still 7–3. That's why I called it a defensive struggle and a close game. If either team took charge early in the third, it might have been over right then and there. We managed a score on a forty-yard drive midway through the period, with Antowain scoring from the one-yard line. Adam's extra-point kick made it 14–3.

The score stayed that way until late in the fourth. That was when Buckley hit Johnson and knocked him out of the game. On the next series Brady was hit by Kendrick Office while backpedaling, fumbled the ball, and the Bills' Jay Foreman fell on it at our seventeen-yard line. Alex Van Pelt replaced Johnson, and he went for it all right away. His first pass was incomplete, but on his second he connected with receiver Peerless Price for a score. Then they went for two points, and Van Pelt found Eric Moulds in the corner of the end zone, lofting the ball nicely over the head of Ty Law. That made it 14–11 with just 2:43 left. So it was crunch time for us. If we went three-and-out, the Bills would have a chance to tie or win it.

We returned their short squib kickoff back to the Bills' forty-five-yard line. Our first play gained just three yards, but then Antowain Smith came through.

He avoided one tackler at the line of scrimmage, and that opening was all it took. From there he ran forty-two yards to the end zone, showing the kind of breakaway speed a lot of people didn't think he had. Adam's kick made it 21–11. That was the game's final touchdown, but the drama in the last five minutes was the reason I said the game was closer than the score. The victory brought us above .500 for the first time, making the upcoming game with the so-tough Rams even bigger. We wanted to keep our momentum going.

Tom Brady took some hits after the Buffalo game, leading some people to question his ability to lead the team, but I was never worried about him. He reminds me a lot of Phil Simms in that he has the patience to wait for the wide receivers to get open. Many quarterbacks become antsy back there and begin bouncing around when it isn't really necessary. Brady stood tall and confident in the pocket. In addition, it had reached a point in the season when we were so focused on our upcoming games that guys were no longer worried about when Drew would return and who would be the starter. Tom was doing well enough, and as a team the New England Patriots of 2001 knew who they were. Everyone was aware of his role and knew that to win we had to be a bunch of diggers and scrappers. We didn't have a lot of big-name marquee guys, maybe didn't even have any future Hall of Famers on the squad. So we knew that to win we had to make it a collective effort, and that meant winning with Tom Brady or Drew Bledsoe behind center. At this point it didn't really matter anymore.

Offensive linemen like Damien Woody and Mike Compton are going to block the same no matter whom they are protecting. Charlie will draw up plays to make sure our receivers get open so the quarterback can connect with them. And, of course, Antowain Smith has to run the ball to make it all happen. With each game we won, and whenever we were successful, everyone contributed and one of our units would do something special. In some games the offensive unit made up for a breakdown in special teams, or special teams reversed a breakdown in defense, or the defensive unit made the big plays to set things up for the offense. While we didn't have a dominating defense that carried the offense, the defense might have been the most solid group at the end of the year and going into the playoffs. When you watch our tapes, you'll see a bunch of physical, so-called no-name guys playing strong football. Because football is the ultimate team sport, you'll never be able to count on a single impact player like Michael Jordan to win games for you. It has to be a collective effort.

As I mentioned earlier, Coach Belichick had his own distinctive ways of motivating us throughout the year. His methods were sometimes subtle, but they were always effective. Lining the hallways from Belichick's office down to the team meeting room and continuing down to the locker room were maybe fifty photos from recent Patriots teams. Many of them were of teams that didn't win much. Before the season started, he removed all the pictures, leaving the walls bare. The only item remaining in the area was a case containing the two AFC championship team trophies from 1985 and 1996. Everything else was gone. Then he said that the only photos that would be put up on the walls were pictures of games that we won, because wins were the only thing deserving to be framed and hung.

As he began putting pictures up, no one would say anything or ask, "Where's my picture?" But as guys saw other pictures going on the wall, they wanted theirs up there, too. These were all hefty pictures, forty inches by forty inches. Once we started to win, there were a lot more defensive pictures going up: Otis Smith returning an interception for the touchdown against the Colts, Lawyer Milloy standing over someone he had hit, Bryan Cox looking down at a guy curled up on the ground. The new pictures were really brightening up the facility and inspiring the team. Coach Belichick hung new pictures Tuesday night so when the players came in to practice on Wednesday they would all want to see what had made the wall.

After the Buffalo game, Belichick put up a photo of Kevin Faulk catching a touchdown pass in the corner of the end zone. I joked with Brady that I kept looking at the pictures and saw receivers making acrobatic catches, but I didn't see the guy throwing the passes. He just laughed. Yet it wasn't only the team's most notable names who made it onto the wall. There was a picture of special teams player Je'Rod Cherry slamming a kick returner to the ground and fullback Mark Edwards blocking for Antowain Smith. Defensive backs coach Eric Mangini was photographed taking his headphones off and waving at Otis Smith like a traffic cop as Otis was running back an interception. He looks as if he's about to go out on the field and block someone. The hanging of these photographs was just another device to create more camaraderie and pride, and it worked.

Then he pulled a switch. Before the Cleveland game he hung a photo from our game with the Browns at Cleveland in 2000. We lost that one, a game everyone thought we should have won. The photo showed me on the sidelines with my head down. Belichick put it up the week before to remind everyone what had happened in 2000 and let them know he didn't want it happening again. That was the only time a negative-themed photo went up on the wall. I know I'm getting ahead of myself a bit because that was the thirteenth game, but I wanted to point out some of the things Coach Belichick did to give the team that little extra push while bringing them together at the same time.

Getting back to the season, we weren't a team that watched the scoreboard. It never mattered what the Jets or Dolphins were doing, because we knew we would get another shot at both of those teams. We felt we were still at a point in the season where we could control our destiny. In other words, keep winning and then beat those guys when it came down to it. We were still on training wheels and needed to take care of the New England Patriots before they would come off. When you start worrying about the things in your rearview mirror, or think about catching up with someone else, then you can lose focus and not concentrate on the business at hand. Everything we did was Patriots, all focused on us as a team—the classrooms, practice field, and on game day.

We felt our defense was improving as a unit and would get better still, that we were coming into our own. You could see it in the way the guys believed in themselves and became more supportive of each other. No matter how you slice it, the defense has to help the offense get things moving. Our job, besides stopping the opponent, is to put our offense in good field position, allow them to play with a short field. Or we can create a turnover and put our offense right back in action. A three-and-out puts their defense right back on the field. All of that helps the offense score more points.

Buffalo had been a good game for us. Everyone said their quarterback had more promise than ours, but he didn't finish the game. They also had a new coaching staff, and that always means it takes time for everything to jell. With all these factors, we were able to win a divisional game, though it was a dogfight. The Falcons game had been won by a pretty similar score, but we beat up on them a lot more than the scoreboard showed. Against the Bills we needed a big Antowain Smith run at the end to really put it away.

Next we had to meet the St. Louis Rams at Foxboro, and they were no picnic. Pretty much everyone—fans and media alike—considered them the top team in the league. The Rams had lost just a single game and were a very fast team with an abundance of talent at all the skill positions. Kurt Warner, their Cinderella-story quarterback from two years earlier, was playing extremely well. Running back Marshall Faulk is considered by some the best offensive player of his time. The high-octane Rams were flamboyant. They threw deep often and had a quick-strike, exciting offense with very speedy wide receivers. Even when they turned it over, there was excitement. They were undoubtedly the NFL's marquee team.

We felt, however, that we were ready for them, and the guys were looking forward to the challenge. This was an ESPN Sunday night game, and we figured the league's schedulers thought it would be a good time to see the Rams produce seven hundred yards of offense and put up seventy points on our defense. I'm exaggerating a little bit, but St. Louis was already the odds-on favorite to win the Super Bowl, and we were against-all-odds to play .500. Though their offense got most of the ink, we felt that their defense was also good, and stat-wise a little more sound than the defense of the championship team of two years earlier.

Then at Wednesday's practice we suffered a real setback. Ted Johnson, our veteran linebacker, who was playing very well, was injured by accident. One of our rookies, Kenyatta Jones, fell on Johnson's knee and hyperextended it. Ironically, the incident typifies Ted's pro career. It seems that whenever he was playing very well he got hurt and couldn't play an entire season. His latest injury couldn't have happened at a worse time, because we wanted to go into the Rams game firing on all cylinders, and now we had lost an important player. Tedy Bruschi was also slightly banged up, and it would force us to go more with the four-three defense, because now we were thin at linebacker. We still had the three-four package, but if we used it, Larry Izzo, our special teams captain, would have to step in.

This was another of those games where the score made it appear closer than it was. The Rams won it, 24–17, but had a 24–10 lead midway through the final quarter. I'm sure they felt they had beaten us because they were the better team, because they were the Rams, but we looked at it as another situation in which we had beaten ourselves. They scored first after a Brady pass went off Kevin Faulk's fingertips and was intercepted, giving them the ball on our eighteen. Warner threw to Torry Holt, and they had a 7–0 lead on a turnover. We got that back at the end of the quarter when Terrell Buckley intercepted a Warner pass and returned it fifty-two yards for the tying score.

On the Rams' next possession Tedy Bruschi intercepted a Warner pass, which led to a thirty-three-yard Vinatieri field goal. Now we led 10–7, and anytime you get a lead on the Rams you're in a position to win the game, but that's also when it started to fall apart. Just before the half they drove ninety-seven yards, with Warner hitting Faulk from nine yards out for the score. However, that never should have happened. We had a solid drive going and had the ball down at their five, ready to add to our lead. Then Antowain got the call and was hit just past the line of scrimmage. It appeared that he fumbled and they recovered, only our side felt he was down before the ball popped loose. We challenged the play, and after viewing the tape, the refs upheld it as a fumble. Antowain felt terrible, especially when the Rams then drove downfield and took a 14–10 lead. I think the way Antowain put it later was that "We had an opportunity to shock the world, and that turnover killed us."

It certainly didn't help. Larry Izzo recovered a Warner fumble in the third, but we gave it right back to them on an interception. They wound up with a field goal and a 17–10 lead. When they completed a seventy-five-yard touchdown drive early in the fourth and went up by 24–10, all we could do was keep playing and try to make it closer. Our final score came on a pass from Brady to Patten midway through the period, bringing the score to 24–17. We were only down a touchdown but couldn't get it. Warner ended up throwing for 401 yards. Brady didn't have a bad day but was picked off twice. Those turnovers combined with Antowain's fumble really hurt us, but then again, turnovers are killers. The funny part was that up to the fumble we were outplaying them. Our offense was moving, and that's often the best way to beat the Rams—have your offense control the ball and keep theirs off the field. If Warner, Faulk, and the rest of those flyers are in there long enough, they'll find a chink in your armor.

Though we were back to .500 again at 5–5, there were some definite positives coming out of the loss. As a team we gained confidence. We knew Antowain wouldn't get into that situation again where he would fumble so close to the goal line. After that happened I think we lost focus. One play can sometimes demoralize a team. If that happened against Buffalo, we were still in it because we'd know it was a rock fight. Against the Rams it was different. We knew how many weapons they had, with all their different formations and shifts. So you had to stay on your "A" game to keep up with them. You couldn't blow opportunities. After the fumble, we tried to calm the guys down because we knew the Rams had that high-powered offense. So we had to shake that blow. In recent weeks the guys had been doing it against nearly everyone, but this time our offense didn't go back out and move the ball, which would have put pressure on their defense. We just kind of sputtered across the board.

In the locker room after the game I remember Coach Belichick putting it right on the line to the team. He broke the game down and said, flat out, that we had beaten ourselves. "There it is, guys," he said. "If you can't see it, I don't know who can show it to you. That was supposed to be the best team the league has to offer. We just didn't show up. We should have beaten that team. No one should feel that we shouldn't have beaten them."

At that time no one really thought we would get a second chance, but the ball can sometimes bounce fatefully. One of the problems in the regular-season game was that we respected the Rams a lot more than we should have. I'm the first guy to say you respect your peers, down to the last man, but by the same token you've got to challenge everyone. We're competitors, and this is a competitive sport. If you are going to compete to the best of your abilities, you can't hold back because you think someone else's abilities are better. You do that and you've picked the wrong occupation. It took a game like that with the Rams to show us we still needed to develop the champion's attitude. We'd had all the confidence in the world going into the game, but I think that fumble near the goal line really did it. Had Antowain not fumbled and had we scored on that play, I honestly believe the outcome would have been different. You can't, however, blame Antowain. Remember, our defense allowed them to drive ninety-seven yards on just eight plays for a touchdown right after that. When something like that happens, you can't stay in shock. It's the job of the defense to come out and slow them down, take the momentum back right away. We didn't do that. As coaches we can't let the team get into a funk and become tentative. We have to do whatever it takes to get them out of it.

I guess we were still learning as a coaching staff, but the one thing we're sure of is that lessons like this won't be lost. The problem was that the loss dropped us back to .500, and at 5–5 time was starting to get short. Just six

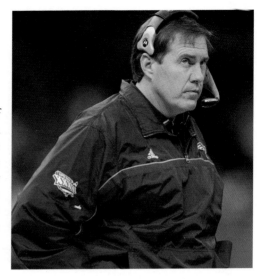

Nothing ever escapes the eyes of Bill Belichick. He's had a reputation for years as one of the hardest-working coaches in the league; and his attention to every detail and every facet of the game is legendary.

Copyright © Andy Lyons/Allsport/Getty Images

This is the man we all call "RAC." I've known Romeo Crennel for many years, and he is an outstanding defensive coordinator, as the 2001 season proved.

Copyright © Amy Sancetta/AP/Wide World Photos

Offensive coordinator Charlie Weis is another one who knows the Belichick system by heart. As with all the coaches, he is an extension of the philosophy and thinking of the head coach, something Bill Belichick has always insisted upon.

Copyright © Elise Amendola/AP/Wide World Photos

Team spirit and camaraderie were trademarks of the 2001 Patriots. After Drew Bledsoe was injured he did all he could to help Tom Brady mature as a quarterback. Here he talks with Tom on the sidelines during a November game against the Buffalo Bills. (That's me in the white shirt with the headset on.)

*Copyright © Damian Strohmeyer/*Sports Illustrated

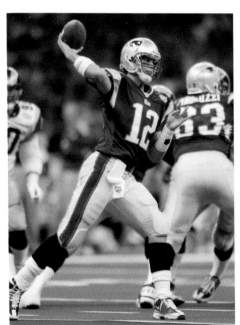

After Bledsoe's injury against the Jets in week two, Tom Brady showed himself to be a second-year quarterback with poise, leadership ability, and a surprisingly accurate passing arm.

Copyright © Ezra Shaw/Allsport/Getty Images

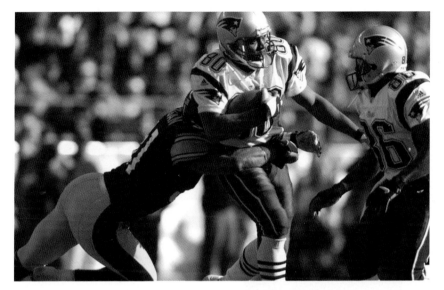

All Troy Brown (80) does is make plays. He was the league leader in punt return yardage and set a team record with more than one hundred pass receptions. Not bad for a guy who began his career by being cut.

Antowain Smith (32) came over from Buffalo and was just what the doctor ordered—a durable runner who could get the tough yards and control the clock. He was simply the big back that the team needed so badly.

Lawyer Milloy (36) is the heart and soul of the Patriots defense. Lawyer is a throwback player, a down-in-the-box safety who loves to hit and hates coming off the field, even for one play.

Copyright © Al Bello/Allsport/Getty Images

Cornerback Ty Law told me he had something to prove after a subpar 2000 season. Then he went out and proved it many times over, becoming once again a vital cog in a team defense that got better as the year wore on.

Copyright © Brian Bahr/Allsport/Getty Images

Veteran linebacker Bryan Cox (51) brought toughness and a winning attitude to the Patriots, impressing everyone so much in his first year with the team that he was quickly named one of our captains, quite an honor.

Copyright © Ezra Shaw/Allsport/Getty Images

David Patten began the season as the team's third or fourth receiver. By the time it ended he was a dependable starter with big-play ability; he played through pain and made enormous contributions to the team's ultimate success.

Defensive toughness was another trademark of the 2001 Patriots. Two of the biggest contributors were linebacker Tedy Bruschi (54) and cornerback Otis Smith (45). I called Bruschi "Mr. Heart" because he played so well despite a lingering back injury, while Otis will battle any wide receiver from the first play of the game until the last.

Copyright © Andy Lyons/Allsport/Getty Images

Everything is accelerated in the playoffs. In our divisional playoff game with the Raiders in the snow at Foxboro, the tension can be easily seen in Coach Belichick's face.

Copyright © Reuters NewMedia Inc./Corbis

Tom Brady took to the snow like a New England native. Despite a slippery field, he was able to scamper past the Raiders' defenders for a key fourth-quarter touchdown that brought victory within our reach.

Copyright © David Bergman/Sports Illustrated

Here's Adam Vinatieri doing it again—booting a clutch field goal in overtime to beat the Raiders and sending us to the AFC Championship game against the Steelers. It seemed that the bigger the field goals became, the better Adam kicked.

Copyright © Ezra Shaw/Allsport/Getty Images

The falling snow makes it look as if Adam is celebrating his winning kick against Oakland all alone. In truth, an entire team, a stadium full of fans, and a city were celebrating with him.

Copyright © Al Bello/Allsport/Getty Images

One of the keys to beating Pittsburgh in the AFC title game was stopping their running game and their star runner, Jerome Bettis (36). Tedy Bruschi (54) and the rest of the defense worked the game plan to perfection and Bettis was held in check.

Copyright © Al Bello/Allsport/Getty Images

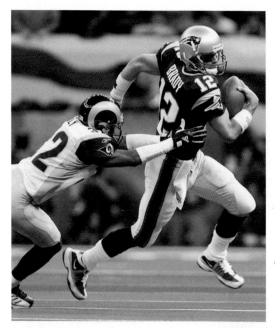

After Bledsoe came to the rescue against the Steelers, Tom Brady returned from an injury to lead the offense against the Rams in the Super Bowl. He soon proved his mobility was back, as he escapes from Rams cornerback Dre Bly during the second quarter at the New Orleans Superdome.

Copyright © Reuters NewMedia Inc./Corbis

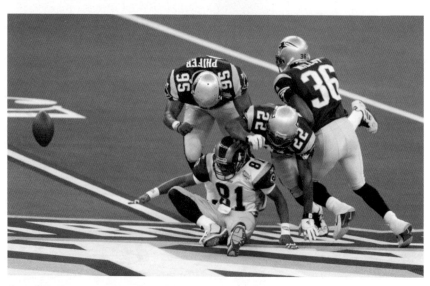

Our objective was to slow the great Rams receivers by hitting them hard and ganging up on them. The plan worked to perfection on this play, with Roman Phifer (95), Terrance Shaw (22), and Lawyer Milloy (36) all combining to make Torry Holt pay on an incomplete pass.

Copyright © Andy Lyons/Allsport/Getty Images

Here's yet another example of how to defend the pass. Phifer (95) runs to the aid of Tebucky Jones (left) and Tedy Bruschi (54) as they sandwich the speedy Az-Zahir Hakim (88). Even when they caught the ball, the Rams receivers knew they would pay a price.

Copyright © Andy Lyons/Allsport/Getty Images

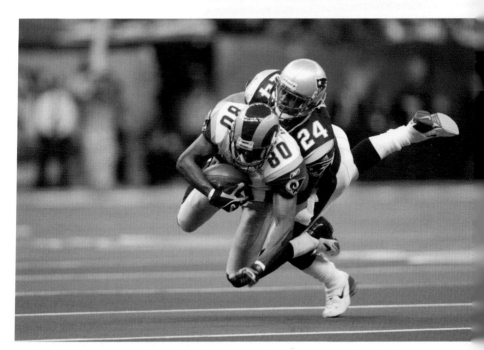

It was no different with one-on-one situations. Ty Law plants a heavy hit on Isaac Bruce (80), stopping him hard after a short gain.

Copyright © Andy Lyons/Allsport/Getty Images

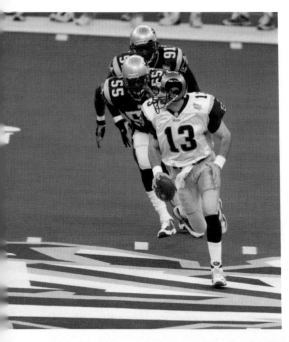

Another part of our game plan was to keep Rams quarterback Kurt Warner (13) from having all day to throw the football. Flushed out of the pocket, Warner has to know that Willie McGinest (55) and Bobby Hamilton (91) are ready to slam him to the turf.

Copyright © Al Bello/Allsport/Getty Images

Stop Marshall Faulk! That might have been our biggest goal when we played the Rams. As great as he is, Faulk was never able to control the game. Here Lawyer Milloy (left) and Tedy Bruschi close in to stop him after a short gain.

Copyright © Ronald Martinez/Allsport/Getty Images

Don't bet against Adam Vinatieri. Not surprisingly, it was Adam who ended the game and gave us the championship with yet another pressure kick. His winning field goal came with just seven seconds left and from forty-eight yards out.

Long snapper Lonie Paxton played a huge role in all of Adam's big field goals. He celebrated against the Raiders by making a snow angel in the snow at Foxboro. Against the Rams, Lonie fell down in the end zone and made the equivalent of a "turf" angel.

Copyright © Brian Bahr/Allsport/Getty Images

I think the coach is smiling here, if only a little. He should. We just won the Super Bowl and there's no doubt about Tom Brady's feelings. He's one happy quarterback.

Copyright © AFP/Corbis

There's little doubt about what the coach is feeling here. We're number one and he has the trophy to prove it.

Copyright © Reuters NewMedia Inc./Corbis

Everybody had a chance to celebrate with the trophy. Je'Rod Cherry, our great special teams player, looked pretty awed as he hoisted the symbol of our victory after the game.

Copyright © Al Tielemans/Sports Illustrated

I never saw so many people in my life as turned out for our victory parade in downtown Boston. Having won a pair of Super Bowls as a player with the Giants, this was my first as a coach. But you never get tired of winning. This one was absolutely great.

For every single player on the Patriots, this made all the hard work worthwhile. While Lawyer Milloy (left) celebrates with the trophy, Tom Brady (center) and Tedy Bruschi (right) have a baseball glove and ball. Wrong sport; right celebration.

In April of 2002, the Patriots were invited to the White House, the continuation of a
long tradition. Owner Robert Kraft (left) presents President George W. Bush with a
Patriots jersey as head coach Belichick looks on. Yes, he's smiling again.

Copyright © Reuters NewMedia Inc./Corbis

As owner Kraft said, it was a good year for a team named the Patriots to win. As
President Bush speaks, a proud New England team looks on. I guess you could say
we won it the old-fashioned way . . . we earned it.

Copyright © Doug Mills/AP/Wide World Photos

Holding the Vince Lombardi trophy is what it's all about. It should be what every single player aspires to. I know when I played I wanted to win it every year. I feel the same way now that I'm a coach.

Copyright © Andy Lyons/Allsport/Getty Images

games left. We had a pretty good New Orleans Saints team coming up next, and another problem stood in the way that could have easily become a major issue and possibly a divisive one.

After the Rams game, the team's doctors had cleared Drew Bledsoe to be activated that week, making him eligible to play against the Saints. Drew had been recovering from his injury since week two, and the questions were already being asked in the press: Who was going to be the team's quarterback for the rest of the year? In the NFL there's an unwritten rule that a starter doesn't lose his job because of an injury. Most times when a star player returns he immediately has his job back. Our situation, however, was more complicated than that, and the last thing Coach Belichick wanted was a quarterback controversy to disrupt the team's chemistry.

Early in the week he announced his decision, and it surprised a lot of people. Without hesitation, he told the press and anyone else who was listening that Tom Brady would remain the New England Patriots' starting quarterback for the rest of the season. Needless to say, it wasn't taken well by many people outside of the team. If the Patriots were to have any chance at all of making the playoffs, they reasoned, the veteran Bledsoe was the man to lead them there. Though the same people conceded that Brady had a done a solid job, they apparently couldn't see a second-year quarterback producing at crunch time, when the entire season might be on the line. Belichick, many said, had made a bad choice that was going to come back and bite him in the ass. Only there was more to it than most people knew.

I can say this now and not really feel bad about it, but Drew simply wasn't ready to take over again. I saw it, and I know Belichick saw it. When you looked at him, he simply didn't appear healthy. Drew isn't extremely muscular, but he's very solid. Yet looking at him, he didn't have the old solid appearance about him. Physically, we could see he wasn't all the way back. He was throwing the ball well and running pretty good, but there's no way to simulate being hit in a game. Drew is one of the tougher guys I know playing this game. He's got great heart and attitude, but I don't think Drew was ready to quarterback the New England Patriots against the Saints. I think his not being ready physically was the number-one reason for Belichick's decision, but there were other reasons as well.

By naming Brady as the quarterback for the rest of the year, the coach was looking at the big picture, what was best for the team. If he put Drew right back in as the starter—a Drew Bledsoe who didn't look physically ready to me—and we lost him again to another injury, leading Brady to return, then we'd have taken a step back. We would have lost everything we had gained with Tom Brady over the last six weeks. We'd lose it as soon as we took him out of the lineup and put Drew back in. Now, if you do it the other way, if you continue with Brady as the starter and lose him to injury somewhere down the stretch, then you have a hungry, experienced Drew Bledsoe in the shadows just itching to get in there. Those quick to criticize Belichick also had to remember that Tom Brady was 5–3 as a starter, playing well, and building character at the same time. So taking everything into consideration, there was a lot more upside to leaving Brady out there as the starter than putting him on the bench and going back to Drew.

I will say this, however. Had Drew Bledsoe been 100 percent ready, had we felt that his body was ready to take the pounding and had the injury been less severe, I think Coach Belichick would have given him the job back at that point. But he had a gut feeling that Drew was not fully ready, and I felt the same way. I feel the decision wasn't based on how well Tom Brady was playing, but rather on Drew's physical condition at the time.

Every player wants to be on the field. At that time Drew had two things pushing him: one, that he's a competitor and two, Tom Brady. No established player wants to see a kid take his job. No one. That was motivation for Drew to continue to get healthy. But nature is nature. If his body was at full strength, and he couldn't take that blow from Mo Lewis, we just didn't think he could take a similar blow when he was fifteen to twenty pounds lighter. The decision that Coach Belichick made was the right one under the circumstances. A lot of people, including those in the media, didn't fully understand it because they didn't look beyond the initial choice. I'm betting, however, that Coach Belichick was looking a lot farther down the line.

He made the decision early in the week because he wanted to nip any controversy in the bud, get everyone's mind back on the Saints, and get Brady ready for the game. Coach Belichick didn't explain everything at the time because if he had, then he would have had to continue talking about it. He didn't want to be answering the same questions week after week. If for some reason Brady started going in the opposite direction over the next couple of weeks, we had ourselves an ace in the hole and, hopefully, by then Drew would be fully ready. NFL pass rushers will always test a returning quarterback. If they know there is a wounded duck back there, they go at him even harder.

Because of Belichick's quarterback decision, the game against the Saints in Foxboro became even bigger. Even though he made things clear, the press hounded the players and others in the team's inner circle all week. Their reaction reminded me of the Terry Glenn situation. Players were being asked which quarterback they would prefer and whether they thought it was right that a quarterback could lose his job because of an injury. As I said, no one really knew the whole story, but the media, not willingly or purposely, can divide you. The last thing we needed at this stage of the season was to be divided. However, Coach Belichick didn't go into the physical aspect of the decision. Rather, he had a kind of politically correct comment, that he was doing what was best for the team. He simply felt at the time that Drew's physical condition was no one's business.

The two quarterbacks were not clones of each other. There was a difference. Brady's mentality was to take whatever the defense was giving him and allow his playmakers to make plays. That was the secret to his success, and his completion percentage would rise as the season wore on. He would gladly dump the ball off to Troy Brown three yards up the field and let Troy turn it into a twelve- or eighteen-yard gain and a first down. Drew has a powerful arm and was always willing to go up top and air it out. There were some games, however, when we needed consistent ball control. So dumping the ball off and getting what we could from short passes was in the best interest of the team. That's what helped us. It wasn't always Brady's decision, but those were the plays that were being called for him. Belichick's naming him the quarterback not just for the Saints game but for the rest of the season boosted his confidence, and it showed on the field.

New Orleans came into the game with a 5–4 record, but could they be a team that was cocky and resting on their laurels from the year before, when they went 10–6 and won the NFC West? Often that kind of moderate success drains a team the following year. Reality doesn't set in, and the players can't grasp the fact that last year was last year. Then it becomes a much tougher job to top last year's performance. The Saints played some big games against the Rams in 2000, splitting a pair in the regular season, then defeating them in the first round of the playoffs, 31–28. They have a young, up-and-coming quarterback in Aaron Brooks, but I had the feeling that sooner or later someone was going to catch up with them. They kind of surprised everyone the year before, not only with Brooks, but with running back Ricky Williams and receiver Joe Horn. They caught a lot of people off guard, but now everyone had a whole year to prepare for them. They had an offense that gave their defense plenty of rest. That brings success to a defense because it allows them to get their breaths and be on the sideline just long enough to stay hungry.

Sometimes they would strike fast, and sometimes control the ball. But in 2001 things weren't working for them that way. Instead of getting a wake-up call, they kept thinking the other team was lucky, that they still had time. It was similar to the situation with the New York Giants that I spoke about earlier. Neither team ever found the sense of urgency in 2001, and when a team doesn't find that, it's destined for doom. It's like I said: if a team is satisfied with *almost* getting there, or *almost* winning it all, then there's no way it will be successful the following year. As it turned out, the hungrier team was the one that played the good, solid game. That team was the Patriots, and the game wasn't even close. We won it, 34–17.

Our defense made sure the Saints didn't get their running game going, turning their offense into a one-dimensional attack. We knew if we just let Aaron throw the ball and not scramble, it would be a big game for us. Offensively, we stayed out of situations where their defense could really crank on third and long. The previous year they were either the leading team or close to the lead in sacks. We kept them off balance with short and medium passes and a strong running game. So their big sackers never had much of a chance to do their thing.

Antowain scored our first touchdown, turning a short pass into a long run to the end zone. In the second Troy caught a TD pass and then Brady hit Charles Johnson for a score. Three TD passes for Brady and a 20–0 lead at halftime. That was the game right there. They came within 10 points twice, but we got the final score with about two and a half minutes left, Antowain running it in from the three. Brady played a great game, completing nineteen of twenty-six passes for 258 yards and four touchdowns. He had really responded to coach Belichick's vote of confidence. Antowain ran for 111 yards on twenty-four carries as the running game continued to improve. Lawyer had a great game on defense with ten tackles and an interception.

In fact our entire defense had been getting stronger over the last three or four games. The loss to the Rams was a setback, granted, especially that one long drive after the fumble. I just think that once they caught us and got us down it was more difficult for us to snap out of it. Before that our guys were showing improvement, especially in their communication. Guys have to communicate and believe in one another on the defensive side of the ball, or it won't work. The entire defense was on a sound footing. Now, as coaches, we didn't have to sit in the booth or on the sideline with fingers crossed, hoping that the guys were going to spot changes and audible and then react. In addition, there was more participation from the players in the meeting room, more helpful ideas and comments, and no selfishness. Every week they were doing a great job keeping everyone involved in the defense. All our different packages and the blitz calls that involved every player helped the guys to really buy into our philosophy.

So we pretty much rolled over the Saints to bring our record above .500 once again. Now we were 6–5 but far from celebrating anything, even though we had beaten them so handily, because we still didn't feel we were out of the fire. We had had those kinds of games early in the year and come up flat the following weeks, suffering some big defeats. In that sense the team hadn't yet found real consistency. Our record spoke for itself. At least we were starting the second half on a positive note, having won two of three and knowing that with the exception of a couple of bad breaks we had also played the Rams very tough. Now, to close out the three-quarter mark of the season, we had to travel to the Meadowlands for our second meeting with the Jets. They were at 7–3, still ahead of us in the AFC East standings, as were the Dolphins. We knew we really couldn't afford another loss, especially to a divisional rival.

As usual, the game with the Jets was filled with subplots that could both motivate and distract our team. There were a few whispers here and there trying to stir up those little monsters again. The story about Cox shaking hands with the Jets' John Abraham just after Drew was hit in the first game was circulated again, and the New York press kept reminding us that we had lost three straight to the Jets. Then they dredged up all the old stuff about Belichick's difficult departure from the Jets, once again calling him *Belichicken*. I always said that Bill Belichick would make a wonderful actor. He doesn't let anything affect him. In the staff meetings he would just joke about the stories. When he enters a now-hostile environment like Giants Stadium, he doesn't have fifteen security guards around him. He just sticks with his normal routine. He'll even say hello to guys in the Jets' organization and to a couple of players. The fans are loud and shouting obscenities at him, and he never budges, never looks up.

During the week there was a sense of urgency and an intense determination to beat the Jets. We wanted this game badly. You could feel it everywhere—in the meetings, on the field, all throughout the stadium. It was a feeling that was coming from everyone, all the coaches, including me. Besides Belichick, a number of other coaches had exited the Jets bitterly, as I did as a player. We weren't angry with the players or some of their coaches. It was simply the total package. To begin with, they were a traditional rival, and when you left an organization and weren't happy with the way they had treated you, well, you pretty much wanted to smash them in the face.

The game plan was simple. Stop Curtis Martin. That was our number-one priority. We were pretty happy that Vinny Testaverde hadn't been dropping back and throwing downfield that much. That was Vinny's strength, something Belichick knew from coaching him in Cleveland. If you played a zone defense against Vinny, he would kill you. You'd have a better chance standing close to his receivers, man to man. He also tended to get a little antsy, because he's a strong-armed quarterback like Drew. He'd try to force the ball. The blessing for us is that he hadn't been just standing back there throwing. We would pretty much know in advance when he was going to throw it downfield. The Jets just didn't drop back and throw it three times in a row unless it was in a two-minute situation. On many of their drives Curtis would be getting the ball two out of every three plays.

How, then, do you stop Curtis Martin? He is a very elusive runner. When the Jets gave him the ball, they allowed him to make his own decisions about whether to cut outside or stay inside. Plays were designed for him, and they tried to spread the defense out, find one guy who wasn't blocked, then let Curtis make him miss and run into the secondary. He was definitely one of the league's better runners. The Jets had three decent blockers, but they weren't the kind of high-caliber offensive line that would get fifteen hundred yards for any back.

Lawyer Milloy and Tebucky Jones had both played with Curtis and were well aware of how he was when he got it going. They looked at it as a challenge and were determined not to let him run uncontested all over our defense. It was like playing against a brother or a good friend. They weren't going to give him bragging rights. Our defense was also bolstered by the return of Bryan Cox, who was activated for the Jets game after missing five weeks with a broken bone in his leg. I think Cox would have gone absolutely nuts if he had been told he wouldn't be playing against those guys. There were two reasons. One, after missing a few games, he simply wanted to go back there and play against them, but I think he also wanted to prove a point to his new teammates. He wanted to let them know, once and for all, that he was unquestionably a New England Patriot. While he called some of the guys on the Jets friends, he wanted to let everyone know "I am a Patriot, and I want to win here."

Because of all these factors, I knew we were ready emotionally. This was simply a game we couldn't lose. Coach Belichick reminded the team during the week that we already had five losses, so each game from this point out would have to be treated as if it were a playoff game. He said what most of us already knew, that we couldn't afford to lose another game, and he told the coaching staff that if we lost we might also lose the team for the rest of the season. It would be more difficult to build their confidence back, and even if we made the playoffs somehow, the team might be so exhausted, so emotionally drained, that chances of winning would be minimal. To the coaches this was an absolute must game, but you can't say that to the players. You have to find ways to emphasize it indirectly, because God forbid if you lose. If the players felt they had lost a must game, a number of them might shut it down. Even if we lost 30 or 35 percent of the team, guys who couldn't get up again for the next games, it would finish us. With our team we needed everybody to win.

For the first half it didn't look as if it was going to be our day. Testaverde came out doing the thing we feared—he threw the football downfield successfully. He completed a thirty-three-yard pass to Santana Moss, then threw to Laveranues Coles for a thirty-four-yard touchdown with just a little more than three minutes gone in the game. Right away we were playing from behind, and they hadn't even turned Curtis Martin loose yet. When John Hall kicked a nineteen-yard field goal before the end of the first quarter, we found ourselves down 10–0. The only scoring in the second quarter was another Hall field goal. Now we were coming off the field down 13–0, playing in their ball yard, and not playing well enough to win.

Our halftime was low-key as always, in spite of the hole we had dug for ourselves. Once again, you never get a fire-and-brimstone, Knute Rockne–

type speech from Coach Belichick. He's a realist. People used to criticize him in Cleveland for not having character and being humdrum to the press. But he has always found it useless to explain football or his philosophy of the game to someone who doesn't really understand, doesn't really want to know, or is going to write what he wants to write anyway. Down 13–0 to the Jets, we followed the same routine, made some adjustments, and again emphasized the importance of the game, telling the team that our entire season was on the line. Belichick reminded them that at 13–0 they weren't out of it, but to win they had to play better. That was enough. Each and every one of the players knew the situation.

Early in the third period the game began turning around, and typical of the 2001 Patriots, we got a big play from an unexpected source. On third down from midfield, Brady threw a slant-in pass to Fred Coleman, who was our fifth wide receiver and had played in the ill-fated XFL. This is a perfect example of how everyone on the team was not only important to its success but contributed in a big way. Coleman turned a short pass into a forty-six-yard gain, carrying the ball all the way down to the four. From there Antowain ran it over, and we were back in it at 13–7. The entire sequence was set up by a Mike Vrabel interception at our own thirty-one and led to the five-play TD drive.

Hall kicked his third field goal midway through the period, upping the lead to 16–7, but once again we didn't quit. Now it was Brady's turn to get hot. He led us on an eighty-two-yard scoring drive highlighted by Antowain's catching a short pass and turning it into a forty-yard gain. That's what I meant by Brady knowing how to let our playmakers make plays. Now the ball was on the twenty-seven, and after several key runs by Kevin Faulk, fullback Marc Edwards punched it over from the four-yard line with just over two minutes left in the third period. Adam's point after made it 16–14. Going into the fourth quarter, the game was still up for grabs.

Midway through the fourth we began driving again, Brady hitting pass after pass, taking just what they would give him. When the drive finally stalled, Adam came on to boot a twenty-eight-yard field goal. With just 6:29 left, we had come all the way back to take the lead at 17–16. The Jets still had time to win and began driving again in the final minutes. Now it was time for the defense to step up. With just over two minutes left, Testaverde dropped back and threw a pass that easily could have put them within range of John Hall's right leg, but Terrell Buckley was Johnny-on-the-spot, intercepting the pass at the thirty-three-yard line, the last big play of the afternoon. That did it. We had won the game by a single point, but that was just as good as winning by fifty.

After such a momentous win our players couldn't resist celebrating. Even Coach Belichick had a rare show of elation on the field. When the game ended, he high-fived and embraced players on the sideline. There was all kinds of joyous screaming going on. Then, to finally end any trace of that sour taste about ex-Jets players, Coach Belichick awarded game balls to every ex-Jet on our roster with the final score of the game painted on it and passed them out at the end of the week. There was no doubt anymore that every last player on the team had just one thing in mind.

I can't count the number of guys who had come up big in the second half. Tom Brady completed fifteen of seventeen passes after intermission. Fred Coleman had made a great run with a pass, as did Antowain. Buckley had perhaps a game-saving interception, while Roman Phifer was all over the field with nine tackles, big Richard Seymour had a sack, and Tebucky Jones had a big day on special teams, besides taking his regular turn at safety. Even Bryan Cox was inspirational. Still not 100 percent, he was in on only two plays. One was on a goal-line stand when they were forced to settle for a field goal. He and Bruschi combined on the crucial stop. On the second play he blitzed and deflected a Testaverde pass. After the game it was apparent that the players were every bit as aware as the coaches that this was a game that had to be won.

Lawyer said it had a playoff game atmosphere, adding that the team was already in playoff mode, something all the coaches knew had to be the case for us to close. Damien Woody and Marc Edwards both admitted the first half had been a wake-up call. No one really had to be reminded of what had to be done in the second half. Bobby Hamilton said something that I have been saying all along. He mentioned that if the same thing had happened a year earlier, that version of the Patriots would have given up. This team, he said, was made up of a bunch of fighters. That's the mentality we had been striving to produce since the start of training camp. We were now two games over .500 for the first time, at 7–5. The Dolphins still led the division at 8–3, and the Jets were 7–4, but if the season ended at that point, we would have been in the playoffs. So we knew we had something going and couldn't afford to let down.

After the game Coach Belichick gave a short talk to the team; it was noteworthy because its theme would endure for the rest of the season. In essence he told the team that every game from this point on would be the most important game we had played in our lives. In any season, your next game is always the most important one. Now, however, everything had become magnified. We still had one more loss than the Jets and two more than the Dolphins. So there was no way we could let down. None of our next three games would be easy. We would begin the final quarter of the season against an improving Cleveland Browns team. Following the Browns would be divisional rival Buffalo again, then an encore with the Dolphins. Finally, we would wrap it up with Carolina, the game postponed by the events of September 11th.

At this point, I saw the Patriots as a maturing team, one that was getting better and gaining great experience playing under pressure. Against the Jets we had proven we could come back in the second half and play clutch football in the fourth quarter. We were winning overtime games and getting important field goals from Adam. The team was also not turning the ball over in the second half, but still creating turnovers. I believe we had twenty-one take-aways in the season after the Jets game. Our special teams were also doing the job, getting us good field position. So everything was starting to jell. All the hard work we had put in early in the season was paying off. As coaches we were becoming more confident in what we were trying to do and felt all the time talking to the players and selling them on our system was finally producing the success we had envisioned.

I want to make mention of our kicking game, especially Adam Vinatieri. Adam reminds me a lot of Matt Bahr, who used to kick for the Giants. I have been around kickers who don't really know what's going on in a game. All they know is that once the offense starts to move the ball within their range they should start kicking into the net and warming up. Some kickers I knew weren't even sure how the team stood within the division. Adam knows. I've had conversations with him, and he's very aware of the situation with our team and with our opponents. He doesn't have the strongest leg in the league, but from forty yards in he's gonna make it. And with the pressure on, don't bet against him from forty-five either.

The entire team knew the importance of Adam, our punter Ken Walter, and Lonie Paxton, our long snapper. It was totally imperative that the offensive line protect them. Everyone knew that if the ten other guys did their job, Adam would make the field goal. He relished those clutch kick opportunities. Some guys want to be the hero, but Adam is not selfish. He wants it because he's part of the team, just as important as the others, but he doesn't want to be put on a pedestal.

So I think it's apparent how this team was coming together, how the season was a steady, upward progression, a learning process, an all-out effort to make this a complete football squad. The victory over the Jets was a tremendous boost for us. It not only erased any doubts about the ex-Jets now being full-fledged Patriots, but gave us a victory over a rival that had beaten us three straight times. I think it's safe to say, though, that our week-twelve victory turned out to be worth a lot more than the previous three put together.

8

Dealing with Distractions

As the 2001 season progressed, the Patriots were slowly bonding as a complete team. We began living the old expression *there is no I in team*, and we knew winning would take a complete effort from everyone, coaches and players alike. Once we could smell the playoffs, especially after the victory over the Jets that had brought us to 7–5, I think that sense of team was stronger than ever. No team, however, has smooth sailing from the beginning of training camp through season's end. There are always going to be problems along the way, difficult decisions that must be made, and situations that, if not handled properly, can lead to dissension in the ranks and a split in that all-important team unity. The Patriots were not free and clear of these potential problems.

Fortunately, our coaching staff and especially Bill Belichick proved themselves capable of handling the problems that arose, dealing with potentially divisive situations, and bringing the team together for the final stretch run and playoffs. I've already talked about the Terry Glenn situation, which began in training camp and continued throughout the first half of the season. Lawyer Milloy helped the team finally put that matter to rest when he told them, "Hey, if Terry is here, then fine, but if not we go on and stop worrying about it." His attitude was simply an extension of Belichick's, the one that says you don't dwell on anything. Put it behind you and go on. The decision Belichick made regarding his choice of quarterbacks was another example. Once he announced that Tom Brady would remain the starter, the speculation and discussion ended. Everyone knew his decision was final, and the press knew there was no sense continuing to ask about it. If you allow the questions to continue, the problem remains.

What many people didn't realize at the time was that Coach Belichick already had some experience handling a potential quarterback controversy. Always one to learn from his experiences, he had to deal with a similar situation during his tenure as head coach of the Cleveland Browns. The longtime quarterback of the Browns then was Bernie Kosar, who had some fine seasons and was wildly popular in the city of Cleveland. Belichick thought, however, that Kosar's best days were behind him and knew he had a young, strong-armed Vinny Testaverde waiting in the wings. Finally he made the decision midway through the 1993 season to bench Kosar and give the job to Testaverde. Talk about a huge distraction. I don't think anyone in the media and in the city of Cleveland would allow that decision to be put to rest.

Cleveland fans are extremely loyal, and to them Kosar was larger than life. Born and raised in Ohio, Kosar always expressed a preference to play for the Browns and called them "his" team. Ironically, he never brought them a championship, but because he had so many good years behind him, the fans put him on a pedestal. It was the same with Drew. He hadn't won a championship, but the expectations were always great. If the Patriots were to win a championship, they'd do it with Drew as quarterback. When a quarterback finds success, fans tend to attach themselves to him. Win a few ball games and pull out a few, and they think they have the next Dan Marino. But Marino didn't win a Super Bowl either. He went to the Super Bowl in 1984, his second year in the league, but the Dolphins lost and never returned to the Super Bowl in spite of Marino's setting nearly every NFL career passing record. He'll go down in history as perhaps the greatest quarterback ever who failed to win a championship.

I think that's something a lot of fans don't understand, but something of which Bill Belichick is acutely aware. It's also one of the things I liked about playing in New York. The fans don't care if you make the playoffs. They want you to win a championship. Some organizations will get caught up in the fact that they have a star quarterback. It's almost as if the first thing they'll say is, hey, we've got Dan Marino. Often, however, those teams fail to do enough work on the other side of the ball or fill the holes that have to be filled to win. Dan, for example, did a helluva job making guys around him better. However, the 1972 Dolphins, the unbeaten championship team, won with a journeyman, Earl Morrall, playing quarterback a good part of the year when Bob

Griese was injured. That's because they mostly ran the football and played solid defense. That was the heart of their team.

John Elway is another example. A great passer, he got to the Super Bowl a couple of times by throwing the ball all over the lot, and his team lost. They relied on his arm too much. Once the Broncos finally established a strong running game, Elway won a pair of Super Bowls just before retiring. While it's often the quarterback who wins the Super Bowl MVP award, behind each one of them you will usually find a running back who had a big game. You simply must have balanced offense to go with a strong defense to win championships in this league. Belichick knew this when he took over in Cleveland. In 1994 he appeared to be building his kind of team and the Browns had a good season, winning 11 games. A year later, however, it began falling apart after owner Art Modell announced in midseason that the team would be moving to Baltimore. That was a distraction even Bill Belichick couldn't make disappear.

The most criticism Belichick had to deal with in Cleveland was when he made the quarterback change in 1993. It was magnified further when he traded Kosar to Dallas at midseason. Ironically, Kosar backed up Troy Aikman with the Cowboys that year and wound up with a Super Bowl ring. As Cleveland's new starter, Testaverde was injured, and the team wound up 7–9, so there's never a guarantee when a coach makes a difficult decision. Ironically, when the Browns made the playoffs in 1994, Belichick had veteran Brian Sipe at quarterback.

The situation, however, was similar to Brady-Bledsoe with the Patriots. In Cleveland, Belichick saw the controversy linger and continue to tear at the team until he traded Kosar. He just didn't want Testaverde constantly looking over his shoulder, and he learned his lesson from it. That's why he was so emphatic when he made the decision before the New Orleans game to name Brady the permanent starter. He didn't say it was for a game or two. He said the job was Brady's for the rest of the season. No looking over his shoulder. In addition, he didn't explain anything about Bledsoe's physical condition. That would have opened it up to more questions. Belichick knows a coach has to act decisively and not allow a problem or a tough decision to become a major distraction.

When we picked the team's final roster during training camp, we looked for guys we all felt comfortable dealing with as coaches for the entire season.

No assholes allowed. If an asshole creeps through the door for some reason, everyone understands. Even if you have two, you can usually deal with it. There will always be a couple, but the majority of our players are just the kind of guys we wanted. When the young guys see Otis Smith, at age thirty-six, running before practice and running after practice, and when they see a bulldozer is required to pull Anthony Pleasant off the field when practice is over, it trickles down. It's contagious. The younger guys don't dare complain or go against the grain.

There were still some personnel problems that had to be handled. Terrell Buckley, for example, was going through a transformation crisis. Because he had been a star in the league and had been a starter elsewhere for nearly ten years, he felt he should still be a starter. However, he had bounced from Green Bay to Miami to Denver before coming here, and the fact that he kept changing teams led people to believe there was a problem. If a player is that good, they would think, he isn't bouncing from team to team or, perhaps he is that good, but he's selfish and difficult to deal with. And there were a couple of times when he was difficult during the year. In the second Indianapolis game, for example, Terrell was angry about alternating with Otis. He was held out for one series when he was supposed to be in, and he got mad. When they tried to send him in again, he refused. So with that Coach Belichick promptly suspended him for the Denver game the following week.

It never really became official, because Belichick didn't want to start something that wasn't going to be beneficial to the team. For that reason, it was never in the papers that Terrell was suspended for refusing to go back in a game. In addition, the game he missed was against the team he had just left. Then, to compound the problem, Ty Law had a problem with his foot later in the week, and the coach had to decide whether to retract the suspension, because now we might need Terrell. This was an example of a situation that could hurt the entire team if it wasn't handled correctly. Finally, during a team meeting, Terrell asked RAC if he could address his teammates. He stood up and admitted he was wrong, that his actions had been selfish, and he apologized for them. Then he said he had been so emotional and got caught up in the game, as we all do, and was thinking of himself rather than his teammates.

I was the first to applaud him for speaking up like that, and I told Coach Belichick that I knew Terrell somewhat and felt that basically he was a good guy. Because of the way he stood up and admitted his mistake, my respect for him went up immensely. For every one guy who stands up the way Terrell did, there are probably fifteen hundred others who would not have addressed it head on, just pouted about it until it got better. Terrell didn't play that week, but he packed up and traveled to the game with us in Denver. The next week at practice he was one of my Dirty Show guys, and you couldn't get him off the field. He was great for the rest of the year. Chalk one up for the coach.

Rookies sometimes present another whole set of problems. Coach Belichick begins talking to them at the rookie orientation meetings, again during the first day of training camp, and once more after the final cut and before the season starts. Belichick is a stickler for trying to keep guys from getting into trouble at crucial times of the year. At the end of June, just before the beginning of training camp in July, there's always an incident with a rookie somewhere around the league. If he can help it, the coach doesn't want one of our rookies to become a statistic. Then during the season you always have your problems—guys caught for DWI, drugs, domestic troubles, solicitation, nightclub incidents. Whenever a player from another team lands in trouble, Coach Belichick brings it up to our guys.

Our final draft pick in 2001 was an outside linebacker from Michigan State named T. J. Turner. He had great size at six-foot-three, 255 pounds, and what appeared to be a world of potential. He was still available on the seventh round because he had injured a shoulder early in his senior year and played in just four games. We knew he was bringing some baggage with him, but we also knew he had talent and figured we could groom the guy. Then, as soon as training camp began, some off-field problems started hampering his development. First his best friend, someone he grew up with, died. Shortly afterward one of his uncles passed away. Apparently there were a few more family incidents. He was getting hit with one thing after another, and you could tell it was draining him. Otherwise he was a likable guy who smiled when you talked to him and practiced hard.

Soon, however, as these things came down on him, he began walking around with a long face. Then the strain really began getting to him, and he started leaving the facility without notice, sometimes before meetings. A couple of times he was dropped off, then called his girlfriend to come back and pick him up. Gone again. We talked to him several times, explaining that he simply couldn't just leave, that he wasn't doing any good for us or for himself, and if it kept up we would have to let him go. The strikes just continued to add up against him until it reached a point where he was distracting the team and we were forced to release him. We were willing to work with him, but he couldn't overcome the off-field problems and make the Patriots his number-one priority. You want to help someone who has those kinds of problems, but he simply can't be part of the team because his focus will never be 100 percent Patriots. Guys with different agendas, no matter what the reason, will become a distraction sooner or later and have to be cut loose.

Our fifth-round pick, defensive back Hakim Akbar from the University of Washington, presented us with a different kind of problem. Akbar made the club, was playing on special teams, was the fourth or fifth safety, and was beginning to make his mark. In fact, at the beginning of the season he was starting to become one of our better special teams players. Then he got into a car accident driving on a mountain road in Rhode Island after the Buffalo game, just before we played the Rams. The impact of the crash threw him from the vehicle. He suffered a fractured vertebra and cracked ribs. It was a serious accident, and we were told there was no way he would return during the season. He just ran off the road at 1:30 A.M. and was charged with speeding, failing to stay in his lane, driving without a license, and maybe one or two other things.

Word spread quickly through the locker room the next day. Coach Belichick met with the coaches first, then told everyone Akbar was in the hospital, that there were still no reports on how he was doing, and that no one needed to call because he still couldn't talk. It wasn't an I-told-you-so situation, because Hakim had some potentially life-threatening injuries and was lucky to be alive. In fact, he was found some forty feet from his vehicle. Needless to say, he didn't play the rest of the year, but he didn't learn his lesson either. He came out to the Super Bowl with us, though he was still on the injured list. Yet he was with the rest of the team and had to abide by the rules. So what happened? He came down late and then on Friday night got caught leaving his room after curfew.

Sometimes I really don't understand guys like this. Hakim was a 210-pound strong safety, and now he looked as if he was down to about 170. He was just starting to come around, and he's caught leaving his room after curfew. The point is that every single man makes up the whole team, whether he's dressing or not. He was in a room with the players, and it was explained to him that he was on curfew too. I know guys who will leave for silly reasons, like they can't miss a party because it's the last one on earth. Don't forget, we're talking about New Orleans and Bourbon Street. At first Coach Belichick was going to send him home. Instead he made him stay there but wouldn't allow him to go to the game. Originally he was supposed to be on the sideline as part of the team.

Ironically, Akbar was one of the better Dirty Show guys, but in my opinion it boils down to relationships and the friends he keeps. Even though I would never try to leave the hotel before a Super Bowl game or to break a curfew, if I did want to go, none of my friends would have let me. They would look out for me and my best interests because they are real friends, not just guys who want to have a good time and encourage you to go with them. If someone asks you to sacrifice three nights of your life because it might change the rest of your life for the better, would you do it? Richard Seymour, our first draft choice, came out of a little South Carolina town. At the end of the year he returned home with a Super Bowl ring, and the whole town had a barbecue in his honor. When we won the Super Bowl in 1990, a running back named Lewis Tillman went home to Mississippi, and the town officials named a street after him. That's something that can change your life. Is it worth sacrificing that for one night out on the town?

In the old days there were party guys who were legends. Back then people often looked at them as heroic when they would return and still play well. Some guys can do that. Today, however, it's looked upon as more of a negative. A young player who isn't established has to be careful. From Coach Belichick's standpoint we're not just protecting the New England Patriots and the Kraft family but looking out for the health and well-being of the players as well. Having a player like that can also be a distraction to the others. Hakim Akbar, in spite of all his potential, was released right after the Super Bowl. He probably had fifteen strikes on him when it happened.

Super Bowl week is undoubtedly the easiest time for a player to get in trouble. There are so many distractions, as well as reporters from all the cities in the league, not to mention parties, people, and plenty of police officers. I remember a few years ago when Green Bay's well-respected safety, Eugene Robinson, was caught for solicitation during Super Bowl week. The cop is the one who earned the extra pelts. Obviously Robinson should have known better, because everyone today is looking to get ahead. It isn't like it was years ago. There's that legendary story from Super Bowl I in 1967, when Green Bay's veteran receiver, Max McGee, who wasn't expecting to play, broke curfew and partied all night. Called on the next day when the starter was injured, McGee became the star of the game, catching seven passes for more than a hundred yards and two touchdowns.

It just doesn't work that way anymore. Back in those days, if fans saw McGee needed help, they would have given it to him, brought him back to the hotel, and then kept the incident to themselves. Today people carry camcorders and cell phones, and any player breaking curfew and stepping out of line won't be a secret for long; it will be national news. For some players it still doesn't matter. Their attitude and mentality make them think they're supposed to be out there, doing these things. Then, when they're caught, they say that people are picking on them. There are guys, however, who don't have anyone looking out for them, unless it's "Slick Rick" or some other kind of alleged friend.

What could possibly be more important than the team, than making a mark for your team and earning your paycheck? I thank the Lord I didn't get in some of those situations. When you hear about a guy like Lawrence Phillips, who has blown one chance after another and has totally squandered his talents, that makes me count my blessings. On top of everything else, the last thing your team needs is a distraction. Let it happen during Super Bowl week and it just becomes worse.

As I said before, we became a stronger team as the season wore on. I already mentioned how the situation with the ex-Jets was resolved. One of the guys who was bothered the most by it was Lawyer Milloy. I talked with him many times about that, about our defense and his role. Lawyer is a very headstrong man with his own opinions, but you can't give in to him. Part of the reason I love a Lawyer Milloy is his intense pride. He's a throwback kind of guy who doesn't just want to win. He wants to dominate teams. When we beat the Colts the second time but still gave them four hundred yards of offense, Lawyer was upset. He felt we were sitting back too much. He didn't realize that sometimes we were better off being very aggressive on defense and other days better off playing possum. Both situations ended up working out for us, but I don't know if Lawyer finally understood or not. He likes to play it one way and is such an integral part of the team that we just have to keep talking to him and working with him. He might grate on us a little bit, but he doesn't become a distraction.

I can take you back to my days with the Giants and Lawrence Taylor. If anyone could be a distraction to a team, it was LT. He was not only our best player but a guy whose name appeared in the papers more than anyone else—and not always for his playing abilities. The recurring off-the-field incidents could have really torn the team apart had it not been for a special quality that Lawrence had. It was something that if had I not seen for myself, with my own eyes, I never would have understood. What I learned, as did everyone else including Bill Parcells, was that under adversity Lawrence Taylor was like a stampede of rhinoceroses. Sometimes he would have so much stress hovering over him that we began to think he might need a week off. Then he would go out on the field and have one of his best days.

It reached a point where we would joke about it: hey, did you read about LT in the paper today? That meant we were going to win that week. A lot of the stuff he did was minor, but he never looked at it as if they were picking on him. He would joke about it, then tell us he had a job to do, that he had to go out and perform. The last thing he ever wanted to do was let the rest of his teammates down. Oh, how he performed. Don't ask me how he dealt with situations when he turned back to Clark Kent. I just know how he was on the football field. No more Clark Kent. He was always the superhero, the guy with the big *S* on his jersey.

I always thought Lawrence was blessed. He could have become like Darryl Strawberry, whose chronic drug problems have been well publicized. I know Lawrence isn't a goody-goody, but he never had a drug problem per se. His last few years in the league he stopped drinking completely. He was simply an amazing athlete. One year on the team flight to Arizona to play the Cardinals, we got to talking mess about bowling. As soon as we landed in Phoenix, we put our luggage on the team bus and jumped in a cab to find the nearest bowling alley. When I bowl, I can fit only the tips of my fingers in the holes. LT cuffed the ball on his forearm like it was a softball, went out, and bowled a 200-plus game and beat me.

Terry Kinard, our safety, knew LT like the back of his hand and used to say he's the one guy he wouldn't bet against with anything. He plays a decent golf game wearing sandals. Someone once bet him he couldn't hit a golf ball out of Giants Stadium with a pitching wedge. He did it. So nothing he ever accomplished shocked me. In practice he would do things that were incredible, and despite everything, he would never distract his teammates. That was because we all knew that no matter what the circumstance, he was going to go out and perform, and if things off the field were not going well, he'd perform even better. Lawrence has always said he was going to live his life as he chose. A superstar like Michael Jordan has always been a little more discreet, more disciplined, because he wanted to savor his image. Lawrence was simply going to be Lawrence.

I think the key to Bill Belichick's dealing with potential problems and distractions—and we saw it all this year from the death of Coach Rehbein to Akbar's car accident—was the way he would coordinate the flow of information between players and the media. Whenever there was a problem, he would address it before the team and tell them exactly what his comments to the press would be. He would then suggest what he would like the guys to say, just so everyone was on the same wavelength. He was not ordering them or putting words in their mouth, but there are just too many times when teams are having problems and players don't really have an idea what is happening. When they're asked a question by the media, they simply don't know how to answer it. Some guys have that tendency to put their foot in their mouth. A player saying the wrong things to the media can cause problems with his teammates or at least make them look at him differently. That kind of situation can also be a distraction and can interfere with the strong-mindedness, concentration, and focus leading to the common goal of winning on Sunday.

What Coach Belichick does is provide direction. As I said, you can't put words in players' mouths, can't *make* them say anything. But if a coach can guide players on how to delicately answer certain questions, then he can eliminate the potential headaches caused by guys who don't know what to say. It always seems the least experienced players, those who don't know quite what to say, are the ones being asked the questions. The media should approach the head coach or the people directly involved, but they always seem to start with those players who aren't clued in. Everyone has to remember that we're talking about a team sport. While you're playing professional football, you have to take your teammates into consideration. If you act or do something out of selfishness, it can affect the entire organization. That's why when you hear all the players sounding like Coach Belichick, it goes back to everyone being an extension. That philosophy applies to every segment of the game.

For example, what if Tom Brady or Adam Vinatieri took a "lesson" from Hakim Akbar and decided to leave the hotel after curfew? We didn't have a backup field goal kicker. If something like that happened with one of those guys two days before the Super Bowl, then we would all be in big trouble. You want guys who are smart enough to view things in a team way. They have to say to themselves, It's not just me who will be affected by this—it will affect all of my teammates. I remember guys asking me during my playing days, "Pepper, don't you ever get sick?" They didn't know that I would tell myself during the season that I couldn't get sick. I didn't care what kind of weather was out there; I just couldn't get sick. I looked at myself as the leader of the defense. I could be banged up and feel as if my whole body was being ripped apart, but there was no way I wouldn't go out for practice. My mindset was that there couldn't be a practice without me. It was my defense. I never even wanted to come out for a single play.

Coach Belichick doesn't take anything away from his players. He has a concept and a philosophy about how a team is supposed to be. Everyone has to be on the same page. If all the defensive guys buy into his philosophy, the defense will jell. The same goes for the offensive side. That's one reason the Rams are so good. They have been called the "greatest show on turf" for so long that they all believe it and feel they have to prove it every week. Good teams are fueled by that kind of confidence and that kind of chemistry. Distractions can tear down quickly what took a long time to build. That's why a good coach has to be able to spot trouble quickly and not allow it to get out of hand. The Patriots had their share of problems and distractions in 2001. We had players who just didn't quite fit. Players expected to help us win were either unavailable or injured. Yet under the leadership of Bill Belichick and with help from a very close-knit coaching staff, we were able to take the team in a singular direction for the entire year while bringing the players closer together as the season progressed. From everything I've experienced and learned, that's the right way to run a football team—in fact the only way to run it.

9

The Final Four Games
A Division Title Up for Grabs

Whenever a team has a shot at making the playoffs, the final quarter of the season looms large. Even if you are leading your division and have a lock on a division title or playoff spot, you don't want to let down for the simple reason that you want to peak by the time the playoffs begin. I mentioned earlier what happened with the 1990 Giants. We won our first ten games, then split our last six. While 13–3 is certainly an outstanding record, we didn't go into the playoffs on a real high and had to battle to get the momentum back. Fortunately, that team was loaded with character and came all the way back to win the Super Bowl. The 2001 Patriots were beginning to show the same kind of character but were in a totally different position at 7–5. We simply had to continue to win. There were no ifs, ands, or buts about it. Just a single loss and our chances of making the playoffs could be over.

The entire team knew our situation was tenuous. We also knew that with two straight wins the momentum was beginning to build, and no one wanted to see it reversed. You want to keep that arrow pointing up. Our comeback victory over the Jets was the perfect catalyst to propel us into the final four games. Each of our remaining games, however, would be important for one definite reason—getting into the postseason—and then for a variety of individual reasons. The Cleveland Browns, our next opponent, were coming in with a 6–5 record. Not only did they still have a shot at making the playoffs, but they were trying to finish above .500 for the first time as an expansion team after the original Browns under owner Art Modell moved to Baltimore and became the Ravens. In addition, they had beaten us the year before, 19–11, in a game we all felt we should have won. So there was a little payback in the offing.

This was the week in which Coach Belichick used reverse psychology and took down a lot of the positive pictures in the hallways and replaced them with photos of the previous year's disappointing loss to the Browns. That was the theme when the players came in on Wednesday morning, just a very graphic reminder not to lose focus as well as forcing the players to remember how it felt losing to Cleveland, a team we were supposed to beat but apparently had taken for granted. There might also have been a little of the revenge factor for Belichick since he had never beaten his former team as a head coach.

In a lot of ways Cleveland had been a training ground for him, the experiences he had there as a head coach all proving valuable once he came to the Patriots. Now, however, the Browns represented just another team standing in the way of our accomplishing our goal. We had a long, hard week of practice, the coaches staying late into the night planning the game to the smallest detail. We worked extra hard with our punt return team, with both the offense and defense in the red zones, and put in the equivalent of a period or two each day on these things. The purpose was not to let up, to create a sense of urgency, one that has to come from the general, the leader of the team. So it's the head coach who had to pass that sense of urgency down to the troops. That's one reason the negative pictures went up. He felt the team had taken the Browns too lightly the year before, and he didn't want that happening again.

Cleveland had started the season very well, exceeding the expectations of many so-called experts. They were doing it defensively, leading the league at one point in creating turnovers. We were also aware that certain defenses gave our offense a hard time, so we knew, quite simply, that our defense was going to have to play better than their defense. Whatever they did to our offense, we felt we had to do twice to theirs. It might mean creating a turnover or playing extra tough if they got the lead. No matter what happened, we absolutely couldn't go into the tank. That, however, wasn't one of my worries. We had toughened considerably since the beginning of the year and now felt we were prepared to handle anything that might occur on the field.

This was what I call a back-and-forth game that turned into a very good win for us. That's because winning the game required contributions from every part of our team. The game got off on a real positive note for us when Adam booted a fifty-four-yard field goal with just over 9:30 left in the first quarter. That's a distance beyond his normal range, and I was told later it was the second longest of his career and the longest field goal ever by a Patriot at Foxboro Stadium. It remained a 3–0 game until there was just under a minute and a half left in the period. Then their kicker, Phil Dawson, tied it with a twenty-seven-yarder. OK, it's an even game with time running down in the first. We can live with that. Then, just seconds later, there was one of those plays that can really take the wind out of a team.

We took the kickoff, and Tom tried to get us moving. He threw a pass toward midfield, and it was picked off by Corey Fuller, who returned it forty-nine yards to the end zone for a score. The kick made it 10–3, and the Browns had scored ten points in less than twenty seconds. As I said, the Patriots had reached a maturity level where there was no longer panic and certainly no quitting. After the ensuing kickoff Tom Brady also showed his grit by shaking off the interception and leading the team on a scoring drive that began on our own thirty-four. It was an old-fashioned, ball control drive that took more than six minutes and featured Antowain Smith converting on a fourth-and-one from the Browns' three-yard line. The first down saved the drive, and seconds later Antowain took it in from the one. Adam's kick tied the score at 10.

It stayed that way until just about three and a half minutes before halftime. Then came a play that really showed once again what kind of team we were becoming. Remember I said that one of the things we worked extra hard at in practice was our punt returns. Boy, did it ever pay off. It started when Roman Phifer sacked their quarterback, Tim Couch, on a third down play to force a punt. Troy Brown drifted back to field the punt at his own fifteen, started upfield, got two great blocks from Lawyer Milloy and Dwayne Rudd, then broke loose. Browns punter Chris Gardocki came over to try to make the tackle and was literally run over by a freight train also known as Richard Seymour. The big rookie had raced downfield to make a crunching block. That was all Troy needed to complete a clutch eighty-five-yard return to give us the go-ahead score.

That's the kind of play that really lifts an entire team, especially the devastating block Seymour laid on Gardocki. It showed us that all the hard work over so many months was really beginning to pay off. The sixty thousand cheering fans didn't really know about Wednesday's practice and how we had worked so hard on our punt return game, putting in all that extra time. Our jubilation was more than just being happy about Troy running back a punt for a score. It was all about the hard work paying dividends. In addition to that, Troy Brown has always been an inspiring player. He was one of those undrafted guys who took years to become a starter at wide receiver. The veterans on the team knew all about his struggles and the way he worked to get to where he is today. There aren't too many receivers in the league good enough to catch more than a hundred passes and still run back punts and kickoffs.

But Troy would never let anyone take him off the return team, and Coach Belichick wouldn't want to do that. He has always known the edge good special teams can give you. In fact Belichick was like that when he was an assistant with the Giants. RAC was on staff with him there as the special teams coach, and Belichick was the only other assistant coach who stayed late in the meeting room with him watching special teams tapes over and over again. His dedication to making our special teams *special* is the reason so many players are willing to do double duty. Tebucky Jones, for example, is our starting free safety and probably the best guy to have in the middle of the field because he covers so much ground. Yet he's also one of our best gunners on the punting team. We know we lose a little bit when we use him as a gunner because he has to burn so much energy running full speed for sixty yards with two guys trying to block him while he tries to elude them and tackle the punt returner, perhaps the most elusive guy on the team. When Tebucky is used as a gunner, we sometimes have to rest him for a play or two, with Matt Stevens relieving him. Tebucky has more range, but Stevens is a tremendous hitter and a smart player who can quickly get guys lined up if they miss the call. So he, too, brings a dimension to the defense and does a great job when Tebucky needs a rest. And he's another reason that the Patriots were really on their way to becoming a complete team.

Of course, we had just a 17–10 lead, so this game wasn't over yet. It took still another big play defensively before the half for us to keep the lead. The Browns appeared to be driving for the tying touchdown when Terrell Buckley intercepted a pass by Couch at our five-yard line. It was his third pick of the year, and all of them came in key situations.

Terrell ran the ball back to the nineteen. Then Brady came on and led a sixty-one-yard drive that stalled at the Cleveland twenty with just three seconds left. From there Adam booted a thirty-eight-yard field goal, which gave us a 20–10 halftime lead. Then we suffered a bit of a letdown. They got a field goal in the third and another at the beginning of the fourth period to close the lead to 20–16 and give them the momentum at the same time. With just under ten minutes left in the game, however, our defense and special teams once again rose to the occasion. Roman Phifer started it by pressuring Browns quarterback Couch and grabbing him by the ankles just as he released a pass. As Quincy Morgan received it, he was clobbered by Otis Smith and juggled the ball. Anthony Pleasant rushed over and grabbed it for his first career interception. He took two steps, then was hit and fumbled, but Otis got to the ball first and recovered for us.

Despite the big turnover, our offense couldn't get a drive going, and we sent Adam out to try a fifty-three-yard field goal. Could he boot another long one? This time we wouldn't find out. Coach Belichick ran a trick play, one we had practiced numerous times, waiting for the right opportunity. The snap came directly to Adam, and he punted the ball instead of placekicking for the field goal. The ball was headed for the Browns' end zone, where it would have been a touchback and brought out to the twenty. But at the last second Jermaine Wiggins came flashing downfield, dove into the air, and slapped the ball back before it carried into the end zone. Our long snapper, Lonie Paxton, downed it at the two, and we had the Browns back where we wanted them, deep in their own territory. It was a great effort by special teams. Now the defense came on, held them to a three-and-out, and when Troy returned the Cleveland punt, we had the ball at their thirty-six with just over six minutes left. Now we were in a great position to put the game on ice.

Six plays and three-plus minutes later, Antowain finally rambled into the end zone from the five. Adam's kick made it 27–16, with just 2:43 left, and that's the way it ended, our third straight win, fifth in six games, and an 8–5 record. This was a big game for so many guys. Troy went over the thousand-yard receiving mark for the season, while Antowain gained seventy-six yards. More important, he was helping us sustain drives and control the clock. That was one of the main purposes of bringing him over here. We needed a big back to do that for us. Tom Brady didn't throw a touchdown pass and was picked off twice, but he did hit nineteen of twenty-eight passes and once again took what a good Cleveland defense gave him. And, of course, we got four more turnovers. I was told after the game that we were now 7–1 when we caused more turnovers than our opponents. The only time we had lost was the first game against Cincinnati.

I was really tickled for Anthony Pleasant when he got that interception. He's one of our old horses, and when he made that pick he had a look on his face as if it was his first year in the league. AP is a guy everyone respects. He's very religious and doesn't like rap and loud music, but to see him happy and all his teammates happy for him and congratulating him gave me a great feeling.

A couple of other quick notes. Bryan Cox didn't play against Cleveland. After getting in for those two plays against the Jets, he was deactivated again because he simply wasn't ready. He was still limping around somewhat, and we wanted to make sure he could give us some time later in the season, especially if we got into the playoffs. The other thing was the return of Terry Glenn once again. Terry caught four passes for sixty-seven yards in his first appearance in eight weeks and just his second of the season. Whenever he's in there he stretches the defense because he can run deep patterns, making it more difficult for the defense to double-team Troy. Unfortunately, his contributions after this game would be minimal. By this time, however, we knew we could win with or without him, so it was no longer a big story if he played or didn't play.

After the game Coach Belichick did his usual great job of not allowing the team to become too happy. We were becoming harder to please now and knew that there was still plenty of work to be done. The victory over the Jets had been a real release, and we were extremely happy because we had finally beaten them. After Cleveland the guys were happy for a variety of reasons. We had again beaten a team with a winning record, which is always a plus. Then there was the matter of what they had done to us the year before. We had kept our focus, overcome some mistakes, made big plays, and won. There wasn't time, however, to rest on any laurels. At this point the one word that might describe the team was simply *next*!

Next was Buffalo again, and it's never easy beating them at Ralph Wilson Stadium in December, when the weather can be a huge factor. Though we had defeated them earlier in the season, it was the old thing about records meaning nothing in a divisional game. The teams simply know each other too well. Even with three straight victories we can't afford to be happy. Because of the ditch we dug for ourselves early in the season, coupled with five losses, everyone understood the importance of each and every game. Once again Coach

Belichick wanted the guys to be very careful when talking to the press. He pointed out that before our game with the Jets their star cornerback, Aaron Glenn, was already talking about them positioning themselves for the play-offs and trying to get home field advantage. Here's a guy with only one play-off appearance acting as if he's been there numerous times. A veteran like Aaron Glenn should know better, because statements like that don't make it easy for coaches. Belichick doesn't want any of his players talking about home field advantage with four of five games left and a lot to be decided. That kind of talk goes no further than the locker room.

A year earlier we played the Bills up there in a heavy snow and freezing temperatures. Adam won it with a field goal in overtime. Even if there was no snow, the Bills played the kind of hard-fought game we had come to expect from them. So while we knew it would be a rough game, and more than likely a close one, we also knew that the last thing we wanted now was to stumble. We had finally worked ourselves into a position where we could not only compete for the playoffs but pretty much control our own destiny. We knew if we won the rest of our games we would definitely be in the playoffs, though we couldn't tell where we would be positioned. If we lost, however, we weren't automatically in. That was just one reason not to lose. In general no team really wants to lose games late in the season, because that's when a ball club is trying to fully jell, establish a pre-playoff identity, solidify the character of the team, and know all the guys who can be called on to make big plays. At the same time you have guys who are playing through injuries, while others are concentrating on getting healthy and coming back. The bottom line is that the excuses from earlier in the year are no longer viable.

Buffalo was coming into the game with an abysmal 2–10 record. Throw it out. There wasn't a single person in the Patriots family who thought the game would be a cakewalk. In fact Buffalo was playing well defensively and had a couple of young cornerbacks who liked to gamble, so they weren't a predictable team, and that made them dangerous. Young guys aren't always smart enough to be fooled. This was certainly going to be another test. The Buffalo weather was cold on game day, but the field was clear and there was no snow. As it turned out, the game was a rugged defensive battle. Unlike the Cleveland game, where the extra practice in certain areas paid off, it didn't this time. In spite of emphasizing our red zone offense during the week, whenever we got into that situation we just couldn't score.

We couldn't trick them and couldn't bully them. It goes without saying that we never go into a game thinking our opponent is going to lie down and allow us to score a lot of points. You just have to take what they give you to win the ball game. What they gave us were field goals. What we gave them were field goals. Adam got the first two. Then their kicker, Shayne Graham, kicked the next three. With just 2:45 left in the fourth quarter, Adam booted a clutch twenty-five-yard field goal to tie the score at 9–9. Adam had made good on all three of his tries. Fortunately for us, Graham missed a forty-three-yarder early, or they might have won it in regulation. Now, for the second straight year, we had to go into sudden-death overtime. That's where the fun really started.

After winning the overtime coin toss and electing to receive, the Bills began moving the ball and appeared to be building a scoring drive, but Otis Smith broke up a third-and-two pass intended for Eric Moulds, forcing them to punt. The kick went into the end zone, and we had to start from our own twenty. Now we began to move. Brady hit J. R. Redmond for thirteen yards, then completed an eight-yard toss to Troy. Antowain carried twice, but just for five yards, though he gave us another first down. Now Tom dropped back again looking for David Patten, who was running down the right sideline. The pass went for about thirteen yards, but as soon as he caught it, Patten was blasted by Keion Carpenter. He fell to the turf, unconscious, with just his head out of bounds, the rest of his body still on the field of play. The ball popped loose and was lying alongside Patten's legs. Buffalo's Nate Clements picked it up and started to run with it, but the refs whistled it dead.

Now here comes controversy. The Bills are all jumping around as if they recovered a fumble. Patten is already coming to on the sideline and wondering what happened. One ref signaled an incomplete pass. Another said it was completed, but Patten caught it out of bounds. In overtime the officials are the only ones who can call for a play to be reviewed, and that's what they did. After watching the play again, they evoked a little-known rule but one that's right in the book. The ref said that Patten had caught the ball, a legal catch. Then he fumbled. As he was falling out of bounds, the ball was still loose on the field, but it then came in contact with Patten's legs just as he hit his head out of bounds and was knocked out. The rule states that if a fumbled ball touches anything that is out of bounds it, too, is out of bounds. Since Patten's head was out of bounds, that made his entire body out of bounds, and since the ball touched his legs before Nate Clements grabbed it, the ball was out of bounds and thus still in the possession of the receiver.

Talk about a break. The Bills didn't believe it, but that was the rule and the ruling. The refs were right. Our offense came back on the field, and on the very next play Antowain took off. He rambled thirty-eight yards all the way to the Buffalo three. Now we were knocking on the door. Brady took a two-yard loss to position the ball in the middle of the field, and Adam came on to kick his fourth field goal of the day, the game winner. A 12–9 overtime win and a 9–5 record. We were finding ways to win, even getting some breaks, and it's especially good to win a divisional game in Buffalo. There were, however, some lingering concerns. There always are.

Whenever you don't score a touchdown you've got to wonder why. I know Charlie Weis wasn't tickled pink with all our points coming on four field goals, but a win is a win. The upside is that it toughened us. Two overtime games now, and we won both of them. By this time the pattern was undeniable; the close games we were losing in 2000 we were winning now, and you could sense more and more confidence building for the playoffs. To credit the offense, they held the ball and put together a drive when we needed it most, in overtime. At the end they put Adam in a situation where he will come through.

That's pro football. You will have some games when you're clicking on all cylinders and some when you stumble. The games when you're going to have that dog bite are usually the divisional games. If you have a game where it comes down to a bunch of field goals, it's usually with a divisional rival. We beat the Jets by a 17–16 score. You expect that. These are all reasons why our 30–10 loss to Miami early in the season was so disheartening. We're supposed to play better against our divisional rivals. In hindsight the players were talking about how rough it always was against Buffalo and were giving the Bills a great deal of credit. We knew we had dodged a bullet, and we respected them, despite their record. No one walked away saying we had played poorly against a team with just two wins. Both teams fought hard. We were maturing and winning, while they were trying to be a late-season spoiler, and that made them even more dangerous.

Next was a big one, the Dolphins again, only this time they would be coming to Foxboro. They were at 9–4 and had a half-game lead. We quickly picked up on the motivational theme for the week, the bad taste they left us with at the end of the 2000 season. I know that game has cropped up a number of times, but that only shows how long it takes to get over a loss like that. Some of us never forget. Lawyer didn't, and he also remembered the things he had said to the team after that game, how it was leaving a bad taste in everyone's mouth, how we were losers, and how he didn't want to feel that way again. This entire season had been a second chance for a lot of us, and every game now had a different meaning. In the week before we played the Dolphins we were all well aware that there was now a possibility that we could win the division; we were playing for more than just a wild card playoff berth. I reminded everyone how they were laughing at us in the locker room the year before and Coach Belichick's main focus of motivation was to show the game tape of our 30–10 loss to them early in the season.

He also reminded everyone what Dolphins running back Lamar Smith had said after the first game. Smith, if you recall, ran for 144 yards on twenty-nine carries, and when asked if he was tired after the game, said, "There's a difference if you're hit hard." He was implying that we weren't physical, and no matter what he said after that the media stuck with that quote. RAC started our Wednesday meeting with the defense reading that quote to the team once again. As soon as he read it, Tebucky Jones stood up and said, "Well, he's gonna know he's been hit this time." That's when I knew we would be ready.

If you look at the box score, it probably seems like a strange game. We scored twenty points in the second quarter and won it by a 20–13 score. It wasn't that close, because their only touchdown came with just under a minute and a half left in the game. Incidentally, that was the first touchdown our defense had given up in fourteen quarters. But I think the game was important for reasons other than the final score. For one thing, we shut down their running game. Lamar Smith had little to say after our defense held him to just thirty-three rushing yards all afternoon.

On our side of the ball Antowain Smith exploded for his best game as a Patriot, rushing for 156 yards on twenty-six carries. Antowain also showed his toughness. He had a bruised leg from the Buffalo game and was doubtful all week, didn't practice much. During the game he returned to the locker room twice to have his leg retaped. Then he put a punctuation mark on his day by popping one for forty-four yards late in the game when we were running out the clock. He also went over the thousand-yard mark for the season and played such an inspired game that he brought the rest of the offense with him.

Defensively, we contained their quarterback, Jay Fiedler, keeping him from scrambling, which is a key to holding them down. Not surprisingly, Tebucky Jones also kept his promise big time. He was banging people all afternoon. He stopped an early Miami drive by slamming into Lamar Smith near the goal line, causing a fumble that we recovered. It was the kind of play that can break a team's back. Later he caused a second fumble, stopping another potential drive with a big hit, and Otis Smith followed suit by clobbering receiver Jed Weaver after a reception, causing yet another fumble. Our defense was on fire all afternoon.

Offensively we scored on a Smith run, a pass from Brady to Patrick Pass, and on a pair of Vinatieri field goals. Even though we didn't get any points in the second half, we still controlled the game with Antowain's running and held them to just a pair of field goals before their last-minute touchdown. Smith's running was the key, because it wore down their defense. Their cornerbacks normally do a great job of harassing wide receivers, jamming them, tugging at shirts, talking a little trash. They're not an easy defense and disguise their coverages well. This was another of those games, much like our game with the Jets a few weeks earlier, where we had something to prove. I don't want to gloat by saying it made up for the other game, but it did make up for the other game, for what they did to us earlier in the year in Miami in the heat. It was pretty apparent that we had grown as a team from that rather distasteful experience.

In the preseason Miami had been picked to win the division. Now we're ahead of them at 10–5. Finally our guys were giving it back to the media a bit, to all those guys who said we would be lucky to finish at .500. The guys had a saying whenever one of the reporters came around. They would shout, "DON'T TALK TO ME!" We really started killing them with that, our way of telling them how wrong they had been about us. The funny part was I don't think we were really getting credit yet for being a good team. Sure, a lot of people were conceding that we would be in the playoffs, but not too many people thought about us getting deep into the playoffs. Probably more of a one-round-and-out thing.

Following the Miami game we had a bye week. That's why there was the half-game difference between us and the Dolphins and Jets. We now had to wait two weeks before playing the makeup game with Carolina, the one postponed after September 11th. Our sentiments about missing a week were kind of divided. Some felt the bye week might help, giving players time to let the bumps and bruises heal. Others felt it was the wrong time to have a bye, giving us too much time to think about Carolina. We also knew now that we had a good chance to win the division. Up to this point every game we won was the biggest of our lives. We couldn't look at it any other way. Once we won a game, however, we wiped it off the slate. The smiles and satisfactions were short-lived. Now we had to look at it as if we were facing our biggest task, regrouping after a week off and having to play a team with just one victory all year. It takes a lot of focus and concentration not to get caught napping.

With a bye week coming up, the players were all shocked on Wednesday when we practiced in full pads. None of them could believe it, and they were all running around asking each other why the hell we had to do this. When they stopped and thought about it, thought about the way we had worked all year, I don't think it was such a surprise. Coach Belichick took the extra week to drill us all over again on the fundamentals. He had a couple of guys who he thought needed work doing tackling drills, for instance. The coaches thought guys like Matt Stevens and Antwan Harris needed work, so they got it. We did a lot of the smaller things in football, the little basics that people neglect and slowly get away from as the season progresses. We continued to emphasize those things.

Before the Miami game, Damon Huard, our third quarterback, did the majority of the scout team work. When we were preparing for the Carolina game, Drew began playing the part of Panthers quarterback Chris Weinke. The Dirty Show couldn't have asked for a better quarterback. He threw passes we knew the opposition couldn't throw, because his arm was so much stronger than Weinke's, yet he was able to emulate Weinke's style and moves, giving the defense the looks it needed. Ever since Coach Belichick named Brady the starter, Drew continued to work hard, get himself back in top physical condition, and make sure he was ready if we needed him. Both guys did a great job. Before the Miami game Damon gave us a great look at what Jay Fiedler would be like. Because he had come from Miami the year before and knew Fiedler, he had his motion and mannerisms all down pat.

I remember Drew playing with the scout team one day, and he began scrambling, something he normally didn't do. This time, however, he ran it in for a touchdown and actually spiked the ball. Guys playing on the scout team aren't supposed to shove it in someone's face like that, and if it were anyone else, the defense would have been really pissed off. Only now they loved seeing that kind of emotion and fight from Drew, and they knew, if we needed him, he would be ready. Not playing eats everybody alive. The bad thing about being the backup quarterback is that you know you won't play unless the top guy is injured. That's one position where players don't alternate, and no one is going to hope a teammate is injured. So it's a tough job, wanting to play, having it eat at you, but knowing you have to work hard to stay ready. Almost every other player has some kind of role on the field during a game, except the backup quarterback.

Drew was aware that there was a chance he wouldn't take another snap in a game for the rest of the season. Yet every backup knows he might have to come into a game without having taken many reps in practice and still perform at a high level and not lose a ball game for his team. Not many backups get as many reps in practice as the starter. There simply isn't enough time. During the season the reps have to go to the guy who is going to be in there. So much of their work, for any backup, is done in the classroom. Even a Terrell Buckley, our third cornerback, is often required to stay focused when he's on the sideline. At any second he might be called on to cover one of the opponent's go-to receivers. For backups it becomes more and more of a mental game. Drew had never played that role at all during his career, yet there wasn't a player on the team who didn't think Drew would come through if we needed him. We all felt we had the best damned backup quarterback in the entire league.

Then, on our bye weekend, the Jets lost their sixth game of the year. We knew now that all we had to do was beat Carolina to win the division. Miami could still finish with an identical record, but we would take the title by virtue of a better divisional mark. So now there was really something to gain. We win the division and somehow get a second seed in the playoffs, then we were guaranteed a bye in the first round and at least one playoff game at home. So there was plenty at stake, and we continued to work hard. During the bye week we had worked on problem plays, things that had been beating us occasionally. The week before the game we went back into pads and put in the Carolina plays so the show team could do its job.

The final score of this one reads blowout, 38–6, but it wasn't as easy a game as the score indicated. For one thing, it was just 10–3 at the half, meaning they were very much in it at that point. In the second half, we started getting turnovers and quick touchdowns. Otis returned an interception seventy-six yards for a touchdown, while Troy ran back another punt, this one for sixty-eight yards and a score. Antowain also had a thirty-two-yard touchdown run, and Troy broke the club record for pass receptions with 101. Not only that. The victory gave us an 11–5 record, a complete reversal of the 5–11 mark of the season before. We had also won six straight games after our loss to the Rams and had won the AFC Eastern Division championship.

Yet there were some things that bothered the defensive coaches. Carolina's Richard Huntley, not exactly a household name, ran for 168 yards on twenty-two carries, an average of 7.6 yards a pop. We were putting too much emphasis on stopping their passing game and didn't respect their runners. Despite the fact that we had gone back to basics in practice, we missed a lot of tackles and made Richard Huntley look like Jim Brown. He did a lot of his damage early, when the game was still close. So even with the big victory and the division title, we, as defensive coaches, knew there was work to be done.

Despite having won the division, we still didn't know who our first playoff opponent would be. The Jets were playing a late game with the Raiders. If Oakland won, they would be the number-two seed behind Pittsburgh, and we would have to play a wild card game. So we didn't have a lot of time to sit back and celebrate. These were small victories, but the war was far from over. We were already on the flight home from Charlotte when we got word that the Jets had defeated the Raiders. The news spread throughout the plane like a hot knife going through butter. While they were no doubt elated, there was only a little cheer from the players. I remember Charlie Weis clapping while Coach Belichick still showed little visible emotion. If you see a smile from him, you better have your camera ready. Still, he had to be happy inside, knowing our first playoff game would be played in Foxboro.

It was funny, because when we had beaten Miami the week before we couldn't be sure if we would have another home game. With our new stadium, Gillette Stadium, scheduled to open in the fall of 2002, that could have been our last game at Foxboro Stadium. Because of that possibility, Coach

Belichick had all the players walk around the perimeter of the field, shaking hands with the fans. I remember Tedy Bruschi and Mike Vrabel coming in and kidding that they never wanted to do that again because it tired them out more than the game had.

So the regular season was behind us. In some ways it was hard to fathom, finishing at 11–5 with a six-game winning streak, especially after starting with two consecutive losses and losing our starting quarterback at the same time. How many times in the early going did we hear and read about the *same old Patriots*. I think we had proven an awful lot to many people, but, as I've said before, if you make the playoffs and lose, you go home on a very sour note. It means your last game was a defeat and you have the entire off season to think about it. My own playoff experience with the Giants taught me that there was absolutely no substitute for winning it all. That's what every NFL player should aim for. Win it all; nothing less matters.

The good thing coming down the stretch the way we did was that many of our guys were getting healthier. Cox came back in the Miami game, still laboring a bit and being spotted in certain situations. I think he was in for maybe six to eight plays. Bruschi was dinged up a bit, but Ted Johnson was back and played well at outside linebacker in a part-time role against Carolina, while Cox saw more action than the week before. There are always more war wounds at the end of the season. Troy Brown and David Patten were both dinged, but it wouldn't stop them. Willie McGinest was as strong as he had been in four years, and our top draft choice, Richard Seymour, was on a tear and dominating. He had been a true impact player. Drew was also healthy and itching to play. If we needed him, we knew he'd be ready.

So it was playoff time. That means you're in the suck-it-up mode—forget about the bumps and bruises and work your tails off. We were lucky in that none of our key players were out for the season. We all felt the team would be ready to give someone hell out there. Now we just had to convince the doubters, the same people who thought we would be lucky to play .500 ball. To some of them, even winning the division wasn't enough proof that things had changed. Fine with us. We had already been doing it all year, and now we were ready to give everyone some more grist for the mill.

10

The Snow Game

Division champs. It has a nice ring to it, but beyond that it represents unfinished business. Everyone, down to the last man, knew we still had a ton of work to do, but because we had won the division, we now had another bye week to await the results of the two AFC wild card games. Because we were off before the Carolina game, we now would have two bye weeks with just a single game sandwiched in between. Right away there were people saying we couldn't afford another off week, that we would lose our momentum. The playoff schedule, of course, was out of our control. We had to work with the hand we were dealt. Right now that hand didn't include the name of our next opponent. It all depended on who won the wild cards.

The AFC wild card weekend had the Raiders facing the Jets in Oakland and the defending champion Baltimore Ravens traveling to Miami to play the Dolphins. We were the number-two seed behind the Steelers, and neither of us knew which team we would be playing the following week. Depending on the outcome of those two games, we could have theoretically ended up playing any one of the four teams. If the Jets topped Oakland and Miami beat Baltimore, we would host the Dolphins. If both Miami and Oakland won, we would play Oakland. If the Jets defeated Oakland and Baltimore beat Miami, we would play the Ravens. The only way we would meet the Jets again would be for the AFC title. Because we knew both the Jets and Dolphins so well and hadn't played either Oakland or Baltimore, we began preparing for them during the bye week. Yet while it was more difficult to prepare for teams we hadn't played, we still had to think in terms of all four teams.

We spent the week pretty much going over crucial plays that had hurt us in the final weeks of the regular season. The Dirty Show ran some of Oakland's and Baltimore's favorite defensive plays to begin preparing our offense.

We also practiced working against their offense. And we watched a lot of tape of both teams. By this time the Advid held enough tape so that we could go back eight or nine games. I watched all the Raiders games just looking for plays where their great receivers, Tim Brown and Jerry Rice, had fumbled the ball. When I found one, I tried to find the reason they had fumbled so that our defense could create a similar situation. Other coaches wanted to see if any of our possible opponents liked running certain plays that we had been vulnerable to in the past. For example, if a deep post play had hurt us the past few weeks and the Raiders had that in their repertoire, then we were gonna run that in practice. Even though we had already played the Jets and Dolphins twice, we ran some of their plays as well. So we were covering all the bases and trying to stay sharp while waiting to see which team we'd be playing.

From a coaching standpoint, our offense preferred to play the Raiders over Baltimore because the Ravens' defense was a little stronger. On the other hand, it was better for our defense to play against the Ravens' offense, which was sputtering, while Oakland's offense was ranked among the top five in the league. Then, while we were waiting, we began hearing stories from the other camps. That's because pro football reporters from cities that don't have teams in the playoffs are sent flocking to the playoff teams' cities in the days leading up to the game. Seattle media, for example, reported from Oakland on the Raiders–Jets game. There were guys from Buffalo and New York City coming to the Patriots' locker room in search of a story. I remember reading about a defensive lineman from the Dolphins saying he wanted to play us again because he knew they could beat us. He was talking as if they had already beaten Baltimore, another victim of the media sharks. Apparently someone forgot to remind the guy that the Dolphins had been in the playoffs for several years without getting out of the first round.

The reporters were everywhere. With us they began bringing up Terry Glenn again, or asking where Andy Katzenmoyer had been. Katzenmoyer was an All-American linebacker out of Ohio State who had been a first-round pick back in 1999. After a pretty good rookie year, he was injured for much of the 2000 season and on injured reserve this past year. Yet there were reporters asking about him. Anything for a story. They were asking guys where they were when Mo Lewis hit Drew, things that had happened early in the year and were long forgotten. They were always looking for blood—anything to stir up something, like sharks going in for the kill. If one guy made a statement that might be controversial or inflammatory, they would all feed off it. The player who gave the story might have had five guys there when he said it, and the next day he'd have twenty-five of them there, all trying to see what they could make of the story and trying to get him to put his foot deeper into his mouth.

For us there wasn't much to be said. We didn't know who we would be playing and hadn't made the playoffs for a few years—not under Belichick's tenure as head coach. We were just happy to be there and glad to have at least one more game at Foxboro. The reporters probably heard the same political answer from everyone on the team: *Happy to be there and happy to have another game at Foxboro.*

With the press Belichick uses his experience. He addresses the team every morning and prepares guys for the questions. He's not really brainwashing the players. He's giving them help. Some guys will get in a situation and don't know how to deal with the reporters. So they panic. Some will take the grilling personally, become offended. So Coach tries to prepare them for certain questions, explaining how the wrong answers will just lead to another question. It's sometimes hard to get a real point across to the reporters because many of them really don't know football.

Reporters today can be attack dogs. A reporter who regularly covers the Jets might not like it that the Patriots are in the playoffs instead of his team. He may have been criticizing the Jets all year, and suddenly he's pissed at the Patriots for keeping the Jets from getting in. If he finds a guy he knows will crack under the pressure of relentless questioning, he won't let up. On our club, if somebody sees another player is not answering properly, he'll come over and lend a hand. I remember my first time in the playoffs my rookie year of 1986. Most of the reporters saved the negative questions for LT or Carson or Banks. Yet as soon as a reporter sensed I was dropping my guard, he'd ask something like "Aren't you guys tired of carrying the offense when they aren't moving the ball?"

Fortunately, I had been watching Carl Banks and paying attention to the way he handled the press. Carl was like a throwback. He knew all the reporters by name. A lot of the quarterbacks are the same way. Even if there was a reporter there for the first time, Carl would get his name. He was totally relaxed when he talked with them, acted like they were all his friends. When you take that approach, they can't load up on you even if they want to. In effect he's working them more than they're working him. I knew I could never get to that point. I'm bad with names, and I didn't have the patience. Carl had them in his pocket. If one reporter threw a haymaker question at him, all the others would turn and look at that guy, as if to say "Why did you want to go there?"

Then there is the preanswered question, such as "Don't you think when so-and-so fumbled the ball it was at a crucial time and didn't help the team?" They're looking for a yes or no so they can build on that and ask more questions. You never answer questions like that; just turn them around. For example, you can say, "When is a fumble not at a crucial time?" We tried to explain these things to guys who came in after 1997, when the Patriots were knocked off in the first round, and didn't know what to expect. The team hadn't made the playoffs since, so this kind of accelerated press coverage during the playoffs is something all the coaches and veterans talked to the younger guys about.

Needless to say, we had a great deal of interest in the Jets–Raiders game. Many of the players got together and went over to Otis Smith's house to watch the game. Not surprisingly, the coaches were working, but we had the TV on while we were viewing tapes of other games. By the way, it's a totally different experience watching a game on tape as opposed to live on television. There are no commentators, the angles are different, and we're watching formations and tendencies as opposed to simply enjoying the game as a game. As coaches we watch games analytically. We don't see the good play as much as the bonehead play that costs a team fifteen yards. Being a defensive coach most of his life, Belichick has always been aware of how damaging defensive penalties can be, and he can cite the high percentage of offensive scoring that occurs after a defensive penalty. So we look for bonehead plays from opposing defenses and work with our defense to avoid needless penalties.

We were doing that as the Raiders beat the Jets, 38–24. So now we knew we would host the Raiders in Foxboro for the divisional playoff the following week. That was a good ball game for us, one we knew would be competitive. They have two future Hall of Famers at wide receiver in Tim Brown and Jerry Rice, and their quarterback, Rich Gannon, was having one of his better years. Rice had a huge game against the Jets after they had done a good job on him the previous week, in the final game of the regular season. Now everyone was writing that the old man was back and, of course, we didn't stand a chance. According to reporters, the Jets had a better secondary than we did, and if they couldn't stop the Raiders, what could the underdog Patriots do?

That week, before the game, *ESPN The Magazine* came out, and guess who was on the cover? Tim Brown and Jerry Rice. That started a precedent that would continue throughout the playoffs. Before we played the Steelers, Kordell Stewart appeared on the cover of *Sports Illustrated*, and when we were getting ready to play the Rams, Kurt Warner showed up on the cover of *ESPN The Magazine*. Each week those pictures were put up in the defensive meeting room immediately, and we used them to challenge and motivate our defense.

I think the majority of our coaches felt all along that we were going to play the Raiders. In that final regular-season game the Raiders blew home-field advantage by losing to the Jets. After playing poorly in that game, I think they were forced to exert more energy than necessary in the wild card game. If they had taken more pains and had beaten the Jets the first time, then they would have been the second seed and we could have been traveling to Oakland. Who knows what would have happened then? So the scenario that had unfolded was a blessing in disguise for us. The Raiders attacked the Jets on all cylinders in the wild card game. Rice and Brown were running free and easy. Now, after traveling from New York back to Oakland for the wild card game, the Raiders had to return to the East Coast and Foxboro to play us. That kind of travel schedule can take something out of a team. It's a grind.

Knowing that perhaps we already had a small edge, everyone was now hoping for cold weather. Bryan Cox told one reporter that he wished it would be ten below with a blizzard the night they arrived in Foxboro and that it would carry right through to the game. We would be playing them on January 19th, so inclement winter weather was a definite probability. During that week temperatures were cold and we practiced at Boston College under a bubble that covers their stadium during the winter months. Ironically, our only exposure to the cold was when we walked through the parking lot at Boston College to and from practice. Yet we were the cold-weather team and hoping for snow. See how much of the game is mental?

Our practice routine remained basically the same. However, weather reports were already saying snowfall was likely by game time. So instead of practicing to defend the Raiders receivers' deep routes, we all agreed to practice more against what we thought would be their cold-weather offense—a lot of medium-range and sideline passes. In other words, they would use more of a controlled passing game instead of the wide open attack they had unveiled against the Jets. We still made our players aware that the Raiders had deep patterns available in their repertoire, but if the weather turned out the way we thought it would, we would benefit far more by working against their cold-weather offense.

What many people don't know is that a lot of coaches today script their plays. In other words, they have their first ten, fifteen, twenty, even twenty-five offensive plays mapped out. It doesn't matter what the situation or where they are on the field, they will still run these plays in the order they're scripted. Raiders coach Jon Gruden likes to script plays that are short and intermediate catch-and-run plays early in the game. So even in cold weather or with snow he can stay with these early scripted plays. In fact Gruden is one coach who won't vary from the opening script at all. Let me give you an example. Athletes like Jerry Rice and Tim Brown, as well as Troy Brown on our team, have the ability to make a play at any time. With Gruden, if the sixth play on the script is a draw play to running back Charlie Garner, he's probably hoping that it comes on a first or second down. Let's say, however, it's the third down of the second series; he's still going to run that draw, because it's on the script. Against the Colts, David Patten ran a reverse on the first play for a touchdown. That was already in Charlie Weis's script as the first play of the game no matter what. The only thing that would have changed it was if our offense had been backed up on the fifteen-yard line.

After the fifteen or twenty scripted plays, a team goes into the play-calling mode since by that time the offensive coordinator should have a strong grasp of the rhythm of the game. In the old days the quarterback called the plays, but now there is so much happening with different defensive schemes and adjustments that you can't ask a quarterback to call plays anymore. Some QBs will call plays in the two-minute drill, but that's about it. In fact quarterbacks now have small radio receivers in the helmets, but they have to be shut off ten seconds before the ball is snapped. During a game you will always see a Gruden or Charlie Weis talking to the quarterback and holding a clipboard or script over their mouths. They don't want anyone reading their lips. In this game, if someone could do it, he would.

As I have said so many times before, the entire Patriots team was now an extension of Bill Belichick. There were people who called our team boring.

We weren't the kind of team to carry on stories or dwell on controversies. No one was cracking, because no one was becoming overly excited about being in the playoffs or acting like kids in a toy store. That's because our mentality over the last six weeks had been that we were already in the playoffs. Each game was of the utmost importance, and Coach Belichick would remind us again and again that this next game was the most important for each player up to this point in his career. Because they are used to seeing championship teams develop gradually, I really think coaches like Phil Jackson, Bobby Knight, or Joe Torre would have been proud of us. They would have understood how we went about taking care of business. We were very serious, but we weren't a bunch of tight-asses. We would BS a little bit with some pranks here and there, just enough to stay loose.

I was really proud of the guys and where they had come from this past year. Now, with the playoffs looming, they were taking a calm, serious approach, the defensive players talking about Tim Brown and Jerry Rice. In our defensive staff meetings Rob Ryan and Eric Mangini keep things pretty loose and lively and make sure we have a little fun while putting in the long hours. Everybody puts in long, long hours. Belichick is known for the hours he puts in and expects the same from his assistants. In fact guys who haven't worked with him don't always know what they're getting into when they interview for a job. I knew him, and so did RAC, so we knew the kind of hours we had to look forward to. In fact, in the sixteen years I've known him I've never seen the man yawn—not once. However, none of the defensive coaches mind the grueling hours. We'll sit up there and crack jokes, talk about other sports or current events, then get back to business. We have a lot of dedicated guys all working for the same thing.

There was a lot of talk going back and forth before the Raiders game. One reason was simply that some of the players knew each other and were friends, so a lot of it was in fun. For example, their star cornerback, Charles Woodson, and Ty Law are good friends, each having played at the University of Michigan. Through the media there was a lot of light ribbing between the two of them about their friendship. Woodson also played with Tom Brady at Michigan, and the two swapped stories about each other through the media. At the same time we knew Woodson was a player we would have to deal with, so we had Leonard Myers emulate him in practice with the Dirty Show. This was good for Leonard, who is a very talented cornerback and has the ambition to be one of the league's elite players.

Leonard really performed well, watched tapes of Woodson in action, and did a lot of the same things that Woodson would do against us. He's close to Woodson's size, a big, strong corner, and he closely mirrored Woodson's movements and gestures. The Raiders have a defense in their third-down package where Woodson plays the middle of the field and eyes the quarterback. In our defense we call that a *position robber*. Woodson stays around the first down marker in the middle of the field and reads the quarterback. If he sees the quarterback looking one way toward a receiver, he reacts quickly and moves toward the play. He can do this with either a matchup zone or playing man-to-man. He doesn't set up as deep as the free safety. Since we like to throw a lot of passes to Troy Brown in that area and Brady is looking for him, we knew that Woodson could give us trouble. So we had to work on our execution and, with Myers playing that position, see how we could beat it. Oakland was very talented offensively. They had some good players on the defensive side of the ball but were more solid on the line and in the secondary, rather than with their linebackers. So we had to prepare to deal with their top defenders and also find ways to exploit the weaker ones.

I've always found that the playoffs, more so than the regular season, will test the mental makeup of a team. The Jets had beaten the Raiders in the final game of the season when Oakland didn't play with a lot of intensity. When the Jets had to travel to Oakland to play them in the wild card game the following week, they were the ones who came in flat. Maybe the trip back to Oakland had drained them, but I've always wondered how a team could come into the playoffs with less intensity and just fall on their faces. I know there have been many blowouts in the Super Bowl, the biggest game of any player's life. To me it just shows that one team is concentrating fully on the game and the other is not, that one team is better prepared than the other.

For the Chicago Bears to have beaten up on the Patriots the way they did in 1985, winning 46–10, there had to be more than just a difference in talent between the two teams. The Bears came to the Super Bowl that year telling everyone that they were supposed to be there, while the Patriots had a convincing act that they were a wild card team that had just played three games. They said they were tired, while the Bears defense was being called one of the best in history. They heard that so much that they began to believe it. It's the oldest trick in the book, taking your opponent out of the game mentally. The Bears played the media masterfully, and come game time the Patriots were already emotionally drained. Their thoughts were more focused on being a wild card team that couldn't win the Super Bowl.

In their wild card game versus the Jets, the Raiders didn't have the home-field advantage. Mentally, they had shot themselves in the foot by talking about having a home-field playoff game way back in week ten. Now they had to shake that off, but it didn't seem as if they really did. Obviously the Raiders wanted it more. The same catch-and-run plays that hadn't worked the week before worked to perfection in the wild card game. In a way, however, it was just as bad for the Raiders, because they had to be wondering why everything they did successfully in the wild card game hadn't worked the previous week. The great thing about the playoffs is that they show the true colors of an athlete. It doesn't matter if he's making $8 million a year or playing for the minimum. The regular-season paychecks have stopped. Now every player has to do it out on the field, and everyone is playing for the same amount of money and with the same goals.

I remember Mr. Kraft stopped me in the hallway one day and asked me what would happen if the game were played in very cold weather and in a snowstorm. I think he was looking for a rah-rah answer, my telling him that with cold weather and snow we should beat them, no problem. I guess it was one of my logical and analytical days, because I said to him that we have just as many guys from warm-weather states, whether they were born and raised there or played college ball in warmer climates. We might have a little advantage having practiced more in the cold, but come game time their body temperatures were going to adjust the same way as ours, and I said I didn't think it would necessarily be an advantage for us.

That's like saying if we went to Florida or California late in the season we probably wouldn't win because we haven't been practicing in eighty-degree weather for a month. That's why I say so much of it is mental. We practiced in the bubble at Boston College, not outside, because we felt we could have better practice sessions in there. No one had to bulk up with clothes, no one was slipping and falling, there was no need for heated benches. So the cold will balance itself out. It's the same as our wilting in the Miami heat early in the season. If you aren't mentally strong, you won't adjust. I always tell guys they cannot run from the hawk. In this case the hawk is the cold wind, the cold weather. He's gonna get you. It's worse if you put on all those layers of clothes and he finds a way in that crack in your neck or sleeve. You're better off just going out, getting your body cold and numb, and playing. The adrenaline rush and excitement should heat your body up enough to do it.

The Raiders have a balanced attack that features the so-called West Coast offense. Some of their pass plays unfold much like another team running a draw or screen pass. They spread the opposing defense out and normally do not rely on the deep ball. The Raiders, however, will occasionally throw deep, and we had their deep plays in our breakdown. Though you will see deep routes from them, with cold weather and maybe snow, you won't see as many deep passes as control passes, the catch-and-run kind. There is also more scripting of plays with the West Coast offense, and I think that's part of the downside of it. They have so many plays in their repertoire that if they hurt you early with a particular play, many times they don't go back to that play because it isn't in the script. As I said, Jon Gruden is a stickler for the script. He'll have his offense script fifteen or twenty plays at a Friday practice or Saturday walk-through. They rehearse them, mentally and physically, and feel there shouldn't be a mental breakdown on those scripted plays. It's like an artist preparing for a play or dance recital. The theory is that once the script gets the offense into its rhythm, the coordinator can call plays from the feel he now has for the game. The only time that early script might change is if the team is suddenly backed up inside its own ten-yard line or explodes early and is operating in its opponent's red zone.

The Patriots, however, don't run a West Coast offense. We might script a few plays early, but Charlie will always have a plan B. The difference in the scripting Charlie does compared to Jon Gruden's is if he sees that a scripted play worked early, he will come back to it. Gruden will stick to the script until all the plays are run. Defensively, the Raiders always want to carry on the tradition started by the team's owner and former coach, Al Davis. That tradition is toughness. However, at this point in the season the Patriots were not going to allow any team to be more physical then they were. If our opponents hit one of our players hard, we were going to go back out and hit three of theirs.

The week of the game, we were once again the underdogs. There were a lot of people who didn't feel we should be the number-two seed in the conference. Hey, we were an eighty-to-one shot at the beginning of the season, and during that last stretch, when we won six in a row, we frustrated the odds-makers by winning games the way we did. Some felt we had backed into the second playoff slot, and while a case could be made for the Raiders backing into the playoffs, our appearance was more of a shock. Even though we had that great winning streak, once the Raiders rolled over the Jets, we weren't supposed to stand a chance. They have two living legends at wideout, Gannon playing like a Hall of Famer and Charlie Garner giving them a strong running game.

Not even the New England media gave us a chance. Our die-hard fans wanted to believe, but deep down I think many of them felt like we still weren't a team capable of winning it all. Maybe next year. Most fans probably felt this would be the last playoff game and last game, period, at Foxboro, and they wanted to get a good look because they felt the next week we would be gone. It would be the Raiders playing the winner of the other game between the defending champion Ravens and the Steelers.

Then, early in the week, the forecasters said that snow was a possibility. The forecast went from cold to maybe some flurries and finally to maybe six inches. We were happy to see that; we embraced it as a psychological edge and ran with it. The guys on our team from Texas, California, and Florida didn't want to see it, but not too many players in our locker room wanted to hear complaints. You want to be on the positive side of the mental game, and the snow would put us there. You still have to play the game, but if enough guys on the Raiders felt the snow was going to affect them adversely, then we'd have the edge before the game even began.

Our basic game plan defensively was to get the ball out of Rich Gannon's hands quickly in crucial situations. If we could do that, it would be a definite plus. The object was to make him get the ball out faster and throw shorter routes. Then we'd have the opportunity to make plays on defense. If we allowed him to drop back, give them time to allow Jerry and Tim to run from one side of the field to the other, that's what could hurt us. The best thing we did was prepare our guys for a cold-weather game and to defend cold-weather plays. We would end up playing those short routes better and better as the game wore on. Another goal was to stop Charlie Garner from going outside. He's an outside runner, so if we kept turning him back in, we'd hold him down. Gannon is also a capable scrambler, and we had to keep him from buying time to find an open receiver. If we pretty much contained those four skill guys, the last thing we wanted to happen was to let somebody else on the team beat us. Our offense also practiced the cold-weather game, which was rather simple. Short passes, screens to everyone, and run Antowain.

When you are playing on a snow-covered or slippery field, there are adjustments that definitely have to be made. It isn't going to be the same game you play on a dry field in warmer weather with great footing. Not by a long shot. Whenever field conditions are frozen or slippery, Coach Belichick will demand that the players go out early and test their shoes. The veterans will do it automatically; the young guys sometimes need to be reminded. Smart players will check every spot on the field, from the sidelines to the middle. The kickers will closely inspect the middle, while the wide receivers report on every area of the field. The information comes back to Belichick in the locker room, and he'll make his suggestions to everyone. Since the middle of the field gets the most foot traffic, that section gradually gets muddied and chopped up like a cattle pen. The sidelines will more likely stay mostly frozen.

Just a couple of examples of how these field conditions can affect the game: Late in the 2000 season we went to Kansas City. The field was frozen the day before. At game time everything from the numbers to the sideline on both sides was still frozen, rock hard. Now it was more difficult for the receivers to get traction. Instead of making sharp cuts, they tended to round off their pass routes. Because of this, a cornerback like Ty Law could now play his receiver inside. He was covering Derrick Alexander that day and knew Alexander couldn't get anything outside him. Because the receivers couldn't run sharp, precise routes, the quarterback could no longer throw to a spot, because he couldn't be sure the receiver would be there. Ty ended up having his best game of the year because he knew just what Alexander could and couldn't do on the field. Being a veteran and knowing these things gives you a huge advantage.

When we saw the snow begin to fall in Foxboro that morning, we were pretty happy. It was going to be our kind of game. Don't get me wrong, both teams have to play under the same conditions. As I've said so many times, though, so much of the game is mental, and I think we definitely had the advantage. It's probably the offensive linemen who like to see a snowy field more than anyone else. Under those conditions the defenders they're blocking simply aren't as quick. In some areas everyone has to step gingerly. Offensive players can use their hands, tug on a defender, and make him lose his balance more easily. At the same time, holding penalties aren't called as much in this kind of weather—to the refs it looks as if everyone is sleeping, because they move more slowly. Linemen have to play up over their feet, keep a narrow base. Their feet can't be too far in front of them. They can't lean with their head or chest too far forward, can't run with their feet too far apart. Do that, and they'll slip. Leverage is more of a factor. If players are more upright, they are easier to block, easier to move out of the way.

In snowy conditions receivers have to run shorter routes. Instead of a fourteen-yard route, they may make their cut at eleven or twelve yards. If the ball is thrown short, they have a better chance to come back and get it. As I said, they can't be as precise with their cuts. That's one of the things you teach and how you can tell which receivers are going to be great route runners. Jerry Rice, for example, was always a great route runner. Even in bad conditions, Jerry would still try to make his cuts. But he had to stand more upright to secure his footing when he was breaking his routes off, and for that reason he wouldn't get as many catch-and-run plays, which is really what he and Tim Brown do best.

A snowy field can be a good game for a runner like Antowain Smith. He's a solid, hard-running, bowl-you-over back, and he likes tough conditions. He knows the offensive linemen can hold on to their blocks a little better and it's up to him to get into the holes faster. You won't see a lot of cuts from the runners, and that's why coaches will teach two cuts only. No runner can make a lot of cuts on that kind of field. If you make enough cuts, sooner or later your ankles will be separated, your feet too far apart, and you'll fall. Long striders especially have a difficult time on slippery surfaces.

Quarterbacks also have to make adjustments. For instance, the quarterback–center exchange is supposed to be the most fundamental play in football. This simple maneuver becomes crucial in snowy situations. In good conditions the quarterback is actually starting to move backward before he has the ball. In the snow the coach will emphasize to the quarterback that he makes sure he has the ball before he takes a backward step. He has to be sure. The center might lose his grip, and while that may mean just a fraction of a second, it slows the time in which the quarterback can drop back. As he drops back, he has to stay conscious of keeping his feet under him. He can lose it at any time until he stops to set up. If his feet slip backward, it can affect his concentration and alter his throw. A smart quarterback will sacrifice the speed of his dropback and not worry about how quickly he can execute play-action passes.

Some quarterbacks drop back holding the ball in one hand. In the snow they should keep both hands on the ball to eliminate the chance of dropping it. Many coaches will tell the quarterback to hold the ball high, around their shoulder, in the snow. That way they won't be swinging it around as much before delivering it. The ball is also heavier once it gets wet. In addition, many quarterbacks like to feel the rotation of the ball as it comes off their hand. They don't get the same feeling in the snow. There aren't as many pure spirals thrown in the snow, and the precision of the passing game is limited. So Tom Brady will have be to doing a bit more of a staredown with his receivers, watching them more closely, because he can't throw to spots as much. He has to adjust.

Defensive linemen must put a strong emphasis on keeping their feet under them in snowy conditions. If they feel they have an opportunity to rush around a guy, however, they have to take it. On running plays the defensive lineman has to make sure he is solid and anchored. He can't let himself be moved or tossed around. Sometimes the defenders have to make piles, because if they get pushed back three or four yards, then the line of scrimmage is moved back. So we teach guys to get on the ground. It may sound silly, even like a nonplay, but it's simple—drop to the ground, drag down your blocker, and make a pile. Like I said, it sounds silly, but it's effective. If the running back decides to go there, he has to jump over the pile to get past. Quick backs will try to avoid the pile and go around it, find daylight. But it narrows the field in which a guy can make a play.

On a snowy field the play of the linebackers is crucial. Sometimes you'll see linebackers having better games in the snow, but sometimes you'll see them falling on their faces in the fourth quarter. I always liked games in bad weather because I felt it brought other guys down to me. Going against a Barry Sanders on a dry field, there was no way you could get him one-on-one. If the weather conditions slowed him just a little bit, though, you had just that much more time to close in on him. If a linebacker isn't in a big hurry and can get to an area where the back is going to make his cut, he can make a lot of tackles. The difficult part for the linebacker in the snow is getting back in coverage. The defensive backs are moving forward to reach their coverage, while the linebacker has to run backward to reach the area where the receiver is going, and he then has to adjust quickly because the receiver is also moving forward. In addition, linebackers are often lighter than the offensive linemen, and if they can't move fast enough they can be tossed around. Again, they have to compensate the same way, with shorter steps, not spreading their feet, as well as being smarter and getting a jump on the play.

Defensive backs also have to use their heads. They must know what the receiver can and can't do under the existing field conditions and make that work to their benefit. Safeties and corners see the field easier, but when they get into man-to-man coverage it's crucial that they don't take the kind of wide, long steps that will get them in trouble. If a defensive back slips, it can be disastrous. In addition, I always try to emphasize the importance of tackling in the snow and cold. You will see a lot of offensive players breaking tackles in these conditions. Players often like to block-tackle, bump a guy hard enough to knock him off his feet. Mentally, a player has to know if his opponent is having the same kind of problem moving on the bad field as he is, but that isn't always the case.

With the kicking game the snowy field shortens field goal range. The ball is a little heavier from being wet, and the footing isn't as sure. The conditions also make the snap and hold more crucial. Lonie Paxton, our long snapper on punts and field goals, has to be sure he has a precise grip on the ball. Ken Walter, our punter and also our field goal holder, has to catch the ball and place it with the laces turned away from the kicker. All this is more difficult on a wet field. The punter also has to be careful not to slip. He has to be sure his foundation foot is planted squarely. So every aspect of the game is affected, but affected the same for both teams.

In general bad weather helps the defense more. Though the offensive players know where they are going, a slippery field brings the percentages for the defense up. At the same time, there are more missed tackles in the snow and cold and wind. That can work for the offense. So there is something for both sides, and the entire game is slowed down. For the offense the emphasis has to be on protecting the ball. Sometimes it helps the receivers to wear cotton sleeves. They may find they can hold the ball better than if they have bare, wet arms. Defensively, we tell guys to poke and pull at the ball as much as possible. When we played the Raiders, it was not only cold and wet but snow-covered as well.

The grounds crew kept the tarp on the field as long as possible, but there was a steady snowfall right from the opening kickoff. While we, as coaches, told the team early in the week that we would have the advantage in the snow, I really didn't think that, when push came to shove, it made for a big advantage. The weather might take something away from Rice and Brown, because they were playmakers. However, they created a lot on their own and, besides, the weather was going to affect our playmakers as well. With the snow falling, most of the players switched from the standard long studs on their shoes to midrange or low studs for better traction.

In the first quarter you could see the effect of the weather right away. They took the kickoff, and on the first play Charlie Garner gained eleven yards. Like I said, Garner likes to make cuts and is an elusive guy. Maybe that woke us up a bit, because we didn't even want to give him a little crack, but right away he ran for a first down. After that our defensive ends and cornerbacks did a good job not allowing him outside. It's called *setting the edge*, and they remained aware of it. After that run for a first down they went three and out. We mounted a nice little drive, going from our own twenty to their thirty-one before we turned the ball over on downs. Brady completed one for nineteen yards to J. R. Redmond, but the rest of the drive consisted of short gains by Antowain and a couple of short completions—the cold-weather offense.

That's how it went for most of the remainder of the period. I noticed that they completed a couple of short passes to the outside, not quite in first down range, but the kind of plays that stretched the ball out and something that could have hurt us. But then they stopped it. I'm sure it was because of the scripted offense. Gruden doesn't like to break the script, and early in the game it hurt them. Once they came off the script late in the quarter, they started to hurt us again with the same plays. We went three-and-out and punted to them with about a minute and a half left in the quarter. They started at their own thirty-five and got a break on the first play when a fifteen-yard penalty brought the ball to midfield. Gannon then threw one of those swing passes to Garner, who gained twelve to our thirty-eight. Now they were in business.

The drive continued into the second quarter. Gannon threw to Jeremy Brigham for ten, hit Rice for twelve, and finally threw a scoring pass to James Jett from thirteen yards out. Sebastian Janikowski kicked the extra point, and we were behind, 7–0. They scored on plays similar to those they had tried earlier. We had been wrapping them up then but didn't do the job on this drive, missing a couple of tackles and paying the price. So the guys who were supposed to have the advantage in the snow were once again going to have to play from behind. Neither team did any damage for the rest of the period as the snow continued to fall. In fact there was no action inside the red zone for the remainder of the period. With the weather getting worse, it was apparent that the game would be low-scoring and the margin for error was getting smaller.

At halftime we still felt good. No way we were feeling out of it or even that the game was going in their direction despite their lead. As expected, both offenses were playing it conservatively, and in a game like this it's often a matter of which team is going to make the first mistake. The snow was still not a concern. Like I said, both teams had to play on it and had to make something happen. We felt that we had given them what they had taken and they weren't going to continue hurting us with a nickel-and-dime offense, as long as we tackled well. The Raiders' offensive playbook is so large, with maybe sixty or seventy different plays. Against most teams we could put a play up on the board and say "Look, this is what they just ran, and this is what you have to do to stop it." With the Raiders, however, you might not see that play again. What we had to try to do was grasp the concept of what areas of the field they were trying to attack. When you get that concept and know pretty much that they are going to attack in a certain way, you can try to adjust.

I still felt good about the game. We missed tackles on a couple of key plays, but that will hurt at any time. I also thought that our offense, which was held down pretty well in the first half, would begin moving the ball in the second half. In other words, the offense would get some points after intermission, but that being the case, I didn't want our defense to allow the Raiders to score again. Because it was still a close game, the offenses could both play at a regular pace. Neither team at this point had the need to score in a hurry.

At the beginning of the third quarter the snowy conditions worsened. Leaf blowers were deployed to blow the snow off the sidelines and yard markers. The snow never let up, and in the second half the flakes were getting larger. We took the kickoff and immediately made a statement, driving from our own thirty-three all the way down to their five-yard line. Brady came out throwing and connected on four passes on the drive. The keys were two passes to David Patten for twenty-five and nineteen yards and one to Marc Edwards for thirteen. We had two plays from the five but couldn't get it in, so Adam came on and kicked a twenty-three-yarder to reduce the margin to 7–3. At this point I thought we were beginning to take over the game.

But I was wrong. Both of their next two drives resulted in field goals by Janikowski, the first from thirty-eight yards and the second from forty-five with less than two minutes left in the period. Now they had a 13–3 lead with just one period left and the snow becoming worse. Janikowski's second field goal really hurt. Though he has a strong leg, I really didn't think he would kick a forty-five-yarder in the snow. The strange part was that even though it was very cold and snowing hard, there was no wind. Wind gusts would have made the kicker's job almost impossible, but with no wind, a good snap, hold, and plant by the kicker was all that was needed. I felt we had been moving the ball better, but we just couldn't seem to put together the nine or eleven plays needed for a solid drive.

Now our defense had to start looking to force a turnover. We wanted them to begin going after the ball a little more, but that's tough in a game like this. In addition, we didn't want a one-on-one situation where the defender goes for the ball, misses, and gives up the long gain. We needed a situation where two or three guys are covering and then one of them can go for the ball. The difference with this team, however, was that everyone continued to look for a way to win. I still felt strongly that somehow, some way, we were going to pull this game out.

Early in the period Troy Brown returned a Shane Lechler punt eleven yards to our thirty-three, but when he was hit he fumbled. That could have spelled disaster if Larry Izzo, our special teams dynamo, hadn't recovered the ball to keep it in our possession. That's when Tom Brady began putting together a solid drive. He began throwing on every play, all short stuff, and spreading it out. Our tight end, Jermaine Wiggins, who had caught just fourteen passes in the regular season, was getting open, and Brady kept going back to him. He caught four passes in the drive that finally gave us a first and ten on the Raiders ten-yard line. After a four-yard pass to Wiggins and his ninth straight completion, Brady surprised the Raiders by running right up the middle into the end zone. With less than eight minutes left, we had finally scored. Adam's kick made it 13–10, and now it was up to the defense to hold them so we would have a chance to win.

After we scored, however, they ate up about four minutes of the clock by moving from their thirty to our forty-four, keeping the ball on the ground and taking as much time as possible. Finally, after Garner lost a yard on first down, Gannon threw a pair of incomplete passes, and they punted to us with just 3:25 left. This time, however, we stalled before we started. After a twelve-yard throw to Wiggins for a first down at our thirty-two, Brady threw three straight incompletes, and we had to punt.

Now time was getting short, just 2:41 left. Our defense knew it was crunch time and did its job, stopping them on a three-and-out at a time when just a single first down could have finished us. After each play we called a time-out. Finally Lechler punted from the Raiders forty-four, and this time I think the snow helped us. His kick traveled just thirty-seven yards, with Troy Brown ready to grab it. What did I say about playmakers? With the season on the line, Troy did what he had done so often, broke a return for twenty-seven yards, bringing the ball back to our forty-six with 2:06 left. Everyone knew this was probably our last chance.

Starting at our forty-six, Brady threw to Kevin Faulk for seven yards. On the next play he ran for five and gave us a first down at the Oakland forty-two. Now came the play that will probably be talked about for years. Brady dropped back again, and right away I could see the play developing. Raiders cornerback Charles Woodson had tried to blitz several times from the strong side, and we kept picking it up. They switched him over to the left side on this play, and there he was, coming again. I knew sooner or later he would rush and try to make a play, because he's that good. Brady didn't see him, and was blindsided just as he appeared ready to throw. Woodson chopped down on his arm, and the ball popped loose. My first thought was Oh, no, don't let it end like this. But that's exactly what appeared would happen when their linebacker, Greg Biekert, fell on the loose ball. The Raiders began celebrating immediately, but I wasn't sure. I thought right away that it was an incomplete pass. Next thing I knew, the officials were reviewing the play via instant replay while everyone held their breath.

No one had to explain the situation. It was simple. If they ruled a fumble, we were done. The season was over. You hate for the entire season to hinge on a referee's ruling. At the same time, however, you want a proper call. You don't want to lose because an incomplete pass was called a fumble. After what seemed like forever, the refs came back out and, sure enough, ruled an incomplete pass. They said Brady appeared to have made a continuous motion with his arm and was pulling the ball down when it was jarred loose. Because of his arm motion—he didn't reload to pass—they called it incomplete rather than a fumble, and we retained possession. We weren't dead yet. It's amazing how the emotions can change in an instant. When the replay led to the call being reversed, our fire was rekindled. It was like ER trauma, when you go flat line, and then with a shot in the chest you come back to life and the line flutters again. To us, when that play was overturned, it was like the beginning of the game all over again. You could feel the confidence level rise, could feel all the energy just turn back on. Everyone got excited. What struck me the most, however, was that while we were pumped and ready to go, the Raiders took the opposite direction and couldn't pull the switch.

When something like that happens, you have to know that that play is over. At the next snap it's *over*! That play could have simply been a what-if had they made one more play. The ball was at the forty-two now, and on the next play Brady completed a clutch pass to David Patten for a thirteen-yard gain to the twenty-nine. We had a first down and were clapping and shouting while the Raiders were still walking around like zombies, just looking at each other and probably still thinking the refs had screwed them and made the wrong call.

All we cared about was that we had a first down at the twenty-nine. At this point Adam would have to kick a forty-six-yard field goal to tie the game. With the snow coming down harder and Adam not being a real long-distance kicker, it seems nearly impossible. That distance for him isn't the same as it would be for Janikowski, who has a powerful leg. Adam would have to fully extend his leg to hope to make it in those conditions. We wanted to get him in closer, but after two incomplete passes Brady tried to run up the middle and got just a single yard. Now, with just twenty-seven seconds left, Adam came on to try a forty-five-yarder. It was all riding on this one—everything we had worked for, our improbable run to the playoffs, getting the home-field advantage. It was all riding on this one kick.

Lonie Paxton made a strong snap, Ken Walter placed it down, and Adam booted a low line drive. It had just enough leg on it and barely cleared the crossbar. It was good! We had tied the game, and everyone mobbed Adam, who had come through for us again just when it looked as if we had run out of luck. Only it still wasn't over. There were twenty-seven seconds left and then, most likely, sudden-death overtime.

Looking back at Adam's field goal, I think it says something about both our team and the Raiders. They still had not put the reversed fumble call behind them. We had learned during the year, when we played the Rams, that you can't dwell on a play once it's over. Remember when Antowain fumbled on the four-yard line and they recovered at the three and promptly drove ninety-seven yards for a touchdown. If we stopped them, it was a whole different ball game, but they scored, and we never recovered or got back in the game. If we still had that mentality against the Raiders, Janikowski's second field goal could have drained us. We learned, however, and they hadn't. On Adam's kick, no one even made a gallant effort to block it. Sure, we did a good job holding them out, but it was a line drive, and if someone had stuck a hand up, he might have tipped it. In a do-or-die playoff game, somebody should have been clawing and scratching to get over that line. But no one did.

After the kickoff and one play in which Gannon took a knee, the period ended and we got ready for overtime. There are some pros and cons about the overtime coin toss. In certain conditions some teams will choose to kick, hoping to pin their opponents back deep, then get good field position after the punt. Conversely, the same thing can happen if you choose to receive. If you don't move the ball and have to punt from deep in your own territory, you're giving your opponents a chance to start from the thirty or forty and perhaps need only thirty yards or so before they can try for the winning field goal. We wanted to win the toss, obviously, and if we did we were going to receive. Adam doesn't normally put his kickoffs in the back of the end zone, and in these worsening conditions chances were he would kick short. That might jump-start the Raiders. If we received, we would put the snow plan, the short game plan, into action and take whatever was open. We won the toss and got the ball.

After the runback, we started from our own thirty-four and Tom Brady went to work. He started with a short pass to J. R. Redmond that netted just one yard, but on the next play went right back to Redmond and connected for a twenty-yard gain that put us into Oakland territory. Brady continued to throw, taking what was open, hitting Redmond again and Jermaine Wiggins three more times. From the twenty-eight he threw for Wiggins again. This time the ball went through his hands, but Patten was right behind him to grab it for a six-yard gain to the twenty-two. Brady had completed all eight of his passes in the drive. Now it was time for Antowain. On three carries he took it from the twenty-two to the Raiders nine. First down. He got it again and took it to the seven. On second down Brady just ran up the middle for two more. Now it was time for Adam Vinatieri once again.

This was a drive that proved yet another point. Remember I had said earlier that while you have to defend a team's stars, like Brown and Rice, you can't allow a lesser player to beat you. On our drive the Raiders were so intent on stopping Troy Brown and David Patten that they forgot about J. R. Redmond and Jermaine Wiggins. These are our emergency guys and also our security guys. They rarely fumble. Like I said, Tom Brady was taking what they gave him, and this time they couldn't really stop us. Brady, J.R., and Jermaine set it up for Antowain, and now Adam was on the field. All he had to do was kick a twenty-three-yarder. I felt if the snap and place were executed well, there was no way Adam would miss. It was over. Sure enough, Lonie and Ken did the job, and Adam booted it through the uprights as the snow continued to cascade down around the erupting stadium. I remember Lonie Paxton running into the end zone, falling down, and flapping his arms and legs to make a snow angel right on the field.

Guys were jumping up and down, cheering, and bowing to the crowd. We all felt this was a game for the history books. It wasn't your average playoff game. There was a good chance that it was the last game ever at Foxboro Stadium and would be remembered forever as the snow game. You couldn't ask for more. It was a game that would be talked about for years, a game that surely delighted NFL fans everywhere. People who watched it saw an exciting, controversial game, with big plays and big hits. It was what football truly was meant to be. The older players saw an old-fashioned snow game come back to life. As the game wore on, we took it to the Raiders and made sure we were headed to the second round. There were plenty of heroes. Brady wound up completing thirty-two of fifty-two passes for 312 yards, an amazing performance under tough conditions. Antowain gained 65 yards on twenty carries and got those crucial yards before Adam's winning kick. On defense Ty Law had ten tackles, while Tedy Bruschi had eight. Everyone contributed, as always, and Adam came through when it counted, as always.

I guess we wouldn't be human if there wasn't a lot of hugging and cheering after the game, but Coach Belichick directed the team back into focus. Baltimore was playing Pittsburgh after our game, so we didn't know if we would have another game in Foxboro if the Ravens won or have to travel to

Pittsburgh. The consensus was that we would rather play Baltimore at home to see what Foxboro Stadium would bring us this time. Maybe another snow game. Anyone who truly enjoys winning championships likes to beat the defending champion at some point. That was the Ravens. You want the guy who's the champion. So in that sense I wanted Baltimore to come over as well.

Either way, we were going to be playing for the AFC Championship. There hadn't been anyone predicting that before the season began, and no one thinking about it when we finished the halfway mark with a 4–4 record. Even though we had now won seven straight games for the first time in franchise history, there still weren't too many people thinking about us as AFC Champions. When Pittsburgh beat Baltimore, 27–10, we knew where we were going, knew where our destiny was taking us. The media and the fans still might not be convinced, but there was a whole locker room full of football players and coaches who were more convinced than ever that this was going to be a Patriots year.

11

Bending Steel
AFC Champions

We beat the Raiders on a Saturday. The next day the Steelers defeated the Ravens to set up the AFC title game against us the following week in Pittsburgh. Though the Ravens were defending champions, they seemed to falter late in the season, began looking like a tired team, as if the energy was no longer there. Had they been a cocky team, I would have guessed that they were taking a victory for granted, figuring they could turn it up a notch when their season was on the line. That's a mistake many teams have made in the past.

Despite their having a couple of showmen, especially their middle line-backer, Ray Lewis, I never had the feeling the Ravens were cocky. Though they still had a very solid defense, the Steelers just had a little more energy than they did. When the Ravens made mistakes on offense, the Steelers jumped all over them, and their defense didn't have that fire to go out and take the game back from the Pittsburgh offense. All along, we felt that this would be Pittsburgh's turn and that we would end up playing them for the AFC Championship.

Right after the Steelers' victory, some of us were watching ESPN Sports-Center, and all the talk was about how the Steelers were already making their Super Bowl arrangements, getting their tickets, making plans to take family down to New Orleans, stuff like that. Coach Cowher, Jerome Bettis, Kordell Stewart—all of them were saying the same thing when they were interviewed. It didn't take long for us to find our ammo. It seemed as if nearly every one of our players had seen the interviews, and that was the hot topic of conversation when they arrived for practice on Monday. In fact about five or six guys came into my office and asked if I had watched it. I was really happy to see how they responded. They all had that same tone in their voice, and I was now fully convinced that our team was mature enough to win the whole thing.

The Steelers had also announced they would not be practicing again until Wednesday. However, we followed our normal routine, and everyone was in first thing Monday morning. Earlier in the season some of the guys might have asked why we were practicing when they weren't. Now no one had to ask. We gave the team a brief look at the Steelers, passed out personnel sheets, and had tapes prepared. Otis Smith, for example, took home tapes of Pittsburgh receiver Plaxico Burress. We had to begin quickly, because playing Pittsburgh wouldn't be easy no matter how you looked at it. We had plenty of work to do with the players and a great deal to focus on. I had to make sure the show team emulated the Pittsburgh defense as closely as possible, and to do that my Dirty Show guys had to be loaded up with all the information they needed. No one worth his salt wants to play in a game of this magnitude and make a mental error. We had all grown up watching football and knew that if you shot yourself in the foot in a game like this it could change the direction of your entire career.

In general I think the Steelers were successful in 2001 due to the strength of their defense as well as the running game led by Jerome Bettis and their other backs. Yet we knew the Steelers were a well-rounded team. They play aggressively with defense still their trademark, and that's what wins championships. In addition they still lived up to that old adage that Pittsburgh was Blitzburg. And Kordell Stewart was certainly in the midst of his best season ever. Even though Stewart might not be a great pure passer, he was still a player who liked to take matters into his own hands. He reminded us of a young Randall Cunningham at Philadelphia. Both quarterbacks could run or pass, and when they started to scramble they often threw deep. That's the fear. The defensive backs begin to come up to support the run, and suddenly there's a receiver behind them catching a deep ball. Add a great running game, and they become a tough team to defend. As good as Stewart is, however, I still had the feeling that Tom Brady was the better pure passer.

Bettis, of course, had been injured part of the year, and we had to go back more than a few games to view him at full strength. Our feeling, however, was that the Steelers were a different team with their other running backs. They were more outside runners, two or three cut guys. Bettis is simply "The Bus," straight ahead and right over you. We weren't sure how much Bettis would play or how effective he would be. Either way, we knew it wouldn't be easy to draw up a game plan against them, because they have offensive plays and weapons that take the game into the schoolyards. Wide receiver Plaxico Burress, for example, is so big and strong that he can push a lot of defensive backs around. He's about six-foot-six and 230 pounds, almost like a modern-day Harold Carmichael, the great Eagles receiver who played for Philly from 1971 to 1983 and was a four-time Pro Bowler. Harold was a six-foot-eight wide receiver and extremely difficult for shorter defensive backs to defend. Fortunately, we have Otis Smith, who's tough enough not to be pushed around and has twelve years' experience going for him. So that's a big plus right there.

Along those lines there was an attempt to spark up some trash talking between Ty Law and Pittsburgh's other wide receiver, Hines Ward. Someone said that Hines was a heavy blocker who loved hitting defensive backs and that they planned to hit our guys hard across the middle. Ty answered by saying that no one on the Patriots was running from anyone, that we might be smaller but we were very physical. This was uncharacteristic of us, answering something in the press, but I guess he felt it was necessary. He also added that we were preparing for a war. The next time he was interviewed, however, Ty told the reporters they were blowing the whole thing out of proportion, that we had a game to play and this whole thing was irrelevant, which is the way we usually handle things. But he also said it in a way to let them know he wasn't backing down from anyone.

Our cornerbacks have different personalities. Otis is our beat-'em-up corner. He can fight with the best of them. Ty is more of a cover corner, who generally takes on the opponents' finesse guys, receivers who can cause problems both short and deep. Otis will take on the receiver who does a lot of dirty work, digging and blocking, and might not get as much credit. But those are often the kinds of receivers who, on a third and eight, catch a pass good for nine yards. Otis will also take on a lot of young receivers, former college stars considered up-and-coming NFL receivers. He'll break them in. He's better at finding weaknesses and beating them. Ty likes to play games with the receiver he's covering. If the receiver likes to throw a lot of fakes—a "wiggle guy," we call him—Ty will back up and let him wiggle. He enjoys the mind game while Otis, with all his experience, pretty much knows where receivers are going before they even go there. So it's great to have these two distinct types of cornerbacks, because offenses generally look for different types of receivers to play those two spots. In the case of the Steelers, both their starting wideouts—Burress and Ward—were big and strong.

In the week before the game the magazines came through for us again. *Sports Illustrated* came out with Kordell on the cover. Up on the bulletin board again. Add the *SI* cover story to the Steelers' previous comments about their Super Bowl plans, and we had all the reminders we needed about what had to be done. It was as if they were passing over the importance of the AFC Championship game, as if beating us was a given. If that couldn't fire us up, nothing would.

Our intensity began to build right away in practice. Because of his superstition, Belichick took us back out to the Boston College bubble to practice, the exact routine we had used preparing for the Raiders. Defensively, we knew we had to prepare Brady for the Steelers' multiple blitzes. I had the show team blitzing him all kinds of ways in practice. We ran one play where Terrance Shaw blitzed, jumped up, and knocked the pass down. The offense ran the next play, and we blitzed again. Once more Shaw tipped the pass. After they called some other plays, Coach Belichick asked them to repeat the second play, where Shaw had tipped the pass. So they ran it again, Shaw blitzed, and got it again. This time Brady got so mad that he went to kick the football, only he missed and fell on his butt. That broke the ice for a minute. I'll say one thing for Tom Brady, though. He doesn't back down from a challenge, and he's as competitive as anyone. He would bet the Dirty Show guys, like Leonard Myers, Je'Rod Cherry, and Antwan Harris, that he would complete a certain percentage of his passes. They would bet every day, and Brady would claim he'd won. I don't think the guys even went back and checked, just took Tom at his word. But again, it was all building a sense of togetherness, the common goal, and getting the guys ready to play.

The Dirty Show did a helluva job. They kept making a stink with Brady about paying on the bet. In fact they shut him down so bad that one day that a couple of guys came up and asked me if I thought they should let up a little on him so he could complete some passes. I was the first guy to say no. If Tom Brady was some kind of chump, then maybe I would have agreed. Only I know that when Brady gets pissed off at himself he shows even more determination and works harder. Plus he knows that the guys are just doing their jobs. Normally, if a play doesn't work in practice, Belichick won't run it in a game. However, if that rule held true in practice this day, they would have had no plays to run. The Dirty Show guys were on fire and having the same luck against the run. Larry Izzo was all over the field, making tackles everywhere, and I'm on the sideline talking mess. We're getting excited, and when that happens more first stringers want to get in and be part of the show team. Bruschi came in; Vrabel was an ex-Steeler and was with us because he was helping prepare for their offense. So we put it on them for two straight days. The offense finally began to move the ball and look decent on Thursday, but these heated practices helped the entire team.

P.S.: Brady wouldn't have a single pass tipped or blocked by the Pittsburgh defense.

It's funny how at this point in the season, with so much at stake, guys don't want anything disrupting their routine. When we flew to Pittsburgh, we heard that a number of club seat ticket holders for our new stadium would be on the flights as guests of Mr. Kraft. A lot of the players are superstitious and like to sit in the same seat on the plane for all away games. We had a larger plane, but some of the players were sent to different seats. Anthony Pleasant, for example, is used to having a whole row of seats to himself, but now he had to double up with somebody. To the naked eye, that might seem like nothing, but when you're playing a game of this magnitude, the last thing you want is a change from what you have been doing all year. That could have been a distraction except that as soon as we got off the plane, the Pittsburgh fans took over and we forgot all about the plane ride.

There were already a few people at the airport yelling at us, telling us "You're in Steeler country now." That wasn't too bad, because we're used to it. Then we got on the bus to go to our hotel, and there were people waiting for us all over, screaming "Steelers, Steelers, Steelers, Steelers!" Now it's becoming tacky but funny. Antwan Harris's mother, who was at the hotel, began screaming back at them: "Patriots, Patriots, Patriots, Patriots!" I told Antwan, "If your mom can drown them out, you can bet what we'll do to the Steelers." All the while we knew what we would be up against. Pittsburgh is a football town, yet you don't expect it to get that tacky. But it did. RAC even addressed it in the defensive meeting room that night. He told everyone not to let the people in the hotel become a distraction. Before I showed my ball disruption tape, I told the story of Antwan's mother drowning them out. Then, at the end of the tape, I showed once more me and William Roberts dancing on the field at the end of the 1986 Super Bowl. I wanted the players to get yet another taste of winning it firsthand.

So now we've got all the motivation we need—the Steelers' interviews on SportsCenter after they beat the Ravens, Kordell's picture on the cover of *Sports Illustrated*, Hines Ward talking about taking it to our defensive backs, and the people screaming at us at the airport and hotel. If that wasn't enough, when we woke up the next morning we got a little more. As soon as our guys opened their hotel room doors, each one saw a newspaper with a front-page headline that read "Pittsburgh's Road to the Super Bowl." There was a big color picture to go with it. This was Sunday morning, game day. Everyone I talked with had seen it, and I could see the looks on their faces. Then, before the game, we found a T-shirt that said "Pittsburgh, AFC Champions." And it had something about the Super Bowl on it. It was the shirt they were going to give out after Pittsburgh beat us. Everything was just getting us madder; we couldn't wait to unload on the Steelers.

When we were writing our last-minute reminders on the board, Coach Belichick took the T-shirt and showed it to Lawyer. He took it and hung it up on the blackboard. The guys had heard all week how the Steelers were already planning for the Super Bowl. Now, with the shirt hanging there in our faces, everyone began saying something, and we were getting pumped. Then, when we went out on the field for our pregame warm-ups, our guys were all stretching, doing the same routine we always did. At the other end of the field we saw Stewart, Bettis, Jason Gildon, and Lee Flowers all standing up while the rest of their guys were on the ground, stretching. Stewart had a towel wrapped around his neck and was skipping back and forth. Even before the game our team was not getting any respect. This was classic. They didn't even seem to be taking their warm-up seriously.

I was standing alongside Rob Ryan, and I looked at him and said, "They just don't have a clue about the hurricane that's about to blow through this place!"

I was so caught up in the moment that I called the stadium Three Rivers, where the Steelers *used* to play. Rob corrected me, saying, "No, no. It's the ketchup place." The Steelers now played in Heinz Field, the naming rights having been bought by the company that makes Heinz ketchup. A quick laugh, but the serious part was that we were still a team that wasn't getting any respect. We don't allow any player to stand outside the team and do their own stretching. Before the game they were saying that Tom Brady would finally meet his match, that their blitzing defense would be coming at him from all over the place. Our special teams coach, Brad Seely, found or heard a stat that said the Steelers had trailed an opponent for only thirty minutes during the entire season, which now stretched for seventeen games. In this league some teams trail their opponent for more than thirty minutes in just a single game. That tells you they were a team that had been playing the entire season with things going their way. No wonder Kordell Stewart was skipping back and forth with a towel around his neck.

That stat was confirmed by a tape that Belichick showed the team the Friday morning before the game. In nine of their games the Steelers defense had either caused a turnover or made a momentum-turning play during the first series they were on the field. They also played with the attitude that if they were losing they could quickly make it up, strike back fast. That theory, however, couldn't have been tested, because they didn't trail much during the year. I can almost see why they were cocky. They had the number-one running attack in the league, while we had been burned by several running backs during the season. Even in our final game, when Carolina's Richard Huntley ran for 168 yards, they probably laughed. He had been in their camp and was cut, yet he burned us. They figured they had three running backs better than he was. It all added up to a how-can-we-lose attitude on their part. When I said to Rob that they didn't have a clue about the hurricane about to blow by, I meant it. I can't honestly say I knew we would win, but I knew we sure wouldn't make it easy for them, and I was certain that they were underestimating our team.

You could see the emotions begin to bubble over during the coin toss. All of a sudden Bryan Cox and Jerome Bettis got into a shouting match. It was so bad that the referee wouldn't even switch on his mike. He was too busy trying to shut them up. Bettis was talking about Cox's leg still being so bad that there was no way he could catch him, while Cox answered by saying the Steelers had two other running backs who were better than Bettis. We couldn't quite hear him on the sideline when it happened, but it fired us up, and we were all yelling "Yeah, yeah, yeah!"

My last thought before the game began was that while Pittsburgh came in known for their defense, I felt that our defense would have to carry our team. I felt as if we had been doing that toward the end of the season, once we began winning. If we were to continue to win at this point, we had to keep doing it defensively. The defense always seemed to inspire the offense and act as a momentum starter.

After we won the toss and elected to receive, Pittsburgh kicked the ball into the end zone for a touchback. We started from the twenty and promptly took a five-yard penalty on our first play. On the second play they blitzed and sacked Brady for a three-yard loss. Then Antowain ran up the middle and was stopped for no gain. Quite an auspicious beginning. On the next play, however, Brady showed he didn't have a case of the jitters because he promptly completed a pass to Troy on the left side for fifteen yards. It wasn't a first down, but it did get our backs a little farther away from the wall. Ken Walter got off a strong kick, and they had to start from their own twenty-eight. When they went three-and-out, our defense had made its first statement of the day.

Then Troy Brown made his first statement, returning Josh Miller's punt twenty-five yards to our forty-five-yard line. The offense still couldn't move, getting the ball only to midfield before Walter had to punt again. The good thing was his kick pushed them all the way back to the eleven. A pair of penalties on our defense helped them get a couple of first downs, but they stalled at the thirty-nine and had to punt again. This time we started from our fifteen, moved out to the thirty-nine with Brady completing three passes, but now it was our turn to punt. Walter again got off a brilliant kick that left them at their own nine-yard line. So far our defense was doing its job. We had now backed them up close to their goal line on two possessions, and this time they couldn't move at all, getting only to the thirteen before a penalty pushed them back to their eight. Now Miller had to punt out of his end zone, and this time Troy Brown was ready.

Miller got off a good punt that Troy grabbed on our forty-five. He started to his left, stopped, did a quick stutter step, then burst right up the middle, taking them by surprise and running the ball into their end zone. Troy and our special teams had done it again, scoring with less than four minutes remaining in the period. Adam booted the extra point, and we had a 7–0 lead. This is what we wanted, to put the team that almost never trailed in a position where they had to play catch-up. One TD certainly won't shift them into panic mode, but at least it brings them to a place they haven't been too often.

In addition, it's a great confidence booster for us, almost like an extra bonus. Whenever you score via special teams or with your defense it's an extra, because the offense hasn't had that chance yet. You alter their game plan a bit, but your defense isn't affected. So we were all happy we got the points, but our objective remained the same: take away their running game and make Kordell throw the ball up the field.

I've got to admit that the Steelers responded well after our score. They started at their own twenty-four. Kordell completed a short pass to Dan Kreider for four yards, then did one of the things we feared. He carried the ball on a predesigned play and ran for thirty-four yards to our thirty-eight. We should have had him but missed at least three tackles. If I recall, Vrabel almost had him, but Kordell ran right out of his shoe, got away again, and completed the run with only one shoe on. Then they got another first down at our twenty-three. Stewart then completed a ten-yard pass to Matt Cushing as the first quarter ended, giving them the ball at our thirteen-yard line, putting them on our doorstep and seemingly ready to tie the game up.

On the next play Bettis rushed up the gut for four yards to the nine, but our defense tightened, and their next snap saw Anthony Pleasant break through and sack Kordell for a two-yard loss. After an incomplete pass Kris Brown came on and kicked a thirty-yard field goal, bringing the score to 7–3. However, I looked at this as a plus. We had fought off their best effort so far, especially after they gained big yards on a quarterback draw, and they came away with just three. We knew Stewart would have a couple of those, and everyone on the field had to be aware and ready to tackle him. We didn't want it to happen but didn't allow seven points to come of it either.

Our next possession produced a first down, but then we had to punt again. When they got the ball, I saw something that, to me, was significant. On a third-and-two play, they gave the ball to wide receiver Hines Ward on an end around. We stopped him for a two-yard loss. It was a trick play that didn't work, but they were already throwing the kitchen sink at us. They also couldn't know that stopping an end run is one of the plays we practice every Saturday, and we react well whenever it happens. To me, however, that also meant they were getting anxious about moving the ball and someone was worrying about them coming away with only a field goal on that drive into the red zone. They should have known that our red zone defense had been very strong during the last three-quarters of the season.

I already had the feeling that our defense had them pegged. Bettis was not going anywhere. We knew his most successful play was a weak-side run, and we had put special emphasis on stopping that. If we were successful, as we had been so far, that meant we were taking a significant part of their offensive game away. On our next drive we moved from our own twenty-two to the Pittsburgh forty before we had to punt once more. Brady completed a twenty-yarder to Troy, who was already having a great game but later in the drive was sacked for a loss of eleven. We punted to them not knowing that within a few minutes the mettle of our team would be tested once again.

There was just 3:39 left in the half when they got the ball at their own twenty. We were continuing to pin them deep in their territory, keeping them from starting a drive with good field position. It got even better when they went three-and-out, as we sandwiched a time-out in between. In fact we pushed them back three yards to the seventeen when they punted. This time Troy couldn't return Miller's kick, and we had to start at our thirty with less than three minutes remaining. After J. R. Redmond rushed up the middle for seven yards, Brady tried a second-down pass, but it fell incomplete. Then came a third-down play that will be remembered for a very long time. Brady dropped back again and fired a sharp pass straight down the middle. Troy caught it on the run and rambled for twenty-eight yards until he was tackled at the Steelers' forty. First down.

Only no one was celebrating. Tom Brady was slow to get up, and when he did he was noticeably limping on his left leg. Apparently, just after he released the ball, Lee Flowers had fallen on the back of his legs. I also think Tom had been nicked up a bit on either the preceding series or the one before that. Flowers's hit just made the injury worse. We took a time-out, and Brady limped off the field. Immediately Drew Bledsoe began warming up. He hadn't played a down since he was injured in the second week of the season. Now he was going to be called on in the most important game of the year, a game that could put us into the Super Bowl. Normally, when the starting quarterback goes down, the other team immediately feels it has the advantage. Only in this case we were confident that we had the best backup quarterback in the entire league. It was a storybook situation for Drew. The only way it could have been better was if it had happened in the Super Bowl.

Of course, Drew still had to perform. He had been throwing well in practice since before the Miami game and, since his injury, had been the perfect professional athlete. In practice, in meetings, hanging out with the guys, he didn't change one lick. He joked with everybody, high-fived Brady after touchdowns, was always talking to Tom, giving him advice. He also continued to work out hard. Knowing he had lost twenty pounds after his injury had to make him feel a little different. By the time we played Pittsburgh he was looking physically a lot more like the old Drew. When he began warming up, you could have put a cape on his shoulders. This, incidentally, was exactly what Coach Belichick was thinking about when he decided to name Brady the starter for the remainder of the season. It was the secondary part of the decision, the knowledge that if we needed him in exactly this kind of situation, Drew would be ready to perform like the All-Pro quarterback he had been.

Like I said, the media had tried to separate the team after the quarterback decision. It was always "Which one do you like better?" But in this situation, against Pittsburgh, Drew was the perfect quarterback to stop the Steelers defense from taking so many gambles, from blitzing like crazy, because they know he likes to take chances and can throw the ball down the field with the best of them. In addition to that, he had a great deal to prove to a lot of people when he entered the game. I just hoped he wasn't too excited, too fired up. None of us wanted him to try to prove too much too quickly. As it turns out, he was perfectly focused, had his mind set on letting everyone know he was back and he was tougher. On his very first snap he dropped back and completed a fifteen-yard pass to David Patten on the right side for a first down at the Steelers' twenty-five. Now everybody was riding high with him.

Then, on the next play, what does he do? He runs to the right sideline, gains about four yards, and just as he's ready to go out of bounds he takes a blow from a defensive back, almost a carbon copy of the play in which Mo Lewis injured him. In fact, when he was hit, he went farther than he had when Lewis hit him. From where I was standing, I couldn't see the whole thing, but my heart stopped for a second. You've got to remember something: you cannot prepare a quarterback for being hit. No one beats up on him in practice, so all the bumps and bruises come in the games. I don't know if Drew wanted to test himself or it was just his adrenaline flowing. I remember how I was when I played. On the first play of the game I had to hit somebody. I think Drew had to get that bump out. Maybe it was just what he needed to get himself loose, to restore all his confidence. After my heart stopped for that second, I saw him pop up and start running back to the huddle, and I knew he was all right.

From the twenty-one, Drew dropped back and hit Patten again, this time on the left side, for a gain of ten to the eleven-yard line. He wasn't wasting any time. Once again he set up to throw and this time found Patten in the end zone for a touchdown. Talk about a dramatic entrance! Everyone was jumping up and down on the sideline, totally pumped. Drew had come in, completed three passes, taken a big hit while gaining four yards, and led us to our second touchdown of the game. Adam's kick made it 14–3, and now the Steelers really had to play catch-up—just the position we wanted them to be in.

With just fifty seconds left before halftime, they tried to make a statement. Stewart completed three passes to bring the ball from their twenty-eight to our thirty-four. They took a time-out with twenty-three seconds remaining, but then we tightened. Stewart missed on his next throw, and a penalty against them brought the ball back to the forty-four. After another incompletion he tried to go upstairs one more time, maybe hoping to get his team into field goal range. Not now. There was Terrell Buckley, the big play guy, intercepting the pass to shut down the drive. Time ran out, and we went into the locker room with the lead that we had wanted.

In the locker room the first question was whether Brady would come back. With Drew coming on and playing so well, there wasn't a huge concern. Had it been the Super Bowl, or if Drew wasn't playing well, Tom might have been able to come back, but he was still hobbling. He couldn't move very well, and while he might have taken some snaps, I think it would have been ugly. Obviously it was Coach Belichick who had the last say, made the final decision. It was a situation where he would talk to the trainer first, but we all pretty much knew that Drew would be going back out. We were leading, 14–3, and were determined to maintain control. Now we wanted to see them squirm, something they weren't used to doing. Some of the things we talked about were keeping Kordell from getting loose and exciting the crowd with a long run and keeping Bettis from breaking anything. The showman-type mentality feeds off the crowd. If we continued to humble them, hold them to two yards here, five yards there, we knew we would prevail. Without big plays we felt we had them just where we wanted them.

Opening the third quarter, we knew that they wanted to score quickly. They didn't want to put together long, time-consuming drives. So they would have to go for the jugular while we were going for the kill. In the second half, we were almost sabotaged by penalties, but fortunately we also kept making big plays. That pattern began immediately. We kicked to them with the ball coming out to the Steelers' twenty-five. Two plays later Stewart hit Hines Ward for a thirteen-yard gain, but on the next play Stewart fumbled the snap and Tedy Bruschi, always the opportunist, made the recovery. With a first down at their thirty-five, we had a chance to really put them in a hole, but Drew cooled down a bit. He completed a short pass for three yards but missed on his next three attempts, and we turned the ball over on downs at the thirty-two. I guess we could have tried a field goal, but it would have been at the outer edge of Adam's range. We could also have punted and tried to stick them inside the ten, but Belichick opted to go for it and maybe put another stamp on the envelope.

Now came a crucial sequence of downs with a series of plays that could have swung the game one way or the other. Stewart started the Steelers' drive by completing a fifteen-yard pass to Burress, bringing the ball to the forty-seven. Bettis then carried twice but got just four yards. We were still holding him down, but Stewart then threw to Troy Edwards for a seven-yard gain and another first down at our forty-two. Now it became interesting. On the next play Stewart threw again, and Tebucky Jones intercepted the pass. Next thing you know, we're all up and cheering as Tebucky brought the ball into Steelers territory, which would have given us great field position. Upfield, however, there was a flag, and the ref was calling for the ball. Unfortunately, Anthony Pleasant had jumped offsides. Nonplay. Talk about taking the wind out of our sails . . . and putting it back into theirs.

Now we had to regroup quickly, because Stewart was ready to throw once more. He fired the ball at Burress, but Otis moved quickly and broke up the play with a hard hit. Flag again. This time they called defensive pass interference, giving the Steelers a first down at our twenty-one-yard line. Eric Mangini, our defensive backs coach, was getting on Otis for taking the penalty, telling him not to get another. I could see Otis was steamed, and he began to walk away. I grabbed him quickly and said, "Otis, just calm down. Stay calm." He just snapped back, "I'm not letting anyone push me around." I knew just what he was talking about. That was the way Plaxico Burress worked. He's too big and strong for most defensive backs. They'll fight him for a while, then quit, and that's when he starts making plays. So I told Otis that he was the only one who could stand up to Burress and fight him, and if he didn't do it Burress would catch ten passes. He just had to be careful and try not to have interference called at the wrong time. I knew Otis would keep doing the job, because he's the kind of guy who never gives in.

Now, however, they were knocking on the door. A touchdown and extra point would make it a 14–10 game, putting them right back in it. So we dug in. Stewart managed a five-yard run between two incomplete passes, giving them a fourth-and-five at our sixteen. Time for the field goal unit. Kris Brown was on to try it, and if that's all they got from the drive, then it was another plus for us, but our defense wasn't about to concede anything. Brandon Mitchell, our defensive end, told special teams coach Brad Seely that he thought he could get penetration on the kick. Seely told him to go for it. It was a play we practiced every week. One guy, in this case Brandon Mitchell, is designated to try to block the kick. Linebacker Tedy Bruschi would set up behind Mitchell and literally push him toward the kicker. At the snap Mitchell charged and Bruschi pushed. Sure enough, Mitchell blocked the kick and it rolled free. But hold on, it wasn't over yet. Our playmaker, Troy Brown, scooped the ball up and started to run. Kris Brown, their kicker, had already built up a head of steam and was about to run Troy down. Antwan Harris was running right behind Troy, hoping to block for him, and when he saw Kris Brown zeroing in, he called out. Troy pitched the ball back to Antwan, who ran the remainder of the distance to the end zone, the second touchdown produced by our special teams. Remember how much emphasis Coach Belichick had put on special teams all year? It was certainly worth it, wasn't it? Antwan said later that all he saw was the goal line and that he was running so hard he thought he would pull a hamstring. Adam's kick made it 21–3 after what was perhaps the most definitive sequence of the afternoon. But with nearly nine minutes left in the third quarter, the game was far from over.

After the kickoff they had the ball at the twenty-one, and this time they responded to the challenge. After an eleven-yard gain by Bettis with a short screen, Stewart dropped back and hit Hines Ward for twenty-four yards, a helluva catch that brought the ball to our forty-four-yard line. Three plays later he completed a short pass to running back Amos Zereoue, who turned it into a nineteen-yard gain. Like I said, we don't mind the short stuff, but once in a while a runner or receiver will break one. OK. That you have to accept, as long as it doesn't happen too often. From the twenty-four, Stewart threw to Ward for nine more, then, uncharacteristically, we committed two straight penalties in the red zone. The first was a roughing call after Ward's catch, and the second illegal use of the hands by Bobby Hamilton. That gave them a first-and-goal from the four. Zereoue gained three, then Bettis took it in from the one. The touchdown call was questionable. I thought we stopped him, but Belichick didn't want to challenge it and use up a replay in case he needed one later. The kick made it 21–10. Now I had to wonder if they were inching their way back into it. Time would tell, and that time came quickly.

We got a solid kickoff return of thirty-five yards by Patrick Pass that gave us the ball at the Steelers' thirty-four and should have ignited a fire. The quickest way, however, to douse a fire is to go three-and-out. Throw in a five-yard penalty and a ten-yard sack, and suddenly we were punting from the twenty-two. Now our special teams faltered a bit when Troy Edwards returned Ken Walter's punt twenty-eight yards, giving them the ball at our thirty-two. It was a sudden change in momentum, and a good team won't let that chance slip away. Stewart completed three of four passes, bringing the ball to the eleven, and Amos Zereoue ran it in from there. They had scored twice in about a four-minute span and were definitely back in it after Kris Brown's point after made it 21–17. We had pretty much worked them over for two and a half quarters, and suddenly they had scored back-to-back touchdowns. Now we needed some help from the offense, because you don't want the defense back on the field after a one-two-three-out. If that happened and they got hit again, they were going to start feeling as if they were breaking down.

On the sidelines we were encouraging everyone, telling them that a couple of key penalties had hurt and they had to expect to give up a couple of plays during the course of the game. If we didn't have those two straight penalties in the red zone, we might have held them to another field goal. Now, as I said, we wanted the offense to go out and build something, to hold on to the ball and not sputter. In fact this was probably their most important possession of the game. Patrick Pass set the tone again with another solid return, bringing the kickoff back twenty-seven yards to the twenty-nine. If there was going to be pressure on Drew to produce, that time was now.

After an incomplete pass across the middle, he went right back up top and hit Charles Johnson for fifteen yards and a first down. We took a five-yard penalty, and then Drew connected again, this time with Troy for thirteen more as the third quarter ended. Now there were fifteen minutes left, the most important quarter of our season. Antowain started it by running three yards for a first down at the Pittsburgh forty-five. He carried twice more for seven yards before Drew completed a six-yard pass to Marc Edwards, giving us a first down at the thirty-two. The drive was serving two purposes as it also allowed the defense to regroup. The offense was doing exactly what we needed, holding the ball. Two carries by J. R. Redmond netted just six yards, and an incomplete pass on third down brought Adam onto the field to try a forty-four-yard field goal. This was important because it would increase our lead to seven points, and whenever kicks are big, Adam seems to make them. No exception here. He split the uprights, and we were up, 24–17, with just over eleven minutes left.

Now we had a little more breathing room since they needed a touchdown to tie it. They started from their own thirty-three. Bettis tried the middle for no gain. We continued to bottle him up as we had all afternoon. Stewart didn't go there again. Instead he connected with Burress for fifteen and a first down at the Pittsburgh forty-eight. He came right back and hit Hines Ward for nine more, but on the next play Burress was called for a penalty on Otis, who had continued to battle him on every play. A pass to Ward netted just five, followed by an incompletion, and they had to punt again. Now the clock was starting to become a factor. Miller kicked to us with about eight and a half minutes left. Not only didn't we return the punt, but we were called for a penalty that put the ball back at the nine. We were in potential trouble here unless we got some yards.

A pair of clutch passes from Drew to Marc Edwards and Jermaine Wiggins gave us a first down at the twenty. After an incomplete and a sack that lost a yard, Drew had a big third-down play. He dropped back and went to old reliable, Troy Brown, who grabbed it and ran for an eighteen-yard gain before he was stopped. First down at our thirty-seven. Now, at least, we didn't have our backs against the wall. Lucky thing, too, because the drive stalled right there, and we had to kick. Ken Walter kicked it high, and Troy Edwards managed just a one-yard return to the twenty-two. So they were seventy-eight yards away with just 4:21 left. Now it was time for the defense to step up. It was no secret what would happen here. We knew Stewart would have to come out throwing. Time to establish a running game was long gone. We hadn't allowed them to run, and, as I said earlier, I didn't think that Kordell Stewart was as good a pure passer as Tom Brady. So, in essence, we had them just where we wanted at this stage of the game.

Stewart went up top immediately and connected with Plaxico Burress for an eleven-yard gain and a first down. Their fans let out a roar, hoping this was the start of something. We didn't flinch, however. On the next play we blanketed the receivers, and when Stewart tried to run, we nailed him for a one-yard loss. His next pass was good for just three yards to Jerame Tuman. Remember, give them the small stuff. That set up a third-and-eight, and now we were ready. Kordell dropped back again and threw over the middle. As he had done so many times during the year, Tebucky Jones read the pass and was in the right spot at the right time. As soon as he grabbed it he was hit hard, spun around, then continued running. He returned it nineteen yards to the Steelers' thirty-four-yard line. Later Tebucky told me he was hit so hard he got dizzy and for the last eighteen yards of his nineteen-yard return he didn't know where he was going.

Fortunately, it was in the right direction. Now we had the ball with 2:41 left, and we were in their territory. Antowain carried twice but gained just two yards. Because the clock was running down, the Steelers were using their time-outs, the second one coming with 2:27 left. Bledsoe then tried a pass, but it was incomplete. With the ball at the thirty-two, Coach Belichick decided to send Adam into the game. In the exact situation earlier in the game, he had chosen to go for it on fourth down. Now he wanted Adam to try a fifty-yard field goal. As I said, that was outside his usual range, but if he made it the game would be on ice. If he missed, they would still have sixty-eight yards to go with just over two minutes left. It was a good gamble, though this time the kick went wide left, even though it had the distance. I always felt that if we had needed that field goal to tie or win, he would have made it. Adam Vinatieri has a way of doing that.

Out came Stewart and the Steeler offense once more, and out to meet them came a Patriots defense that loved these situations. Our confidence was sky-high, and everyone was looking now to finish the job. It took just two plays. Stewart's first pass was incomplete. On the second he dropped back and looked for the big guy, Plaxico Burress. Otis was underneath him, where he had been all afternoon. With the big receiver out there and knowing Otis's ability, Stewart threw high. Only this time he threw it too high. It sailed over

Burress's head and into the hands of Lawyer Milloy, who was playing behind him in case Burress had made the catch. Lawyer returned it eleven yards to midfield. With 2:02 remaining, we had the ball again, and now we were all pumped.

Time to kill the clock, and, as usual, Antowain Smith came up big. He was the icer. With the ball at the fifty, he was stopped for a loss of a yard. On the next play, however, he burst over the right side of the line, powered his way into the secondary, and ran for nineteen huge yards, bringing it all the way to the Steelers' thirty-two. They called a time-out with 1:42 left, but we all knew the numbers. With a first down, all Drew had to do was take a knee three times and let the clock run out. While he was doing that, the celebration began on the sideline. The clock ticked away for the Steelers as it officially crowned the New England Patriots AFC Champions! We had beaten them, 24–17.

Now it was payback time for the guys. They were screaming at the fans, telling them to cancel their Super Bowl reservations: "Call me at Foxboro. I can use your reservation." This was so exciting. I got a real big kick out of the Raiders game because we needed that one to push on, but beating Pittsburgh in their backyard was a double high. When I played in Cleveland in 1994 and we had a chance to do something, we lost to them three times. Our team, however, had really done the job of putting them away. I was just so happy for the players, watching them jump around. They rolled out a stage for the presentation ceremony as Mr. Kraft and Coach Belichick went up to receive the AFC Championship trophy. At the same time, I remember the Steelers' Joey Porter yelling that he wanted to fight Bobby Hamilton. Losing isn't always easy, is it?

A few minutes later came the part I really enjoyed. Remember before the game, when I found the T-shirt that said "Pittsburgh, AFC Champions"? When we got to the locker room, I grabbed that shirt off the blackboard and threw it on the floor. Then I told everyone who came in to step on it, and that's what they did, one after another, stepping on that shirt. There was a big storage room right next to our locker room, and in it they had boxes and boxes of the shirts. They must have planned to give those bad boys away after the game. When we were coming in, there were guys on forklifts with the door open, putting the crates of shirts back in the storage room. I grabbed Lawyer and told him they were all Pittsburgh's AFC title shirts, and he said they would make a great bonfire.

When Coach Belichick came into the locker room, he followed everyone by stepping on the shirt. Otherwise he was Belichick, short and blunt, right to the point. He said he was happy about another total team effort, but we still had more business ahead. He told everyone he would have itineraries ready on the flight back to New England. "Let's shower and get out of here," he basically said to the team. So we left that night for the return to Foxboro. Before we left, however, we heard an interview with Kordell Stewart in which he said the best team doesn't always win. That just let us know how much it had really hurt them, that we had really shocked them with our victory, and that, too, made us feel good.

There was something else, however. When I heard his remark, I felt that Kordell didn't really understand professional football. Maybe on paper the best team didn't win, but football isn't like baseball, basketball, or hockey. Championships are not decided by a best-of-seven series. In pro football it's one day. It's how well a team comes together on that given day. You have one chance, one opportunity to make a play. I still live with the personal demons from Super Bowl XXV, when the Giants were playing Buffalo and I ran Jim Kelly down from behind during the last drive. When I was chasing him, the question went through my head as to whether I should try to strip the ball or make the tackle. I chose to make the tackle. To this day I wonder what might have happened if Scott Norwood had made that field goal. If I had stripped him, there wouldn't have been a field goal try. If I missed . . . I had played for the security of the game, not the gamble. I still think about that today. That's what I mean by one opportunity to make a play. We made the plays against the Steelers. It didn't really matter which was the better overall team. On this day the better team was the New England Patriots.

Everyone had played a role in the victory. Before he was injured, Tom Brady completed twelve of eighteen passes for 115 yards. He was on his way to a fine game. Then Drew came in and connected on ten of twenty-one for 102 yards and that important touchdown. He did it while under a tremendous amount of pressure and was playing for the first time in three months. Antowain gained just forty-seven yards but had a big run at the end. Troy Brown had eight receptions for 121 yards and had that great punt return. Special teams had been outstanding, and our defense came up big whenever it had to. Otis and Ty held their big receivers in check, while Tebucky, Lawyer, and Terrell Buckley all had interceptions. Again, a total team effort.

On the flight back to New England I felt it was time to share my experiences as a player with some of the guys because this was the time it would have the most relevance. We were now going to be getting ready for the ultimate show, the game's biggest stage, and that was one reason I was there. I had bed check in Pittsburgh, and the coach with bed check always sits in the back of the plane coming and going. If a defensive coach is back there, then an offensive coaching assistant sits back there with him. Ned Burke was there, and we take care of any player's needs or questions.

I had a whole group around me—Rod Rutledge, Kevin Faulk, Bryan Cox, Bobby Hamilton, Brandon Mitchell, Fred Coleman, Roman Phifer, Mike Vrabel, Jermaine Wiggins, Leonard Myers, maybe a couple of others. I told them about sacrificing just a few days of their lives and not being seduced by the distractions they would find in New Orleans. Everyone said, "Yeah, sure," and I said I didn't have a crystal ball and wasn't going to tell them that if they partied we wouldn't win the Super Bowl. Then I reminded them what we had been saying all year about taking care of business and asked them how they would feel if they didn't have the energy they wanted come game day. They could party all they wanted if they won the Super Bowl.

How often do you see guys proudly wearing AFC Championship rings, I asked them? That's embarrassing. They're wearing AFC rings because they didn't win the Super Bowl. To me, I said, Carolina winning just one game all year isn't as bad as our losing the Super Bowl. People will forget faster that Carolina won just a single game than that we lost the Super Bowl. I can reel off the names of every Super Bowl winner and loser, I told them, but I can't tell you which team had the worst record all those years. I also wore my Super Bowl rings, and on the plane Bobby Hamilton took them and walked up and down the aisle, showing them to all the players. This is what it's all about. Winning or losing, the Super Bowl is priceless, but you want to do everything that is possible to win it. The entire team wasn't there to hear me, but enough of them were so that I knew the message would get out to the others. Oh, yes, it certainly would.

12

A Victory for the Ages

When we defeated the Steelers, I think we upset not only the odds but a lot of people as well. I really had the feeling that nearly everyone in the media, as well as the commissioner of the National Football League, wanted a Steelers–Rams clash in the Super Bowl. These were considered the league's marquee teams, both exciting, with the Greatest Show on Turf Rams butting heads with "The Bus," Kordell Stewart, and the Blitzburg defense. That was the matchup that was most conducive to the pregame hype, would generate the greatest amount of interest and undoubtedly the highest televisions ratings. Then along came the lowly Patriots to upset the apple cart. The Rams were still there, however, and, not surprisingly, installed as heavy favorites, even though we had given them a good game early in the season. In fact, I think the knowledge that we had played them tough and felt we could have beaten them gave us an early boost of confidence as we began to get ready.

Ever since I was young, the concept of the Super Bowl has been attractive to me. It has the ultimate *right now* feeling. Sudden death. Do or die. One game for the championship. In that respect the Super Bowl is always a game seven. Football being a more physical and vigorous sport than the others, I think the entire concept excites the nation, and that's why so many people watch every year. New Orleans was an ideal site for this kind of event, only this year there was a big commotion because the original date had been pushed back a week due to the events of September 11th. Now everyone in the city was scrambling because a lot of reservations had to be changed, from hotels to car rentals, not to mention that the Super Bowl had overlapped with Mardi Gras.

When it comes to the playoffs, I always felt the guys who made the difference were those who were the hungriest, often the guys who were playing not only for a championship but for the financial incentives. We were already used to playing with everything on the line, and a good number of our play-ers—especially the free agents—had incentives in their contracts. In 1990 I damn near doubled my base salary in incentives when the team won the Super Bowl and I made the Pro Bowl, so I could identify with these guys. They hadn't come this far to lose.

The players came in about 1:00 P.M. on Monday to load up the buses for the trip to the airport and left for New Orleans later that day, accompanied by Coach Belichick. The assistant coaches stayed behind and didn't leave until Tuesday night. We had to remain because all our computers and the Advid system were at Foxboro. We needed the equipment to work on our game plan. Every NFL team sends some video equipment and computers to the Super Bowl site. Once we arrived there, we had Jets cameras in our defensive meet-ing room and equipment from Kansas City in the linebackers room. Every-thing had been set up by our video man, Jimmy Dee, who had gone down early. This is done because the teams still playing can't break down all their own equipment in a day and get it to the city hosting the game.

Now we were facing our ultimate challenge: the Rams. Tedy Bruschi made a comment right before we played the Jets for the second time that I had never forgotten. He referred to the remaining part of our season as *Godfather II*. He said we had to take care of the family business. That meant taking care of the Jets, Buffalo, Miami, settling all matters within our division. That's where we had to have the better record during the regular season. The other teams, the Raiders and Steelers, didn't fall under the heading of family business. They hadn't done anything to us, but we had to take care of them as well so we could reach the final team on the checklist—the Rams.

It's crazy, but when the players left for New Orleans on Monday I truly missed them. It was only for a day, but it seemed like three or four. It was as if my kids had suddenly been taken from me. When we finally arrived, every-one was hugging and high-fiving each other. It really felt as if we had all gone down there on a mission and with a common goal. We were there to take care of the family business and do it as a team. A couple of the players approached me and reminded me what I had told them on the plane. They told me they didn't have a curfew Monday night, the only night there wouldn't be one, but they had stayed in anyway. A few of them visited with family, then returned to the hotel. After Monday, however, family and friends can be distractions, and we want to alleviate that as much as possible, so everyone stays together.

Tuesday of Super Bowl week is always media day. Everyone is obligated to do interviews, even the assistant coaches, who rarely do them during the year. Then Tuesday night we met with the players and began work in earnest. There was a midnight curfew that night and an 11:00 P.M. curfew the remainder of the week. The coaches' work began on Monday after the players left. We went over our first meeting with the Rams very carefully, evaluating them as we did every opponent throughout the year. We looked at the things we'd done right, those we'd done wrong, what we hadn't done enough, and what we could have done better. Of course, the defensive coaches were looking for ways to stop them, defend them better than we had the first time around.

We knew full well that they ran multiple offenses with skilled personnel, using a lot of shifts and motions. They did it, however, without a pattern, without rhyme or reason. Some teams have a formation and then shift to another formation. The Rams' preshift formation didn't fit their offensive scheme or the plays they ran. It was almost as if their offensive team was free to line up wherever they wanted before the shift. They knew where they had to end up, so the look before the shift was meaningless. If we say on offense, for example, red formation, shift, blue formation, we actually have a red formation. They have a dummy formation, shift to blue, the formation from which they run a play. That makes them very difficult to defend.

If the Rams used a regular offense setup, with two running backs, two wide receivers, and a tight end, then we would play a regular defensive alignment. However, if they brought in an extra wide receiver, we would counter with an extra defensive back. Our strategy was to react to whatever they did. Because we had blitzed so much in the first game with them, we decided to bluff this time. When we did decide to blitz, we were able to disguise it very well because they were looking for the same kind of blitz formations from the first game. At the same time, we didn't want to play new defenses that would confuse our guys. When the Rams went through all their shifts and motions, our guys would have to adjust. The easiest way to do that was to play man to man, have the defender stick with his man wherever he goes, or sometimes play a zone, where the defenders stay in the zone no matter what they do.

We also felt we hadn't been as physical in our first meeting as we should have been, especially against their go-to guys, like Marshall Faulk, Isaac Bruce, Torry Holt, and Ricky Proehl. Things happen for a reason. Perhaps we just didn't have a good enough game plan to win that first game, but that made for a better situation in the Super Bowl. Now we were playing for a lot more than we had that Sunday night in November. We decided that week not to try to outsmart them, rather just to go out and let the guys be physical. In the first game our strategy was to blitz from the back side, try to make Kurt Warner get rid of the ball early or hit him. They picked some up, and when Warner got rid of the ball early, he did it successfully. Playing at Foxboro in November, they had a cold-weather game plan. They threw a lot of short passes early on, and that helped negate our blitzing. It wasn't so much that they adjusted to the blitz as it was that they were making plays, like that long drive after Antowain's fumble. They made the plays, and we didn't.

We worked very hard Monday at Foxboro on the game plan so that we were a little ahead of ourselves, which was good, because we knew when we reached New Orleans that the schedule and media obligations on Tuesday would be heavy. We needed to get as much done as possible on Monday and Tuesday morning before we left. Then we gave the game plan to the players on Wednesday. Creating a game plan for the Rams was not easy. They had excellent offensive weapons and, like I said, knew how to move them around. Isaac Bruce was the ringleader of the receivers. Marshall Faulk could line up as a wide receiver instead of a running back and be just as successful. Many feel he is the best offensive player in the game today. I'll tell you one thing: Marshall is not a nice guy on the football field. He has a toughness about him to go with his many skills, and that's what separates him from other talented players.

We were all in agreement that we were gonna "butch" Marshall Faulk. That meant our outside pass rusher would shove him as he was coming out of the backfield without the ball on a pass play. Many times the running back likes to clip the defensive end, and we weren't going to let him do that. It's the same strategy the Giants used against Buffalo running back Thurman Thomas in Super Bowl XXV. We would sacrifice something from the pass rush to block the running back. If Faulk were to run real wide, then the defensive back would simply cover him. If he ran a route through the line, the orders were if he came close to you, you hit him. You hit Faulk first, then you went after Warner. It's legal to hit him within five yards of the line of scrimmage. The purpose of it was to frustrate him and also to slow him down on pass routes.

What we also didn't want was our linebackers to be caught moving backward to stop twenty-yard in-cuts while Warner dumped the ball off to Marshall with room to run. That was the last thing we wanted. By bumping him, the linebackers have more time to read the pass route. A linebacker can cover a stumbling Marshall Faulk, but not a Marshall Faulk coming out of the backfield at full speed. I remember a good friend of mine, someone who had played football with me, noticing that. He had seen Marshall running out of the backfield at full tilt and getting open, but then he saw that in our regular-season game Marshall was being slowed at the line before he could take off. I'm always glad to hear something like that from someone who knows football.

In fact there was a play caught on our highlight tape. Marshall was near our sideline when one of their passes went incomplete on the other side. Before the play stopped, Mike Vrabel hit him in the back and knocked him down. He popped up, looked left and right, then uppercut Mike in the chin. I told you he had a mean streak on the field. Vrabel, however, just kept walking and talking to him. Marshall had punched the right guy. If he had punched Lawyer, there would have been a fight on the sidelines. If he had punched Bruschi, a fight on the sidelines. Vrabel had a different approach. He knew we were getting to him and probably kept talking trash to him, saying something sarcastic.

We would keep the same aggressive approach against the Rams the second time around. The night before the game I told the guys that we were putting all the Rams on "butch" call. We had to hit everybody, all the time and all game long. I also told them—and this came from my experience with the Jets—that I didn't want to see anyone knock a guy down and then have someone else from our team come over and help him up. There's nothing worse when you're trying to implement the intimidation factor and someone on your team helps an opponent up. To me, you're showing you're scared. To help a guy up hurts you more than it helps. I can remember when I played at Ohio State, Earl Bruce, our coach, wanted us to help guys up. He thought it was the sporting thing to do. So I got to talking trash while I was picking them up. I would tell them, "Get up, don't stay on the ground, get back into the huddle and get the ball again. That way I can knock you down again."

But I also remembered the AFC title game the Jets played with Denver in 1998. We were knocking them down and talking trash, but Victor Green and Corwin Brown kept helping them up. Too many times. They were really hurting me so badly when they continued to do that. I recall asking Mo Lewis, "Did you see that?" Everyone doesn't have my philosophy, of course, but an awful lot of people came up to me after the Super Bowl and said that there were a bunch of Pepper Johnsons out on the field against the Rams. That made me feel good.

Another question before the game was, once again, which of our quarterbacks would start. Many people felt Drew should continue after his showing against the Steelers, that he was back and would have the best chance to lead us to the title. Tom Brady, however, had made a rapid recovery from his ankle sprain, which was relatively mild. Once again Coach Belichick made his decision early and decisively. He named Brady the starter with Bledsoe pitching relief, if necessary. Again, the thinking was that Drew would have a little more fire coming off the bench than Tom. In addition, to bench a healthy Brady at this time would appear to be a demotion. As always, Belichick was trying to do everything he could to avoid a controversy as well as a potentially divisive issue.

There were already many stories in the papers about what the Patriots would do with Drew in the upcoming off season. That started as soon as the playoffs began. Everyone was scratching the surface to stir up something. Our feeling was to let Brady finish out what he had started. Any question about our quarterbacks and their future would have to happen after Sunday. Once again, Drew did everything he could to prepare to play in the Super Bowl if he was called on, while Tom did everything possible to stay in there and win a Super Bowl. Drew threw the ball when he could. He got a few more offensive snaps in practice than the backup normally would. Instead of Brady getting a large majority of snaps in a twelve-snap sequence, Bledsoe would get four. Normally he might get only two.

Offensively we wanted to force the Rams' linebackers to make open-field tackles. I don't think their unit was as weak as the Raiders', but we knew they had missed a number of tackles in the open field. Most of all, however, we wanted them to play our game. Belichick said exactly that before we even left Foxboro. "We're not going to get in a shootout with them," he said, "scampering around like chickens with our heads off, trying to match their speed or trying to match them score for score." Do that, and we come up short. We all knew that. So no matter what happened, we had to make them play our game. One thing we needed was a running game. Antowain had to come up big so we could control the pace and keep the offense on the field.

As I said, it was really a blessing for us that we had played them during the regular season. We didn't feel we were cooking on all cylinders defensively in that game. We had guys banged up then and were a much different defense from the one they would be facing in the Super Bowl. We really believed that. Offensively we had success moving the ball against them in that first game and just didn't capitalize on that early advantage. We went into a funk after Antowain's fumble and their subsequent ninety-seven-yard drive. We planned for the Super Bowl with the feeling that twenty-one points would win it for us. If they got to thirty points, chances of our winning would be slim and none. The Rams are streak shooters who like to fast-break. They can score easily a couple of series in a row, then just when you think they're done they hit you with yet another bomb. They can also put together long drives, like they did against us the first time, and have so many different guys who can make the big play for them. There's so much you have to take away from them to be successful.

Then, wouldn't you know it, when *ESPN The Magazine* came out that week, there was Kurt Warner on the cover. Wow. That's the trifecta. First Tim Brown and Jerry Rice, then Kordell Stewart, now Warner. Every team we played against in the playoffs had their star on the cover of a magazine. None of our players made it. Yet we kept winning. Once again, the magazine cover was right up there on our bulletin board. An omen? We would find out. There was another one as well. During the week our team was staying at the Fairmont Hotel. I found out that every year New Orleans had hosted the Super Bowl the team that stayed at the Fairmont had won the game. That was fine with me. The last time the Patriots went to the Super Bowl in New Orleans was in 1996. They didn't stay at the Fairmont that time.

Before the game some of the veteran players spoke briefly. But it was nothing out of the ordinary, just the same routine we used before all our games. Bobby Hamilton and Otis Smith went around the locker room high-fiving teammates. So did Bryan Cox and Lawyer Milloy. Even though it was the Super Bowl, our guys were treating it as business as usual. RAC went over the key reminders for the defense. Stick to the game plan. Don't crack if they make a big play. Coach Belichick had reminded us at the coaches' meeting that we, too, had to keep our cool, that we couldn't lose our composure on the sidelines, but it didn't hit me until the game started that it was imperative for me to stay calm.

That's because I was totally psyched. I think I would have paid someone a couple of thousand dollars just to let me wear the uniform for a play or two. It's funny, but up until the Raiders game I had kind of calmed down. I wasn't as bad as I had been in 2000. With more responsibility this past year, I started living more through the guys, became more relaxed as the season wore on. Then came the Raiders game in the snow. That brought back all kinds of memories. I remembered growing up with snow in Detroit. When school was called off because of a snowstorm, we would go out and play football all day long. So snow always meant football to me in those early years. I lived three doors from the freeway. While they were building it, we would play tackle on the dirt piles because the park was too far away. Normally we would play tackle on the grass and touch on cement, but when there was a bad snowstorm, it was tackle everywhere, even on the street when it was deep enough.

The Raiders game also took me back in history to the classic Vikings–Packers battles played out on snow-covered fields. That was something I had looked forward to when I came into the NFL. I told the players, especially the guys from the warm-weather states, who couldn't relate to playing in the snow, that they had an opportunity now, and there would be kids watching them who would look forward to games like these in the future. All this came back to me before the Raiders game and, along with it, the urge to play. I knew I couldn't play, of course, but I began feeling that same kind of wild excitement I used to get before big games, and as a coach I had to keep my composure.

A perfect example of how pumped I used to get was my first Super Bowl as a rookie in 1986. I was so excited that they said I had a concussion in the second quarter. Yet no one had hit me. I remember talking to another linebacker and saying I couldn't remember the defense. He told the head trainer, who began asking me questions, and they actually held me out a couple of series. Even today I can't remember the play when George Martin sacked Elway for a safety. I've seen it on tape, but don't remember even though I was on the field. That's how pumped I was. I never wore a neck roll when I played, but if you see the tape of me dancing with William Roberts after the game, I had a neck roll on. I don't remember who put it on me or when. Even my mother didn't remember my hitting my head. They explained later that it was the result of my being so excited and caught up in the game.

By 1990 I was one of the leaders on the team and one of the guys who helped carry the defense. Coach Belichick, who was the Giants' defensive coordinator then, put a lot of responsibility on my shoulders that season, and I knew I had to stay cool for him, that I couldn't allow myself to have one of those overexcited blackouts again. But before every game I still needed to run my head into somebody, hit someone on that first play. Now that I'm coaching, I had to keep telling myself the night before and the day of the game, right until the kickoff, "Pepper, do not go crazy." So I stayed in the locker room watching a DVD, a comedy, just to relax. Then I read the press guide, the game-day program. If I had sat there doing absolutely nothing, I would have become overly excited. I simply had to look around that locker room at the players and just allow it to wash over me again that I was coaching now, and these were my guys, players I had imposed my will on, and now I had to allow them to go out there and do it. That's when I realized I was finally able to pass the torch mentally, while watching them get ready to play. McGinest was stretching, Buckley jumping up and down, and I knew Pepper Johnson had to remain on an even keel.

So I tried to go into the extra-super-cool role, walking around and asking my guys if they were OK. They seemed to be at the moment, but it's not like you can see their chests busting through the shoulder pads. Belichick always stays true to form. Before he starts clapping his hands and giving a lively speech, he'll talk quietly about what got us here—hard work, implementing the game plan, playing our game and not our opponent's, not getting caught up in the hype, the screaming, the excitement of the event, and all the cameras. He told everyone it was business as usual. Speaking like that, he had a calming effect on the entire team. If he had become overly excited, the players would have been surprised and probably not quite as confident. Seeing a calm and businesslike Belichick gave everyone the impression that things were under control.

Then game time was here.

My final reminder to my guys before they went out was to make contact, whether or not a guy had the ball. Let every one of them know we were there. If a guy falls down after making a catch, I said, don't just touch him down; fall on him with all your weight. Hit, hit, hit. Do that, I told them, and we'll wear them down.

At game time the Rams were introduced first. Not surprisingly, their offensive unit got the individual attention, coming out one at a time, with Marshall Faulk and Kurt Warner hearing the loudest cheers as they ran through the long gauntlet. We, however, did it very differently. Even during the season, when we opted to come out as a unit instead of individuals, the non-starters and other units would join the cheerleaders in making a gauntlet. At the Super Bowl there was no gauntlet. Our entire team, to a man, came out together, as if to tell the entire world that, win or lose, the New England Patriots were going to do it as a team.

They won the toss and elected to receive. When Yo Murphy took Adam's kickoff at the one-yard line and promptly returned it thirty-eight yards, many people probably figured the rout would soon be on. Then Warner, on their second play from scrimmage, hit Torry Holt over the middle for eighteen yards, and they were already in our territory at the forty-three. Faulk then carried for the first time, and we stopped him for a gain of just one. That's what we had to do. A ten-yard penalty set them back, and on a third-and-nineteen Warner tossed a screen to Faulk, but we stopped him after just eleven yards. We were happy to give him the dump-off pass, knowing he wouldn't get the first down. Holding them was a great start for us. Had they driven right down the field and scored, it might have opened the floodgates, creating the kind of momentum that can make their offense look like a runaway train. Instead they had to punt.

Our first drive began at the three, our backs to the wall, but Tom Brady and Troy Brown quickly made a statement. Brady threw over the middle with Troy grabbing it and taking it out to the twenty-four, a twenty-one-yard gain. Then Antowain ran for nine yards and Brady threw to Troy again for ten more. We had our second first down at our own forty-three and had quickly shown we could move the ball. Then the drive stalled, and four plays later Ken Walter punted into the end zone, giving them the ball at the twenty. Neither team had drawn blood in the first series. When they got the ball, they began driving in small chunks—eight-yard pass, two-yard run, three-yard pass, three-yard run, eleven-yard pass. We would rather make them work like that then give it to them all at once.

But when Warner completed a fourteen-yard pass, they were in our territory at the thirty-nine. They moved it to the thirty-two, and Jeff Wilkins came on to boot a fifty-yard field goal, giving them the lead, 3–0. We knew Wilkins had the leg to make fifty-yarders, so we weren't shocked. As I said when we played the Steelers, it's much better to give up three than seven. On their drive we simply weren't putting together three solid defensive downs. We would play well for two, then give up a first-down play. Remember, to beat them you've got to get their offense off the field fast and hope that yours can stay on longer. Yet giving up the three points is like a small victory for us. With the Rams, many times two drives lead to fourteen points, so holding them to three was quite acceptable at this point.

It didn't help, however, when our offense returned and went three-and-out. That's what we didn't want, because now the defense was right back on the field. You can't go to the Super Bowl and just be running around chasing them. We had to make sure they didn't get the big play. In that respect we still had them where we wanted them. We noticed they were keeping extra guys back to block, waiting for the blitz, yet sometimes we rushed only two guys and were dropping everyone else back. Though we always go into a game with our blitzes set, we were determined not to blitz as much as we had against them the first time. We wanted to make Warner find the open receiver, get him the ball, then see if he could hold on to it while being hit hard by two guys for a short or medium gain.

After our three-and-out they started from their twenty-two and moved out to the thirty-seven when the first quarter ended. When play resumed, they got their first big play, a twenty-nine-yard connection between Warner and Az-Zahir Hakim that brought the ball to our thirty-nine. From there they could move only five yards in three plays, and Wilkins missed a fifty-two-yarder. So we had held them once more and now had the ball back at our thirty-four. We managed to move it to just the forty-seven when Walter had to punt once more. The kick was returned to the nineteen, and the Rams' offense came out on the field once again. Now came a key series, one that showed just how quickly things can change in a football game.

Starting at the nineteen, Marshall Faulk carried twice, first for six yards, then for fifteen on his best carry of the night. They had a first and ten at their forty, and to many it appeared that Faulk was about to begin rolling. Then Warner dropped back to pass, and this time we were blitzing. Mike Vrabel was coming from the back side, and when Warner turned to look for his receiver, Isaac Bruce, Vrabel was in his face with his arms up. Warner still tried to make the play, but he didn't release the ball properly, and the pass went behind Bruce, where Ty Law was running. Bruce tried to plant his feet and come back. Too late. Ty grabbed it and went right down the sidelines, running forty-seven yards untouched for a score. We were so excited on the sideline, yelling and screaming as Ty ran past us. Terrell Buckley lost it for a second and actually starting running onto the field in front of Ty. If the refs had seen him, they easily could have called a penalty, but I think he caught himself in time and stepped back. Still, he had moved down too far and was also out of the designated area where the team has to stand. Close call.

Now we had done exactly what we were hoping for. Defensive pressure caused a turnover, and we took full advantage. A turnover can't get any better when it results in a score. It not only clipped their wings a bit but also gave us the lead, as Adam's kick made it a 7–3 game at the 6:11 mark of the second quarter. I think Ty's interception really inspired the defense. Then, next time they got the ball, they managed one first down, then had to punt. We didn't have a long drive, but the offense stayed mainly on the ground and ate up some four minutes of the clock before punting back to the Rams from our thirty-one. They started from their fifteen this time, and in less than a minute our defense came up big once again.

They quickly got a first down on a run and a penalty, bringing the ball to the twenty-five. Warner then dropped back and threw a quick slant over the middle to Ricky Proehl for a gain of another fifteen and a first down at the forty. They were running their two-minute offense and looking to get a score before the half. Once again Warner dropped back and went to Proehl a second time. It looked as if it was going to be about another fifteen-yard gain. What happened next might sound surprising, but this is the way I saw it. Proehl caught the ball in the middle of the field, so there was no way he was going to get to the sidelines to stop the clock. He got past Terrell Buckley, but Antwan Harris was playing the robber position in the middle of the field. Now Proehl was heading straight for Antwan, who was also running toward him.

Proehl must have felt he was going to be hit hard by Antwan, because he didn't make any attempt to get past him. Instead he started to go to the ground to stop the play. Az Hakim had done the same thing on the series before while Terrell was guarding him. Terrell just leaned on him a bit, kind of touched him down. We wanted our guys to drop on them when they did this. Antwan didn't mess around. As Proehl was going down, he put his helmet right into his arm, jarring the ball loose. Fumble! Terrell reacted quickly, picked it up, made a nice move, and returned the fumble fifteen yards, back to the Rams' forty. This was a dream for our defensive unit. We now had a second turnover; the first had been taken back for a score, and this one put us in position to score. Was this ever what we wanted to see. In fact it was typical of the makeup of our team all season long. Now we were doing it on the grandest stage of all, the Super Bowl. We still hadn't been moving the ball the way we wanted offensively, but now the defense was handing it back and hoping the momentum would continue.

I think the offense came out with a lot of adrenaline pumping. They knew the opportunity we had given them. Brady wasted no time. On the first play he went to Troy, who ran it to the twenty-four for a gain of sixteen yards and a first down. We were already within Adam's range for a field goal, but we wanted more. With 1:12 left in the half, the Rams took a time-out, but it didn't phase Tom Brady. He went right back upstairs and completed an eight-yard toss to Jermaine Wiggins, who brought the ball to the sixteen. After an incomplete pass, Kevin Faulk ran the ball eight yards to the eight. Brady took the next snap and dropped back. He fired into the right corner of the end zone, where David Patten made a nifty catch, just keeping his feet in bounds. Touchdown! The Rams held up the celebration when they challenged the play, but Patten knew he was in. He was on the sideline yelling to them, telling them it was a score, and seconds later the ref came out and raised both his arms. Adam kicked the extra point, giving us a 14–3 lead with just thirty-one seconds left. All they could do after the kickoff was let the clock run out. Halftime.

I'm sure much of the football world was shocked by the halftime score. Our defense had held the mighty Rams offense to just three points in the first thirty minutes of the game. The Greatest Show on Turf had pretty much stalled, while we had played the opportunist again, converting a pair of turnovers into a pair of touchdowns. No one, however, came into the locker room feeling we had the game wrapped up. We knew they would come back. They weren't the number-one team in the league without good reason. Halftime was longer than usual because of the lavish entertainment program, so we had a little more time to think about what had happened. Coach Belichick was calm, as usual, telling everyone that the Rams would not go quietly. They would, he said, give us their best shot, and we still had to expect a struggle. He also talked about their shifts, the way they had been running plays across the middle with some success, and he felt we would see more of Marshall Faulk in the second half. Basically, though, he wanted us to continue to do just what we had been doing, especially on defense.

We received the third-quarter kickoff, which Patrick Pass took three yards deep in the end zone and then returned all the way to the thirty-two. After we got one first down on a thirteen-yard burst by Antowain, the offense stalled and we had to punt it away. Up to this point we really had thought we would have done better offensively. The Rams, however, were making plays defensively, covering our deeper routes well and making tackles we thought would give them trouble. Yet we knew we had to keep punching and continue to protect Tom Brady. We just wanted to bleed the clock and not allow them to get into a pass-rushing mode with us, while continuing to go after them on the defensive side of the ball. We would have liked to see a few more plays on offense, but we stayed with the game plan and continued to hit hard, trying to wear them down. The result was that the entire third quarter became a real struggle for both teams.

After a penalty they started from their own eight and right away showed signs of life. On two successive plays Warner completed a twenty-yard pass to Az Hakim and then a twenty-two-yarder to Bruce. Tack on a nine-yard penalty, and they were at our forty-one and driving. Then our defense toughened once more. A sack dropped them back seven, followed by two incomplete passes and a five-yard penalty that forced them to punt. We came right back with a seventeen-yard run by Antowain and a twenty-two-yard end around by David Patten, but like them, we just couldn't sustain the drive. Four plays later it was our turn to punt. The great Super Bowl shootout was turning into a defensive struggle. Ken Walter's punt rolled into the end zone, and they started from their twenty once again.

With 6:40 left in the third quarter, Faulk began their next possession with a twelve-yard run up the middle for a first down. After he gained six more, they went right back to him, and he ran for another twelve. First and ten at midfield. Suddenly Faulk was doing it on the ground, and we didn't want that to continue. We tightened it up and on the next play stopped him for no gain. That forced Warner to go back to the air, but his pass to Torry Holt gained just five yards. Now they had a third-and-five at our forty-five-yard line. The next play was going to be a slant back to Holt, the kind of bang-bang play they love to run. Only this time Otis Smith was ready.

First he jammed Holt in the chest so firmly at the line of scrimmage that it blew the timing of his route. When Warner released the pass, throwing to the spot Holt was supposed to be, only Otis was there. He grabbed it and ran down the left sideline with Richard Seymour running toward him. We always tell our linemen to keep running after an interception. Seymour had been pressuring Warner, and after the ball changed hands he started running to the sideline toward Otis. Warner also ran over to try to make the tackle. When Otis cut back to try to go inside Warner, he ran right into Seymour. Pow. Without that he might have scored. Seymour was just doing what he was told, looking for someone to block, but when Otis came to the sideline the first thing he said was "Next time, please tell Seymour to get the hell out of the damned way."

Now, however, we were having fun. At this point we could not have asked for anything more, to be playing the St. Louis Rams in the Super Bowl and having fun defensively. Otis had run the ball back twenty-five yards before bumping into Seymour, and now we had a first down at their thirty-three. Brady came out with the offense and promptly hit Troy with a pass good for eleven yards and a first down at the twenty-two. Then we stalled a bit, and Adam had to come on to boot a thirty-seven-yard field goal, which he made with ease, giving us a 17–3 lead with just 1:18 left in the third period. Though I said the defense was having fun, we were also aware that two touchdowns for the Rams were nothing, not with the weapons they had. A missed tackle or blown assignment on Faulk, and he'd be gone. A missed tackle on Isaac Bruce, and he'd be gone. We still wanted to see more coming out of the offense because, as I've said so many times already, the best defense against the Rams is a good offense.

After Adam's field goal the Rams knew they had to ignite their offense. They started their drive from the twenty-three with 1:05 left in the period, and this time they began moving the ball. Fortunately, it wasn't the long-strike variety. They would drive seventy-seven yards and take some six and a half minutes off the clock, bringing the game solidly into the fourth quarter. It was a crazy drive for them, nickel-and-dime stuff. Gain a yard, lose a yard. Some teams would become impatient in this situation, especially one with the striking power of the Rams, but they didn't. They took what we gave them. In this kind of situation they simply continued making plays, and we couldn't put together three straight defensive plays to stop them. It turned into a twelve-play march. Once they reached the three, we really made it hell for them.

The Rams' goal line offense is scary. Every week they have a new gimmick on the goal line, changing personnel, sometimes using two or three tight ends or putting a tight end in the backfield. Other times they'll spread it out with four wide receivers. I was so proud of the way our defense handled this situation. We just kept stopping them and should have been out of it three times.

Lawyer dropped a potential interception. Ty almost had one at the back of the end zone. Their receivers were running pass routes and couldn't get open. That's a victory in itself. Then with a fourth-and-three at the three-yard line, Warner tried to take it in himself. Roman Phifer blasted him at the line of scrimmage, jarring the ball loose. All I could see was Tebucky Jones picking it up and nothing but open field in front of him. The game breaker, right there for the taking. Sure enough, Tebucky reacted in a flash and ran untouched ninety-seven yards to the end zone. We were all set to erupt on the sidelines when someone heard the ref's whistle and saw the flag.

Talk about having the wind knocked out of us. Apparently Willie McGinest had held Marshall Faulk, the maneuver that allowed Phifer to get to Warner. The play was brought back, the penalty giving them a first down half the distance to the goal line. So they had it at about the one and a half, and our defense had to come back out. Now we were tired. They tried running Faulk, but we threw him back for the loss of a yard. On the sidelines we were all screaming at them: "Show us something!" "What else you got?" Then they shot us in the back. Warner rushed it up the middle and finally got it into the end zone. I thought we still should have had him, but not this time. If we didn't get the penalty and Tebucky's run had counted, I think we would have won it big, maybe by 30–3, something like that. As I always say, though, the Lord works in mysterious ways. Wilkins's extra point made it a 17–10 game. Now we needed something from the offense.

Unfortunately, what we got was a three-and-out, and Ken Walter had to punt from the thirty-three. After that long drive, that great goal-line stand, the emotion of Tebucky's near touchdown, the defense had to go right back on the field to face a Rams offense that was now fired up and would be gunning to tie the score. The punt pinned them back to their own fourteen, and a penalty on the next play brought it back to the seven. But then they started a sustained drive that would keep our defense on the field for another four exhausting minutes. After they got a first down at the nineteen, Warner and Ricky Proehl connected on a big one, good for thirty yards to the forty-nine. A ten-yard pass to Jeff Robinson brought the ball to our forty-one. If nothing else, they were getting close to field goal range. Faulk next ran it to the thirty-eight, but then our defense came up big once again. Otis broke up a key pass intended for Torry Holt, and then Willie McGinest made the huge play, chasing down Warner and sacking him for a loss of sixteen big yards, effectively taking them out of field goal range. Three plays later they had to punt. The ball went into the end zone, and we took over at our twenty, again looking for some offense. There was just 3:44 left, and any kind of drive could have eaten up the clock.

Only not this time. Three plays netted just five yards, and we had to punt once more. We felt we had dodged a bullet on their drive, but now the defense had to try to hold them again. At this point even a field goal would be bad, and we didn't want to give up anything. Though the offense was still having problems, we were all together on the sidelines, all going into the locker room together no matter what happened. Then came another bad break. Ken Walter shanked the punt, something he hadn't done at all during the playoffs. For the most part he was booming the ball. Now, however, they had the ball at their forty-five-yard line with just 1:51 left. Suddenly the game had real drama. It became even more pressing when on the first play Warner threw a simple crossing route underneath to Az Hakim. We should have tackled him right away, which would have kept the clock running, but he got away, ran for eighteen yards, and then went out of bounds. First down at our thirty-seven.

Warner wasn't wasting any time now. On the next play he went to Yo Murphy for an eleven-yard gain and another first down at our twenty-six. Now came another key play. This was something we had worked on forever during the course of the week. It's like a pick play. The Rams had four receivers in the game, two of them wide left, the other two wide right. The outside receiver runs a pick on the inside defender. Then the inside receiver goes outside, and Warner throws him the ball. The play worked to perfection, because we didn't execute well. Our two defenders were tied up with the pick, and Warner fired the pass to Proehl, who turned it upfield. Tebucky was still tired from his ninety-seven-yard run that was called back and then from being out on the punt team. The three-and-outs didn't help either. Proehl was able to cut back on both Tebucky and Terrance Shaw and took it all the way in for a touchdown. Wilkins's kick tied it with just 1:30 left.

After we had led for nearly the entire game and come *this* close to putting it away with Tebucky's run, had it not been called back, they had rallied and tied it. Looking back, Proehl taking the ball in from twenty-six yards out was a blessing. Suppose they took another three or four plays to score. Then perhaps there would have been thirty seconds left, and it definitely would have been an overtime game. At least we had a minute and a half to try to do something. No way anyone on our sideline was going to quit. We had come too far, and I still had a feeling about this game.

There's an old schoolyard theory that goes like this. Anytime you have a team with superstars, and a team that's supposed to win cheering when they *tie* the score, you know you've got them—you know you're doing something right. They were jumping up and down on their sideline, but the game wasn't over, and they shouldn't have been in that situation in the first place. In my eyes it was as if they were just happy to save face. That wasn't the only thing I was feeling. Like everyone else on our sideline, I was mad now. I didn't want to lose this one, and I'm telling you with all honesty, I still had the feeling that in some kind of way we were going to win. We had played too hard. We had defended everything they threw at us and had played them too well to come up short. As we had hoped, we had been able to play our game and had kept it low-scoring, just as we wanted. Up to now our offense had been very conservative. Now, however, Brady would have to throw.

Troy was able to return Wilkins's kickoff only fifteen yards out to the seventeen. So with 1:21 left, we were eighty-three yards from the end zone and about fifty yards from giving Adam a shot at a long field goal. Brady started things with a five-yard pass to J. R. Redmond over the middle. On the next play he went right back to J.R. and gained eight more. First down. After an incomplete pass Tom found J.R. for a third time, this one good for eleven yards and a first down at our forty-one. On that play J.R. stretched his body out in the air to get out of bounds and stop the clock, another of those little things that help win ball games but that few people notice. Now everyone was fired up, everyone was helping each other, everyone on that field was scratching and clawing for an extra yard.

Brady brought us to the line again. This time his pass fell incomplete, but he didn't blink. On the next play he threw it out to the left flat to Troy, who came up big once more, getting a couple of blocks and taking the ball twenty-three yards to the St. Louis thirty-six, then getting out of bounds to stop the clock once more. Now we were in business. Adam was already warming up, kicking into the net, but we still needed a few more yards. Once again Brady stayed cool under fire. He dropped back and calmly hit Jermaine Wiggins over the middle for a gain of six yards. Now the ball was at the thirty, but the clock was ticking down. We rushed up to the line, and Brady spiked the ball with just seven seconds left. Time for just one more play.

As he came out onto the field, every eye in the Superdome was on Adam Vinatieri, but I don't think he saw or heard anyone. He was just concentrating on what would be the biggest and most important field goal attempt of his life from forty-eight yards out. There was a statistic that I'm sure very few people knew. Adam had never missed a field goal in a dome. He's a South Dakota guy, used to cold weather, and he proved just two weeks earlier he could make them in the snow. But he'd never missed in a dome. Whether they knew this or not, I'm sure the Rams had a sinking feeling just seeing him come onto the field. They probably figured overtime was a lock, especially with the way our offense had been going. Now, however, the three most important guys on the field were Lonie Paxton, the long snapper, Ken Walter, the holder, and Adam. As I said, all three had to execute perfectly.

Paxton's snap was perfect. Walter set it down, spun the laces, and Adam stepped up and swung his leg through the ball. As soon as it left his foot, he began jumping up and down. He knew. We all watched, and in a few seconds we all knew. The ball cleared the uprights with plenty to spare. Even if Wiggins hadn't gotten that final six yards, that kick would have gone through. He gave it enough leg to make it from fifty-four to fifty-six yards out. We had done it. We had beaten the Rams and, as Lawyer Milloy would say, we shocked the world. The New England Patriots had won the Super Bowl and were world champs!

As everyone began running out on the field, I couldn't help noticing Lonie Paxton. When Adam kicked his field goal in the snow to beat the Raiders, Lonie had run into the end zone, fallen onto his back, flapped his arms and legs to make an angel in the snow. Now, in the comfort of the Superdome, he did the same thing. He was lying in the end zone, flapping his arms and legs like mad, making a turf angel, I suppose. By then all the guys were screaming and jumping around, and I had the look of a proud father on my face. I had told the guys before the game that if we won I was going to go to the middle of the field and dance, just as I had in Super Bowl XXI and Super Bowl XXV with the Giants. Only I didn't do it. The first thing I did, after I thanked the Lord, was look for Bill Belichick to congratulate him. A couple of guys were hitting me on the shoulders. Then I just stood there with my arms crossed and watched our guys celebrate. Wow! They did it. We did it. My eyes didn't see a single Rams player on the field. There was plenty of confetti, but I couldn't have seen a Ram if I had wanted to.

Then any thought of dancing ended when the stages were rolled out onto the field for the award ceremony. There was so much happening that we didn't even come together to say the Lord's Prayer like we always did. Guys were busy doing interviews, running to find their families, and still busy congratulating each other. There was no way we could come together, and we wouldn't actually see everyone as a team again until we went to get on the plane the next day, and even then there were some guys who didn't ride back with the rest of the team. However, no one was about to quibble about that now.

After the presentation guys were running around with the Super Bowl trophy. Tedy Bruschi was high-fiving everyone. Roman Phifer grabbed his son and put him on his shoulders. He said to me, "Pepper, man, I love you. You said this was going to happen." I really felt good for him. He had always just missed the playoffs when he'd left teams before. In fact he had spent much of his career with the Rams, and they had won the Super Bowl the year after he left. Now he had come to New England and not only made the playoffs but helped beat the Rams in the Super Bowl. I remember Lawyer running up to McGinest and just screaming. By then I was trying to find my family. Because of tight security, only one family member with tags could come on the field.

My mother had her tag but was so nervous she didn't even come down. And my son, Dionté, couldn't come down early because he had a wrestling match in which he qualified for the high school city championships. He was a sophomore at Eastmore Academy in Columbus, Ohio. He flew out the Sunday morning of the game and walked to the stadium with my mother. It would be a double victory for me when a week later he won the city wrestling championship at 189 pounds and I was there watching him. Could anyone ask for anything more?

It's funny, but I felt the same way after the Super Bowl as when I watched my son win his championship. In both cases it was like a proud father watching his sons. I was so happy at the moment we won the game, but I really couldn't put it into words then. My family and friends seemed happier than I was, and I found myself trying to figure out this feeling. It was different from when I was a player. A big difference. As a player all the hard work—the sprints, the weightlifting, the bumps and bruises, the pain—it all goes away when you win. You're screaming for the moment. When you win the Super Bowl, the price you have paid all year long hits you at once. I could move a building but don't know if I could have picked up a mouse. That's the feeling.

As a coach it was a different feeling, a strange one for me. I was close to the last person to leave that night. I sat in the locker room and let it all soak in. I was trying to see everyone, congratulate all the guys. Mr. Kraft came in, the coaches' wives came in, and I was still waiting for my family to show up. Coach Belichick, of course, was ecstatic. The last time I had seen him that happy was when we won the Super Bowl in 1990. This wasn't like beating the Raiders or even the Steelers. There was a little fist-pumping then, and a smile, but the business voice returned very quickly. Here it was more like *Yeah, baby*.

To close the story of the game, that final drive that led to Adam's dramatic game-winning field goal resulted in Tom Brady being named the game's Most Valuable Player. He had completed sixteen of twenty-seven passes for 145 yards and a touchdown. Not spectacular numbers, but he took care of the ball and produced when the game was on the line. Once again, however, it was a total team effort. Antowain was steady the entire game, finishing with 92 yards on eighteen carries. Troy led our receivers with six catches for 89 yards. Ty, Lawyer, and Tebucky Jones were our leading tacklers, and that showed me that we had defended their passing game well. They were making stops before their speedy receivers could break away. And none of them went deep. There were so many key defensive plays that I can't name them all, but I was damned proud of all those guys. Remember before the Pittsburgh game when I told Rob Ryan that the Steelers weren't aware of the hurricane that was about to blow through? The Rams weren't either. The defense spent a great deal of time on the field and did one helluva job. Maybe the best way I can describe the entire playoffs is to say that during the season we had eleven *wins*. In the play-offs we had three *victories*!

We flew back home Monday night. When we reached the stadium, there were people all over the place, probably enough to fill the entire place if they were allowed inside. The parking lots were loaded. People were hollering, screaming, and cheering. Every father probably had a kid on his shoulders. The next afternoon they gave us a parade in downtown Boston. It went for three miles, and I never saw so many people in my life. There must have been more than a million people along the route. They were in buildings, hanging out of windows, in the trees, on top of the buildings. There were signs all over the place. I remember laughing at one that read "I'M GLAD WE HAD BILL

BELICHICK AS OUR COACH AND NOT JOHN MADDEN." During the telecast of the game, Fox television announcer John Madden had apparently predicted that we would run out the clock on that last drive and take the game into overtime instead of going for it all. The fans remembered that one, especially after we proved him to be totally wrong. Then again, a lot of people had been wrong about the New England Patriots all season.

It was a cold day in Boston, very cold. When we had to sit for the ceremony, they were giving us hot packs to put in our gloves, but it was worth every minute of it. After all, we're a cold-weather team. It's not supposed to bother us, especially not on a day many of the fans and probably some of the players thought would never come. This was a team, however, that had begun to believe in itself early in the season, even when no one else did, even when we weren't given a chance to make the playoffs. The real joy of it for me was watching it all come together, having a role in building a defense that could compete with anybody, a defense that had pride and a physical presence and didn't fear any team, not even one considered a juggernaut that was expected to run us off the field in the Super Bowl.

Maybe that was what failed to sink in right after the game when I said I didn't know how I felt. I had experienced winning the Super Bowl as a player but not as a coach. It took some time for me to realize that my joy was now reserved for others rather than myself. I was happy for the players and proud of what they had done. I also found that it gave me a great deal of satisfaction to watch this group of players come together as a team. That, more than anything else, was the essence of the 2001 New England Patriots. From Coach Belichick to the coordinators and assistant coaches and right down to the last player, we were a unit, an extension of one philosophy that led to a common goal. Winning. We were also a group of guys who wouldn't allow anything to distract us from achieving that goal. In the end it all worked, and that, for me, is the greatest satisfaction of them all.

The day after the big parade, Coach Belichick scheduled a staff meeting for all of us. Everyone was pretty much still riding high, still in the celebration mode. Belichick came in, and as soon as he started to speak we knew. The business voice was back. Listening to him, you never would have thought we had just won the Super Bowl. In reality, however, it was as if that almost didn't matter now. We had things to do and plans to make. We were already back at work and rightly so, because in the NFL the next season is never very far away.

Epilogue

When it comes to team sports, I've always been a strong believer in the old adage that you're only as strong as your weakest link. With the New England Patriots, the least-recognized player on the team still contributes in a positive form or fashion. Even if a player's role is only special teams or he isn't activated for a game, he has to do his homework and contribute to the study of the tapes. You never know when that player is going to pick up a tendency or see something that no one else has seen, and Bill Belichick always makes sure that each and every player has an assignment every week.

The following are the players who were members of the 2001 New England Patriots. This is how I view their contributions to the overall success of the season and ultimately the Super Bowl championship.

You'll notice that a good number of players on the team are denoted as domino players. Playing the game of dominoes became another way in which our players came together, bonded, forged a special kind of unity and camaraderie during the 2001 season. Otis Smith brought the first set into the locker room, and once I saw the game beginning to grow, I put two more sets in Otis's locker. Before long over half the players looked forward to sitting and playing dominoes before meetings, during breaks, at lunch, after practice, or whenever they could squeeze it in. The games were boisterous and competitive, with the guys organizing a regular tournament during training camp.

The numbers kept growing during the season, and the games continued right through the playoffs. I would join the game on Saturdays after practice. When I played, I beat them all and came away with the nickname "The Dominologist." A bunch of big, tough professional football players hunched over a table playing dominoes may make a strange picture, but with all the meetings, the rigorous practices, the pressure of the games, and the overall battle to survive, dominoes provided a healthy outlet and a way for the guys to compete without getting any more bruises than necessary. Unfortunately, I can't say the same for the dominoes. There were times when they went flying all over the place. Camaraderie and competition will do that sometimes.

Joe Andruzzi (offensive lineman)

Joe came from a small college, Southern Connecticut State, and, like many others from small colleges, was probably told he would never make it. Yet he earned a starting job after three seasons as a backup by virtue of a great off-season workout program in 2001. Started all sixteen games at right guard and continued to improve throughout the season.

Drew Bledsoe (quarterback)

Drew Bledsoe gets my vote for true leadership, and that's really what it's all about. It's easy to lead a team when things are going well, but when adversity strikes, can you still step up? Drew proved he could. Before I met him, I thought he was a guy clinging to his fame who tended to be selfish. Once I joined the Patriots, he proved me wrong. Drew is very likable, down to earth, easy to approach, and he really showed me toughness. In the 2000 season a lot of quarterbacks would have shut it down if they had been hit as much as he was. He didn't. In 2001 he worked very hard to overcome a serious injury and be ready when we needed him. Then he stepped up again.

Tom Brady (quarterback)

Last season was Tom's career, so far. When I think of Tom Brady, I remember his rookie year, when he would watch the defensive team's tapes to use in his show team work. He always wanted to improve and give us the right looks. Tom is another guy I watched in the off-season workout program become faster and stronger and develop better coordination. His hard work was all geared to make him a better player.

Troy Brown (wide receiver)

Here's a guy who started his career by being cut by the Patriots, then picked back up, and who was looked on as a career backup receiver and punt returner. Before last season someone said he didn't have the strength to play regularly and would always be a third receiver. Yet all Troy Brown does is make plays. He led the league in punt return average and set a team record with 101 receptions. To me he was by far our most valuable player. Domino player.

Tedy Bruschi (linebacker)

This is "Mr. Heart." Tedy was slated to be a backup when the season began. He stepped in when others were hurt and became part of our three-man inside linebacker rotation. He finished the season as our starting middle linebacker and continued to play outstanding football despite a lingering back injury. Domino player.

Terrell Buckley (defensive back)

"T Buck" was another true veteran. He had been a starter throughout his career before joining the Patriots as a free agent in 2001. Alternated with Otis Smith at the beginning of the season before settling in as our nickel back and became the best pinch hitter in the league. He had to have the best ratio for making big plays during the time he was in the lineup.

Matt Chatham (linebacker)

A true member of the Dirty Show and a surgeon of tight ends. Matt was designated to break down every tight end we played against during the season, and he found out things about them that our scouts didn't even know. He has continued to improve in the two years he has been with the Patriots.

Je'Rod Cherry (defensive back)

The demolition man. Je'Rod is one of the best gunners in the league on the punting team. He continues to make plays on special teams that put him on a par with anyone in the league.

Fred Coleman (wide receiver)

The hero of the second Jets game, Fred caught a quick slant and took it forty-six yards. He then recovered an onside kick and held on despite a huge hit. He also gave us that fourth wide receiver who could make major contributions on special teams as well. Domino player.

Mike Compton (offensive lineman)

The practical joker of the locker room, Mike has even played a couple of pranks on his position coach, Dante Scarnecchia. Compton also brought leadership to our offensive line that had been sorely lacking. He was a teammate of mine with the 1996 Detroit Lions, and he's our shotgun center as well as our starting guard.

Bryan Cox (linebacker)

"Mr. Attitude." I know the feeling Bryan had coming to a new team and then at the end of training camp being voted a captain by his peers. That says a lot about what he brings to the table. In this day and age it's hard being cool, sitting in with the guys, and remaining a student of the game. BC stuck by his guns and challenged all comers, as well as helping to motivate the entire defense into developing character. Domino player.

Marc Edwards (running back)

A hungry fullback who wanted to prove a point—that he could play the game. He found a home with the Patriots during the off season, then found his role with the team, and the rest is history. Domino player.

Kevin Faulk (running back)

Arguably might have the best hands on the team. Even with his abundance of talent, he improved so much during the off-season conditioning program with speed, endurance, and strength that it surprised even the coaches. Kevin became more confident in himself, and, as a result, we had more confidence in him. Domino player.

Bobby Hamilton (defensive lineman)

For a so-called non–pass rusher, Bobby led our team in sacks while playing only on first and second downs. At the beginning of the year I prayed to have a team of Bobby Hamiltons. The Lord heard my prayer and blessed us. Bobby is an overachiever who will always play hard. For all the reasons people said we couldn't finish 8–8, Bobby couldn't play defensive end. But he played left defensive end, usually against the biggest tackle on the opposition, and he stood them all up. To me that sums up Bobby. He constantly produced, even when people counted him out, and he kept doing it throughout the year.

Antwan Harris (defensive back)

Before the season I nicknamed him "Puddin'," as in Jell-O pudding, because in Belichick's tackle drill he was run over. But after the 2001 season, when he scored a TD in the AFC title game and caused a fumble in the Super Bowl that set up David Patten's touchdown, we would never call him "Puddin'" again. Domino player.

Damon Huard (quarterback)

Damon is a backup quarterback that every team would love to have. Normally, when you have a third-string quarterback, he's an ERW guy—*e*at, *r*ide, and *w*arm up. But Damon works harder than anyone else on the team and is always prepared. A player-coach.

Larry Izzo (linebacker)

Special teams captain. Look what fell out of the sky! When Larry came on his recruiting visit, Coach Belichick told me that if I let Larry leave New England without verbally committing to a contract I might not have a contract myself. That's how important we knew he would be to the team. Domino player.

Charles Johnson (wide receiver)

Another true veteran who never complained and came to work with an uplifting attitude every day. He also had some big games. Domino player.

Ted Johnson (linebacker)

Can anyone tell me why I like this guy so much? We're both named Johnson, both have the initials T.J., and both wore number 52. My first year in the league my jersey read T. Johnson. As for Ted, there isn't a guard in the league who can block him without holding. Domino player.

Kenyatta Jones (offensive lineman)

Kenyatta might be our most athletic offensive lineman. His continued presence in 2002 will definitely make our offensive line stronger.

Tebucky Jones (defensive back)

"The Hard-Hittin' New Britain." Our safeties all bring fear to opponents crossing the middle. Right when a receiver thinks he is safely behind our linebacker, Tebucky lines him up and—BOOM! He hits harder than most linebackers, yet his most memorable moment from 2001 might have been running down the Colts' Marvin Harrison from behind.

Ty Law (defensive back)

Controversy. Ty always has something brewing. His name is always on the coach's lips. At the end of the 2000 season Ty told me he had something to prove. He dedicated himself with his personal trainer during the off season, then came out and kicked butt all season long. Domino player.

Matt Light (offensive lineman)

The karaoke singer. Matt was a rookie in every sense of the word. In the beginning he was late to meetings, was hardheaded, and kept using my private bathroom, though his coach, Jeff Davidson, let him. He was spoiled and always gave me a problem on the kickoff show team. But when it came time to play football, he made me forget the headaches. He was a delight to watch perform.

Arther Love (tight end)

The quiet storm. Arther was the type of guy who gave our defense hell in practice.

Willie McGinest (defensive lineman)

"Big Mac." Another real man and a true veteran. A lot of guys would have curled up after a newcomer, Cox, was named captain. Willie stayed strong, didn't complain, and came back strong after off-season back surgery. He played well in those situations when he was called on, then turned it up and had perhaps the most outstanding playoffs among all the defensive players. Domino player.

Lawyer Milloy (defensive back)

Lawyer is the heart and soul of the defense. We go on his count. All our guys are self-motivators, but Lawyer gives them that little extra push. He takes our defense to another level and has an Energizer-bunny motor in him, playing hard on every single down and never wanting to come off the field. Domino player.

Brandon Mitchell (defensive lineman)

"B. Mitch" is a pup still trying to find his place in the league. He was well groomed by ex-Patriot Henry Thomas in acting the part of a professional athlete, not just a professional football player. Brandon made a remarkable recovery from a knee injury in the 2000 season. Domino player.

Leonard Myers (defensive back)

"Crash." Leonard has an uncanny way of driving a car and doesn't go more than six months without some kind of accident. Though still waiting for his time to shine, he's already one of the premier defensive backs in the league. I will be highly disappointed if he doesn't have a successful career in the NFL.

Stephen Neal (offensive lineman)

"The Wrestler." Still learning the game after an outstanding collegiate and amateur wrestling career. Stephen re-signed late in the season and is now rededicating himself to professional football.

David Nugent (defensive lineman)

"The Big Nuge." David might be pound for pound the strongest guy on the team.

Riddick Parker (defensive lineman)

My Krispy Kreme partner. Riddick is a special guy, similar to Brandon Mitchell, a hardworking player who understands the importance of being in the league, the honor of being in the league, and how important it is not to abuse the privilege.

Patrick Pass (running back)

I'm still waiting for him at the bowling alley. We bowled last year on Thursdays, and when I started beating up on him too bad, they changed the day to when I couldn't make it. Patrick arguably might be our most gifted back.

David Patten (wide receiver)

David is definitely one of the most pleasant guys to be around. He's also a receiver with big play ability. David stepped up in a way no one expected when he was needed the most. Labeled as injury prone, he played through the pain, and his contributions were enormous.

Lonie Paxton (long snapper)

"The Snow Angel." Another great guy who contributes to the character of the team. Despite having a limited but important role that receives little attention, Lonie is nevertheless one of the hardest workers on the team. Domino player.

Roman Phifer (linebacker)

One of the nicest guys you ever want to meet. Also a guy I couldn't have been happier for after he made the difficult decision to leave California and his children to be with the Patriots. Never in the playoffs before despite a long and successful career, he shed the label of "the jinx" given him by Bryan Cox and played an enormous role in the team's run to the Super Bowl.

Anthony Pleasant (defensive lineman)

"The Chief." I'm so happy for AP, who had the best year of his career. Watching him—a teammate of mine in his early years—get his first career interception this past season was one of my most memorable moments in football . . . and his as well.

J. R. Redmond (running back)

I've seen J.R. grow faster in two years than any other player. Though he served as our third-down back most of the season, he was also our best blocking back. Another star in the postseason and a hero in the Super Bowl.

Greg Robinson-Randall (offensive lineman)

I call Greg "Three Names," and his teammates call him "Baby Face." Our most durable offensive lineman the past two years, if he continues to improve as he has already, he could be a Pro Bowler in the near future. Domino player.

Grey Ruegamer (offensive lineman)

The offensive lineman every team would like to have. His versatility allows him to play center as well as both guard positions. The offensive lineman most likely to start a fight in training camp. That's why I like him.

Rod Rutledge (tight end)

Rod really began to excel once he accepted his role as a blocking tight end. Then he went out and made us know why.

Richard Seymour (defensive lineman)

"First Rounder." I didn't know much about him before he was drafted, but I sure know a lot about him now. He's as much a gentleman off the field as he is a beast on it. His rookie year started slowly because of injuries and simply learning how to be a professional athlete. By the end of the season Richard became—as they say down south—a full-grown man.

Terrance Shaw (defensive back)

Another veteran player at the turning point in his career. Was a solid substitute corner all year. Domino player.

Antowain Smith (running back)

I played against "Big Twan" and thought he was just another big back. This season he showed he could catch, had more game speed than he had been given credit for, and had the heart of a lion. He played with pain toward the end of the season, but he knew the only way we could win was with him carrying the ball. Domino player.

Otis Smith (defensive back)

"O.T.I.S." This is my younger brother. Sometimes I think I'm the only person who sees Otis's true value to our team. I give him credit as a brother, while the others just pat him on the back because he does his job. Being the second corner in this era means you will see a lot more passes than the first corner. Otis is always ready. Ask any wide receiver who has played against him. Led our team in interceptions. Domino player.

Matt Stevens (defensive back)

We used Matt as a substitute for Tebucky Jones. He follows the mold of our starting safeties by being very aggressive. We got more from Matt than we thought we would when we signed him. Great guy, a wannabe soccer player, and a Revolutionary War expert.

Adam Vinatieri (place kicker)

"The Big Four." Not only does Adam fit the mold of great personalities on the team, but he makes you sleep well at night because you never have to question whether he will make the pressure kick. Domino player.

Mike Vrabel (linebacker)

Fellow Buckeye. The best guy you could have around to make light of an ugly situation, but he won't take crap from anybody at any time. "Vrabs" turned out to be a diamond in the rough for us. I thought he would be a role player, but he ended up dominating tight ends, provided blitz pressure, and was a fine third-down pass rusher. He definitely fit the mold of our linebackers with his versatility. Another excellent free agent. Domino player.

Ken Walter (punter)

This kid was our ballboy in Cleveland. Second in the league in net punting average and first in percentage of punts inside the twenty-yard line, which is a lost art. Joined the team after the start of the season and became not only a top punter but an excellent holder for Adam as well. Not bad for a kid from Kent State.

Jermaine Wiggins (tight end)

He's East Boston's finest. I will always remember Wigs by the tape Coach Belichick showed of him playing high school basketball and football. Seeing is believing. Wigs is one of the guys who would always find a way to get open, which made him one of our postseason heroes.

Grant Williams (offensive lineman)

A quiet guy who's a true veteran. He was always ready, in the same mold as Damon Huard.

Damien Woody (offensive lineman)

Perhaps one of the most underrated players in the league. Should be a Pro Bowler at center or guard. Manhandled nearly everyone he played against. He is our best offensive lineman.

The following players either began the season with the Patriots or were placed on injured reserve at some point during the year. In my mind they all contributed to the winning effort in one way or another: Hakim Akbar, Kole Ayi, Bert Emanuel (Domino player), Rob Holmberg, Curtis Jackson, Lee Johnson, Andy Katzenmoyer, Ben Kelly, Adrian Klemm, Marty Moore, Jace Sayler, Torrance Small (Domino player), Maugaula Tuitele, and T. J. Turner.

The unsung heroes of any championship are often the coaches. This was definitely the case with the 2001 Patriots. Our coaching staff did an outstanding job from the start of training camp to the final gun of the season. As mentioned many times in the course of the book, the entire coaching staff became an extension of the work ethic and philosophy of our head coach, Bill Belichick. Other members of the staff were Romeo "RAC" Crennel (defensive coordinator), Jeff Davidson (offensive line assistant), Ivan Fears (wide receivers), Eric Mangini (defensive backs), Randy Melvin (defensive line), Markus Paul (assistant strength and conditioning), Dick Rehbein (quarterbacks; deceased), Rob Ryan (outside linebackers), Dante Scarnecchia (assistant head coach/offensive line), Brad Seely (special teams), Charlie Weis (offensive coordinator), Mike Woicik (strength and conditioning), and coaching assistants Ned Burke and Brian Daboll.

None of what happened during the 2001 season would have been possible without the direction and leadership provided by our owner, Robert Kraft, and his family.

Index